... clear and practical
... ...nance. It thoroughly explains
... financial statements, tools, and concepts; fundamental
financial instruments and transactions; and global financial
participants, markets, and systems. This fully revised third edition
captures the most important aspects of a changing financial
landscape, including:

- updates on key areas of the financial system, including default
  experience, corporate finance trends, growth in dark pools,
  hedge funds, foreign exchange, and derivatives, and changes to
  the international regulatory and central banking framework;
- further real-world examples/studies that introduce, or expand
  upon, a range of practical topics; 12 updated studies are supplemented by new cases related to reinsurance, central bank
  quantitative easing, and digital currency and payments;
- a comprehensive glossary containing key terms discussed in
  the book.

Each chapter is accompanied by an overview and summary,
illustrations and tables, real life case studies, and recommended
reading. *Finance: The Basics* is essential reading for anyone
interested in the fascinating world of finance.

Erik Banks is an experienced practitioner and regular contributor to the literature in the field of financial risk management,
traded markets, banking, and regulation. He has spent over
25 years in international banking, working at major financial
institutions in New York, London, Tokyo, Hong Kong, and
Munich, and is the author of over 20 books on risk, derivatives,
markets, and governance.

THE BASICS

FINANCE

THE BASICS

THIRD EDITION

Erik Banks

LONDON AND NEW YORK

Third edition published 2016
by Routledge
2 Park Square, Milton Park, Abingdon, Oxon OX14 4RN

© 2016 Erik Banks

Routledge is an imprint of the Taylor & Francis Group, an informa business

First edition published by Routledge 2007
Second edition published by Routledge 2011

British Library Cataloguing in Publication Data
A catalogue record for this book is available from the British Library

Library of Congress Cataloging in Publication Data
Banks, Erik.
    Finance : the basics / Erik Banks. — Third Edition.
      pages cm
    Revised edition of the author's Finance, 2011.
    Includes bibliographical references and index.
    1. Finance.   I. Title.
    HG173.B3363 2015
    332—dc23   2015009251

ISBN: 978-1-138-91976-1 (hbk)
ISBN: 978-1-138-91978-5 (pbk)
ISBN: 978-1-315-68767-4 (ebk)

Typeset in Aldus
by Keystroke, Station Road, Codsall, Wolverhampton

MIX
Paper from
responsible sources
FSC
www.fsc.org   FSC® C013056

Printed and bound in Great Britain by
TJ International Ltd, Padstow, Cornwall

CONTENTS

PART 3
Participants and marketplaces   **209**

FINANCE IN ACTION CASES

FIGURES

TABLES

PREFACE TO THE THIRD EDITION

The topic of finance is dynamic in its evolution and important in its application. To be sure, much of the foundation of finance is well established, providing a stable framework for decision-making: basic financial concepts such as financial statement construction and analysis, time value of money, risk versus return, diversification, short- and long-term financial management, and capital-raising, for instance, are all part of well-accepted daily financial practice.

But much of the financial landscape continues to change around us. The continued innovation taking place in the financial markets, the growing accumulation of wealth around the world, the increasingly global movement of capital and assets, the advent of advanced communications, networks, and computing, the changing views of regulators, and the periodic onset of financial crises necessarily mean that certain dimensions of finance are also subject to change. Our goal in this third edition is to capture the most important of these changes and discuss them in a clear and practical manner. Readers of this edition will benefit from a series of additions and improvements:

- updates on key areas of the financial system, including default experience, corporate finance trends, growth in dark pools, hedge funds, foreign exchange, and derivatives, and changes to the international regulatory and central banking framework;

- further real-world examples/studies ("Finance in action" studies) that introduce, or expand upon, a range of practical topics; joining previous studies are new examples centered on reinsurance, central bank quantitative easing, and digital currency and payments;
- additional worked examples and explanations in each chapter;
- expanded and updated chapter readings and external references for further consultation on individual topics;
- a concise and comprehensive glossary containing key terms discussed in the book;
- an updated Appendix listing Internet resources that provide valuable information on different aspects of the financial topics discussed in the book.

As in the first two editions, this version attempts to convey the fact that financial markets and concepts are quite universal; although some practical and definitional differences may arise between the USA, the UK, Germany, France, Japan, Singapore, Australia, and so forth, the fundamentals can be applied in any jurisdiction. To that end, we have tried to mix into our examples a range of countries, currencies, and terms, so that this book can be seen as truly cross-border in nature.

ABBREVIATIONS

ATS	Alternative trading system
BA	Bankers' acceptance
BBA	British Bankers' Association
BP	Basis point
CAPM	Capital asset pricing model
CD	Certificate of deposit
CDO	Collateralized debt obligation
CF	Cash flow
CP	Commercial paper
EBIT	Earnings before interest and taxes
ECP	Euro commercial paper
EFT	Electronic funds transfer
EMH	Efficient market hypothesis
EMTN	Euro medium-term note
EPS	Earnings per share
ETF	Exchange-traded fund
EURONIA	Euro Overnight Index
FV	Future value
FX	Foreign exchange
GAAP	Generally Accepted Accounting Principles
GDP	Gross domestic product
GP	General partner

IFRS	International Financial Reporting Standards
IPO	Initial public offering
IRR	Internal rate of return
LBO	Leveraged buyout
LIBOR	London Interbank Offered Rate
LP	Limited partner
M&A	Mergers and acquisitions
MBO	Management buyout
MTF	Multilateral trading facility
MTN	Medium-term note
NASDAQ	National Association of Securities Dealers Automated Quotations
NAV	Net asset value
NPV	Net present value
NYSE	New York Stock Exchange
OTC	Over-the-counter
P&C	Property and casualty
P&I	Principal and interest
PP&E	Property, plant, and equipment
PV	Present value
ROA	Return on assets
ROE	Return on equity
SG&A	Selling, general, and administrative
SPE	Special-purpose entity
UIT	Unit investment trust
WACC	Weighted average cost of capital
WMCC	Weighted marginal cost of capital
XOL	Excess of loss

PART

CONCEPTS AND TOOLS

THE WORLD OF FINANCE

CHAPTER OVERVIEW

In this chapter we will consider the basic definitions and concepts of the financial world, the meaning and scope of finance, and how it impacts daily activities. We will then consider the goals of finance, which center on how a firm maximizes value, ensures proper liquidity and solvency, and manages risks. With this background in hand we will then discuss the financial process, a cycle based on financial reporting, planning, and decision-making, and consider how market factors can impact the cycle. We will conclude with a brief overview of the book, describing in general terms the concepts/tools, instruments/transactions, and markets/participants discussed in subsequent chapters.

DEFINITION AND SCOPE OF FINANCE

Finance is the study of concepts, applications, and systems that affect the value (or wealth) of individuals, companies, and countries over the short and long term. The study is both qualitative and quantitative, and we shall consider both dimensions in this book. Once we understand the essential elements of finance, we can identify the motivations and goals that drive specific actions and decisions.

Finance affects the daily activities of people, organizations, and entire nations. Though financial dealings have existed for centuries, their presence and importance have become even more apparent in an era characterized by growing wealth accumulation, consumption, and investment. Indeed, the penetration of finance is so thorough that we needn't look far to see its impact: consider that on any given day many of us are likely to be aware of economic growth, unemployment and inflation estimates, stock prices and deposit quotes, oil and gold price trends, credit and mortgage loan offers, corporate earnings announcements, and takeovers and bankruptcies. A financial transaction occurs every time we place savings into a deposit account or the stock market, make a purchase with a credit card, or take out a loan to buy a car or a house. A financial transaction also occurs when a company borrows money from its bankers or issues bonds to investors or acquires a competitor. And a financial transaction occurs when a government agency issues bonds to finance its budget requirements, sells state-owned assets to the private sector, or changes its interest rate or tax policies. It's easy to imagine that, when each one of these individual transactions is multiplied by thousands or millions of similar transactions, asset prices and capital flows can change and affect the fortunes of individuals, companies, and countries.

While finance can obviously affect a whole range of participants – from countries to companies, to individuals – we will focus our discussion on companies. The corporate focus is useful because companies drive much of the financial activity that impacts all other participants.

THE GOALS OF FINANCE

A company exists to produce goods and services, and doing so successfully leads to the creation of an enterprise with value. In fact, a company operating in a capitalistic free market economy aims to maximize the value of its operation. Naturally, this is just one primary goal – we can easily imagine that a company may also try to pursue other goals, such as building market share, delivering top quality customer service, establishing competitive leadership, creating an international presence, developing brand name recognition, introducing new and exciting products, promoting employee/community support, and so forth. Ultimately, however, a company seeks to create a maximum level of enduring enterprise value. As we shall see, this overarching goal can be accomplished by maximizing profits, managing liquidity and solvency, and taking proper account of financial and operating risks.

MAXIMIZING PROFITS

Companies seek to maximize value (wealth) while adhering to certain social, legal, and regulatory constraints. When markets are left to their own devices – under a *laissez faire* system, where free markets dominate and government involvement is at an absolute minimum – companies can produce goods/services at will, and consumers can freely select which ones to buy. In such free market systems companies try to attract consumers in order to produce and sell more goods/services as efficiently as possible. How can a company become stronger and increase its wealth? The obvious answer is by increasing its profits, or the income that remains after expenses have been paid: a company that makes more money is more valuable than one that makes less money, all other things being equal, and if it can do so continuously, over a long period of time, it becomes stronger.

Let's consider a simple example to help frame the discussion. Assume that a hypothetical company, ABC Co. (which we shall revisit throughout the book), produces certain goods, which it sells to its customers. In order to produce these goods it has a staff of workers, sources raw materials locally, and owns a factory (which it depreciates, or reduces in value, on a regular basis as a result of normal "wear and tear"). The purchase price of the factory is paid by taking out a loan from a local bank. The rest of the company's assets (i.e. items that it owns) are kept in a short-term bank deposit. The revenues earned by selling the goods are used to buy raw materials from abroad, repay the interest and principal on the loan, and pay the salaries of the employees, the rent on the office space, and taxes to the government. The remaining balance, net income (or net profit), is then reinvested in the business or paid out to the owners. This simple example raises a number of important questions about how the company operates and how it attempts to maximize its profits. For instance, does the company maximize profits by:

- Buying raw materials from abroad rather than locally?
- Borrowing from the local bank rather than issuing bonds or stock?
- Purchasing the factory instead of leasing it?
- Depreciating the factory on an accelerated basis rather than a straight-line basis?
- Renting the office space instead of buying it?
- Keeping its remaining assets in short-term bank deposits rather than long-term securities?
- Reinvesting net profits rather than paying them out to the owners?

The correct answers are not immediately apparent, mainly because we need to understand more about the company, its financial structure, its operating environment, and the competitive marketplace. And, of course, we need a proper suite of financial concepts and tools so that we can evaluate the issues and alternatives; we shall consider these concepts and tools in subsequent chapters.

Let's now extend the example one step further, to demonstrate that the scope of finance is very broad. Assume that ABC Co. wants to expand its operations and decides to buy a competing firm. To arrange the acquisition, it borrows from its local bankers. Once the acquired company is fully integrated, the firm invests in factories located around the world, which allows it to source raw materials in each local marketplace, produce goods in a local setting, and then sell them to the local consumer base. Half of any profits it earns are reinvested in the local operations, while the other half is repatriated to the home office.

Once again, we can ask whether ABC Co. maximizes profits by:

- Acquiring a competitor instead of growing only through internal resources?
- Using loans instead of stock to buy the competitor?
- Making a series of long-term investments in local markets instead of concentrating production in the home market?

- Sourcing raw materials in each local market rather than arranging a single centralized purchase agreement for all markets?
- Retaining 50 percent of its local profits in each local operation and repatriating the other 50 percent to head office?

The correct answers are still uncertain because we again lack the necessary tools and information.

So, how does a company actually create profits? Broadly speaking, it can do so by investing, speculating, or restructuring. Let's consider each one.

Generating revenues and profits is accomplished primarily by investing in productive resources – plant and equipment, technology, intellectual property, human resources, and financial assets. We can define investing as the commitment of capital in a venture, project, asset, or security in order to create more value. Investment may be focused on physical assets, like the purchase or construction of a factory, the development of a power plant, or the purchase or lease of a fleet of ships. Automobile manufacturers, airlines, energy companies, steel companies, and others regularly invest in such physical assets. In other cases investment is based on the purchase of securities, such as stocks and bonds that are also designed to generate a return. This is an "indirect" form of investment in productive assets, as the company buying securities (perhaps for its investment or retirement benefits portfolio) is actually contributing its capital to the firms that have issued the securities; those firms, in turn, are likely to be using the proceeds to invest in the hard assets and projects we have just mentioned.

Some firms try to make profits by speculating. Speculating, like investing, is a method of committing capital in order to generate a satisfactory return. Speculative activities are generally centered on a company's purchase or sale of securities, financial contracts, or select physical assets (commodities, real estate), rather than the direct purchase of productive assets used to create goods and services. In fact, specialized institutions like banks and investment funds are actively involved in speculative activities.

A firm can also create or expand profits by restructuring corporate operations. It may do so by changing its business through a corporate finance transaction such as a merger, acquisition, or joint venture, or by selling a subsidiary no longer considered essential to corporate strategy. It can also do so by restructuring its balance sheet, perhaps repaying some of its debt by issuing stock. A company pursuing such strategies hopes to expand the revenue base, lower costs, and/or increase operating efficiencies – any, or all, of which can help generate profits.

MANAGING LIQUIDITY AND SOLVENCY

While a company may wish to maximize its profits and its value, it must first be in sound financial condition. A company that has been weakened by bad decisions or a difficult operating environment is interested primarily in surviving from month to month and is unlikely to be thinking about ways of expanding its earnings power and value. Accordingly, it must make sure that its foundation is strong. In financial terms this relates primarily to two key areas: liquidity and solvency.

Liquidity is defined as a sufficiency of cash (or assets that can be quickly converted to cash) to pay bills and cover any surprises or emergencies. In fact, managing liquidity is critically important, as any mistake can turn a company's fortunes almost immediately. Firms that lack enough cash to cover their short-term outflows and those that rely on only a few sources of external funding that can be withdrawn by the providers are at greater risk of financial distress than those that keep a prudent amount of cash on hand and arrange external financing across a broad range of markets, instruments, investors/lenders, and maturities.

Companies manage liquidity by spacing their liabilities (or amounts owed) over time (so that not everything comes due at once), keeping some portion of their assets in the form of cash or short-term securities (such as government treasury bills), and establishing proper financing arrangements. For instance, if ABC Co. has a £10 million credit line with its bank and is presented with unexpected payments of £5 million, it can pay the charges using the credit line and carry on with its operations. Naturally, it will have to repay the money it has borrowed to meet the emergency payment, but it will have more time to do so (perhaps up to several years). Or, instead of using the bank facility, ABC

Co. may sell £5 million of short-term treasury bills that it holds in its portfolio expressly for emergencies. The result is the same: avoiding a liquidity squeeze by arranging in advance the right mechanism to deal with any potential anticipated or unanticipated problem. Naturally, proper management of liquidity raises certain questions:

- What is the best type of liquidity credit facility for a company?
- Should liquidity be accessed by preserving more cash and short-term assets on the balance sheet (internal), arranging more bank credit lines (external), or both?
- If assets are to be used, is a discount to the value of those assets necessary in order to provide a better reflection of the cash liquidation value?
- Do liquidity needs change during a given season or do they fluctuate according to the broader economic cycle?
- How much enterprise value is lost by being too liquid, i.e. holding too much non-earning cash on the balance sheet?

The finance framework helps a company answer these questions and develop the right kind of program to ensure a liquidity crisis is avoided. While liquidity planning is an essential process for all companies, it is especially critical for small- and medium-sized companies that often lack the resources and credit access enjoyed by large firms.

Solvency, the second major element of a sound financial foundation, is defined as a sufficiency of capital (or permanent/semi-permanent funds) to meet unexpected losses. Companies generally operate their businesses with a certain amount of equity capital and retained earnings (and certain classes of long-term debt) to protect against potentially large and unexpected losses that consume its resources. By preserving this buffer, a company tries to ensure that it can operate as a "going concern," even under dire circumstances. For instance, if ABC Co. has a capital base of £250 million that supports £1 billion of assets and it generates a loss of £150 million as a result of negative judgments on a lawsuit, a portion of its capital base will be depleted, i.e. the buffer falls from £250 million to £100 million. While this is clearly a dangerous situation and ABC Co. will need to rebuild its financial position as quickly as possible, it can still continue operating. If the company didn't have enough capital funds to absorb the loss, it would become technically insolvent and have to file for bankruptcy. In order to manage solvency properly a company must consider the following:

- How much of a capital buffer is needed to protect the firm under various normal and stress scenarios?
- Should that buffer be expanded through internal resources, externally, or both?
- What is the best mix of capital and how much will it cost to raise each portion?
- Do regulators demand a minimum level of capitalization?

Once again, the finance framework helps answer these questions in a manner that is rational and consistent.

MANAGING RISK

Since finance is concerned with a series of fluctuating variables and dynamic decisions, it is keenly focused on risk – which we define as the uncertainty or variability surrounding a future event. In a risky world a company must weigh all of the costs and benefits arising from a short-term or long-term action designed to boost profits and value. If a firm absorbs too much risk, it may suffer losses or financial distress, or even failure. Conversely, if a firm takes too little risk, it may miss the opportunity to create profits or accumulate market share. While taking risk can help a company achieve its goals, at some point incremental risk-taking may not be sensible. The marginal benefit gained from each incremental risky project or investment may decline, to the point where risk and return are misbalanced.

Risk comes in many different forms, including operating risk, financial risk, legal risk, and environmental risk; each of these can be decomposed into even more granular classes.

Risk can be managed through hedging (i.e. neutralizing), risk reduction, and risk diversification; some risks can also be mitigated by loss controls, which are pre-emptive behaviors that reduce the likelihood that perils will occur.

Before creating a risk management strategy, ABC Co. must again resolve various questions:

- How much risk should the company take in each class?
- Is this risk core or ancillary to the business?
- Is the company being properly compensated for taking risk?
- Should the risk be transferred, reduced or eliminated, or should it be preserved?
- How much does it cost the company to shift or eliminate particular classes of risk?

The definitive answers to these questions will again depend on a company and its operations, its comfort and experience with risk, and the nature of the markets/opportunities.

THE FINANCIAL PROCESS

A company trying to maximize the value of its operations faces many financial decisions. Financial decisions depend on a standardized process that provides continuous feedback. The process can be viewed as a three-stage cycle that is driven by the financial goals that a firm hopes to achieve. It begins with a review of the company's financial position (financial reporting/analysis) and is followed by the development of short- and long-term plans (financial planning), which leads to the execution of certain actions (financial decisions). These decisions will yield results that affect the firm's financial position, allowing the cycle to begin anew. The process is thus continuous.

FINANCIAL REPORTING/ANALYSIS

Financial reporting/analysis relates to the structure and trend of a company's financial position, most often conveyed through three key financial statements (or accounts) that are prepared and distributed every quarter or year:

- Balance sheet: a point-in-time reflection of a company's assets, liabilities, and capital.
- Income statement (or profit and loss statement): a cumulative reflection of a company's revenues, expenses, and profits.

- Cash flow statement: a cumulative reflection of the cash flowing into, and out of, a company.

These key statements are supplemented by other information, including financial footnotes and detailed management discussion and analysis. This reporting/analysis is done via established accounting rules, such as the International Financial Reporting Standards promulgated by the International Accounting Standards Board, which inject uniformity into the process. Through the reporting mechanism, internal and external stakeholders can determine how a firm, such as ABC Co., has performed over time (and versus its competitors) and what its financial position is at a particular moment. We will review these key financial statements in more detail in Chapter 2.

FINANCIAL PLANNING

Financial planning is the second phase of the financial process. It helps define the actions that a firm needs to take over the short term and long term to meet its goals.

Some aspects of financial planning deal with an immediate time horizon, generally 1 week to 1 year. These issues center on daily management and progress of corporate operations, such as:

- Working capital (or liquidity) management: managing cash, short-term assets and liabilities.
- Hedge management: rebalancing financial/operating risks through the use of various types of instruments intended to protect against losses.
- Funding management: arranging financing through a loan or capital markets.

Other dimensions of financial planning are based on longer-term actions. Such strategic financial management is critical to the methodical expansion of corporate operations and the long-term creation of enterprise value. Issues in this category relate to:

- Capital investment: managing long-term investment projects, research and development, and capital expenditures.

- Capital structure: identifying the optimal blend of debt, equity, and off balance sheet funding.
- Mergers and acquisitions: creating opportunities through corporate combinations or restructuring.
- Tax planning: optimizing operations to reduce the tax burden.
- International strategies: managing operations in, and expanding into, offshore markets.
- Dividend policy: developing a proper policy to pay dividends to investors.
- Risk management: creating a consistent, long-term, approach to the management of financial, operating, and legal risks.

While short- and long-term planning are essential to the continued success of any company, they can lead to different goals: plans (and subsequent decisions) that are based on the short term tend to focus on near-term profitability; those of a longer-term nature center on sustainable enterprise value creation over multiple reporting periods.

FINANCIAL DECISIONS

A company can make decisions once its financial position is well understood and its tactical/strategic plans have been formulated. Decisions are made by using specific financial concepts and tools, such as risk/return trade-off, risk diversification, cost of capital, time value of money, net present value, and investment rules, all of which we will discuss in Chapter 3. Concepts and tools help a company objectively understand the impact of translating plans into actionable decisions.

The three dimensions of the financial process are thus part of a continuous cycle: a firm examines its financial position, develops short-term and long-term plans and makes decisions to put the plans into motion. The next set of financial statements will reflect some aspects of decisions that have been taken, and can be used as the basis for further short-term and long-term financial plans and decisions. Figure 1.1 summarizes this cycle. Naturally, a company must make its short- and long-term financial actions meaningful and must also be flexible enough to adapt to changing circumstances.

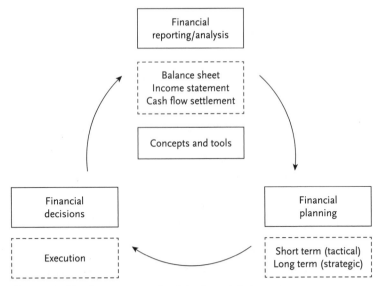

Figure 1.1 The three-stage cycle of the financial process

EXTERNAL AND INTERNAL FACTORS

External and internal forces impact the financial actions and activities of a firm operating in a complex economic world. Every company is influenced, directly or indirectly, by macro-economic factors: economic growth, productivity, employment, inflation, interest rates, currency rates, commodity/input prices, consumer confidence, and so forth. It may also be impacted by the state of the industry in which it operates, competitive pressures, availability of substitutes, and regulatory restrictions. A company must generally react or adapt to these external forces: since they are so powerful and pervasive, they are typically beyond the control or influence of any single company (or industry) and must therefore be viewed as factors that shape the operating environment. Assume, for instance, that ABC Co. is operating in a macro environment characterized by healthy growth, strong consumer confidence, and robust demand; all other things being equal, ABC

Co.'s ability to sell products will be greater than if the economy is in recession. Similarly, if several new competitors have entered the same industry, ABC Co. may feel heightened pressures that force it to change its pricing or marketing tactics. It can react or adapt to, but cannot change, the competitive environment.

Internal forces are equally important in dictating a company's path to success. These may include a company's financial strength and resources, its access to cash and financing, its approach to strategic ventures, its ability to respond to pricing/costing changes in the face of fluctuating supply and demand, and the quality and experience of its leadership. Each one of these factors is within a company's control and can be changed over the short or medium term, generally unilaterally. For example, ABC Co. may believe that raising additional capital to expand its operations or purchasing a smaller rival may give it the competitive edge it requires. Or, the company may believe that it needs a stronger marketing team in order to boost its sales, so it may choose to hire top sales producers from a competitor. It can take these actions on its own, hopefully improving its fortunes as a consequence.

THE COMPLETE FINANCIAL PICTURE

We've now introduced several theoretical elements of the financial world: definition/scope, goals, and process, along with the impact of internal/external forces. Assembling these gives us a complete picture of the financial world.

To review, we know that finance is the study of how companies (and individuals and countries) can increase value or wealth. By using financial concepts and tools in a three-stage financial process, a company attempts to achieve its financial goals in a disciplined manner. Maximizing profits and managing liquidity, solvency, and other risks helps a firm operating in a free market economy achieve the overarching goal of value maximization. But the financial process is dynamic and subject to the effects of internal and external factors, so any process that is implemented to fulfill financial goals must take account of these factors and adapt to them through a continuous feedback process. This financial picture is summarized in Figure 1.2.

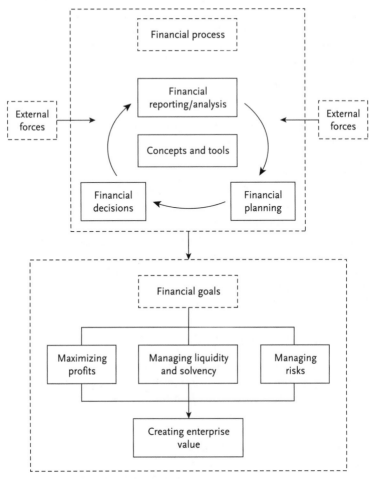

Figure 1.2 The complete financial picture

OUTLINE AND STRUCTURE OF THE BOOK

Finance is clearly vital to the activities of companies, individuals, and sovereign nations. The question is how to deal with the topic in a manner that is comprehensive – but also manageable, relevant, and interesting. To accomplish this goal, we will approach the subject by focusing on three broad areas, or "pillars": concepts and tools, instruments and transactions, and participants and markets. By exploring finance in this way, we'll be able to cover the key micro and macro dimensions in a logical manner.

We begin by considering concepts and tools. This provides the essential background needed to understand the mechanics of finance and helps clarify the company-wide issues that we'll consider in subsequent portions of the book. We will start with an examination of corporate financial statements, focusing on:

- Financial structure and reporting: the nature and use of the balance sheet, income statement, and statement of cash flows.

With an understanding of financial statements and how they can be used as part of the decision-making process, we will then turn our attention to fundamental financial tools. There are many well-established principles and tools that can be used in quantifying and evaluating many of the issues that companies face:

- Risk considerations: the nature of risk and return, risk diversification, and value maximization.
- The price of capital: the determination of interest rates/yield curves, stock prices, and the weighted cost of capital.
- Time value of money: the use of present value and future value.
- Investment decisions: the use of net present value, internal rate of return, and decision rules.

Once we've assembled this financial "toolkit," we'll explore the nature of financial instruments and transactions that let companies achieve particular goals. Our intent in this second pillar is to demonstrate how specific assets, liabilities, off-balance-sheet contracts, and restructuring transactions are used to advance the progress of companies and their stakeholders. Our discussion will focus on:

- Common and preferred stock: the nature and use of equity-related instruments.
- Loans and bonds: the nature and use of debt-related instruments.
- Investment funds: the nature and use of investment mechanisms that incorporate multiple assets.

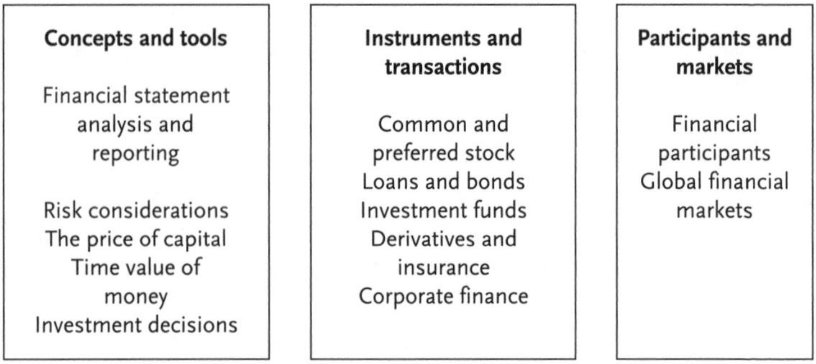

Concepts and tools	Instruments and transactions	Participants and markets
Financial statement analysis and reporting Risk considerations The price of capital Time value of money Investment decisions	Common and preferred stock Loans and bonds Investment funds Derivatives and insurance Corporate finance	Financial participants Global financial markets

Figure 1.3 Three pillars of finance

- Derivatives and insurance: the nature of risk management and the use of instruments to manage, transfer, hedge, or assume risk.
- Corporate finance: the nature and use of corporate restructuring transactions.

We will then examine the third pillar of finance – the macro picture. Specifically, we will consider how key participants and markets support, and are supported by, activities at the micro level. We shall do this by describing:

- Financial participants: intermediaries, end-users, and regulators.
- Global financial markets: macro-structure of the markets, macro variables, monetary policy, and the nature of the twenty-first-century marketplace, including financial crises, which can sometimes disrupt the plans and goals of companies.

The three pillars that constitute the world of finance are summarized in Figure 1.3.

CHAPTER SUMMARY

Finance, which is the study of factors that impact the wealth or value of participants, is an essential component of daily life in the business world. Financial dealings and transactions are prevalent throughout modern society, affecting individuals, companies, and entire countries. A company's overarching goal of increasing value can be achieved by meeting a series of important financial goals, including maximization of profit, prudent management of liquidity and solvency management, and rigorous management of financial and operating risks. The standard three-stage financial process, which is based on financial reporting, short- and long-term financial planning, and financial decision-making, allows a company to work towards its goals in a methodical fashion. Any decisions taken by financial managers must take account of a series of internal and external market forces; companies are generally required to react to external factors, but can more readily influence internal factors.

FURTHER READING

Banks, E., 2010, *Dictionary of Finance, Investment and Banking*, London: Palgrave Macmillan.

Brealey, R., Myers, S., and Marcus, A., 2013, *Fundamentals of Corporate Finance*, 11th edn., New York: McGraw Hill.

Fama, E., 1972, *The Theory of Finance*, New York: Holt, Rinehart and Winston.

Melicher, R. and Norton, E., 2011, *Introduction to Finance*, 14th edn., New York: John Wiley & Sons.

2

THE FINANCIAL STATEMENTS

CHAPTER OVERVIEW

A company attempting to maximize profits, maintain proper levels of liquidity and solvency, and prudently manage risks must first understand the state and trend of its financial position. In this chapter we consider the process of standard financial reporting, analyze the structure and use of the three main financial statements (balance sheet, income statement, and statement of cash flows), and discuss how financial statement ratio analysis can be used to decipher the financial strengths and weaknesses of a firm. We will conclude by considering how financial statements are used in the decision-making process.

FINANCIAL REPORTING

Financial reporting – the process by which a company prepares and presents its accounts – is a key element of the modern accounting framework. Reporting leads ultimately to the creation of financial statements that let managers, investors, creditors, credit rating agencies, regulators, and other stakeholders evaluate financial strength or weakness. Naturally, a degree of uniformity in approach and presentation must exist in order for statements to be useful. If no standards existed, then every company would simply do as it pleased, making it impossible to compare performance across companies – or, indeed, within a company, if it decided to change its standards every year.

Regulators and industry bodies have developed and refined standards of financial reporting over the years. Though these can vary across some national systems, the essential process of financial reporting and presentation is the same: every company posts transactions that affect its daily operations to relevant ledger accounts according to pre-defined rules or guidelines. The major guidelines are set forth via Generally Accepted Accounting Principles (or GAAP, promulgated in the USA by the Financial Accounting Standards Board) and International Financial Reporting Standards (IFRS, managed on a global basis by the International Accounting Standards Board). These accounts are then aggregated into unaudited trial statements over certain common reporting periods. An external auditor independently audits (or examines) statements to ensure conformity to established standards. The end goal is the uniform preparation and distribution of the financial statements that we discuss below every 3, 6, and/or 12 months. Figure 2.1 summarizes the financial reporting process.

KEY FINANCIAL STATEMENTS

We can capture the essence of a company's financial position through:

- The balance sheet: a "point-in-time" representation of assets, liabilities, and capital.
- The income statement: a cumulative record of the firm's profits and losses.
- The statement of cash flows: a cumulative record of the firm's cash inflows and outflows.

Let's consider each in greater detail.

THE BALANCE SHEET

A company that is in business to produce goods or services requires assets (items of value that are legally owned by the

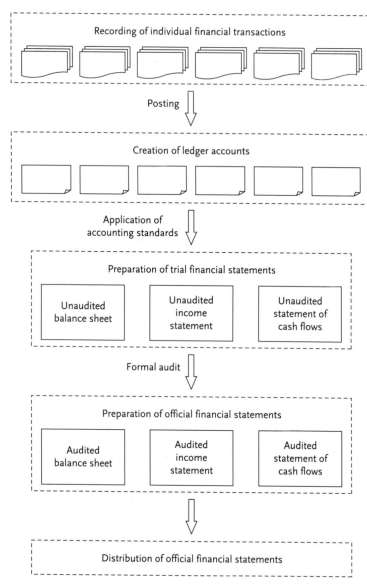

Figure 2.1 The financial reporting process

company), which it funds through liabilities (amounts that are owed by the company to others) and some form of equity (amounts representing an ownership interest in the company); let us note that the terms capital, shares, and stock can also be used to refer to equity. These three broad categories, presented in a statement known as the balance sheet, are linked together by an important accounting relationship, which says that:

$$\text{assets} = \text{liabilities} + \text{equity} \tag{2.1}$$

If this equation holds true, then the balance sheet "balances." The relationship makes intuitive, as well as financial, sense. If a company possesses some asset, it has either purchased that asset using its own capital resources (i.e. equity) or external resources (i.e. a bank loan, which is a liability) – or both. For instance, if ABC Co. has a computer (an asset) worth £10,000, it may have borrowed £10,000 to buy the computer (a liability), it may have purchased the computer outright from its own capital (equity), or it might have used some combination of the two (i.e. it has paid off half of the computer's value – £5,000 of equity – and borrowed to finance the difference – £5,000 of liabilities). This example balances, per [2.1]. It is relatively easy to see that we can extend this process to include all of ABC Co.'s assets.

We can also rearrange the equation above to gain some understanding about the equity (or net worth), of the firm:

$$\text{equity} = \text{assets} - \text{liabilities} \tag{2.2}$$

This tells us that the actual value or worth of the company is the difference between its assets and liabilities. Thus, if ABC Co. has borrowed £5,000 to buy the £10,000 computer, its equity (or net worth) in the asset is equal to £5,000 (i.e. £10,000 – £5,000). Again, we can extend this across all accounts to find the equity value of the firm. A critical point to note is that, when assets are worth less than liabilities, the firm has "negative equity" and is considered insolvent. Thus, if the computer is really worth £2,000 and the company borrowed £5,000 to buy it, its equity is equal to –£3,000. Not surprisingly, financial managers are heavily focused on ensuring that the value of assets always exceeds the value of liabilities.

Though the actual number of asset accounts in a large firm can reach into the hundreds or thousands, we can condense them into a smaller group of key accounts:

- Cash and short-term securities: accounts that form the company's asset-based liquidity (i.e. cash and cash equivalents), which is an important part of liquidity management. A company needs to keep a certain amount of liquid assets on hand to pay bills as they come due, or to meet unexpected payments.
- Accounts receivable: a form of credit extended by the company to its customers. For instance, while customers might receive goods/services from the company immediately, they may take 30 to 180 days to pay for them; this is precisely equal to the company making short-term loans to its customers.
- Prepayments: payments made by a company for goods/services to be received at a future time. For instance, a company might prepay all of its property and casualty insurance premiums at the beginning of the year, even though it receives the benefits of insurance coverage throughout the year. Other kinds of accounts can be prepaid, such as rent, taxes, and so forth.
- Inventories: accounts comprising the items needed to manufacture physical goods that are ultimately sold to customers. Inventories are generally classified according to their stage in the production process, such as raw material, work-in-progress, and finished goods. Inventories have to be managed smoothly so that there is no disruption in the production process and enough finished goods are available for sale.
- Property, plant, and equipment (PP&E): all of the physical infrastructure that a company needs to run its business, such as computers, office buildings, trucking fleets, factories, assembly lines, and so forth. Since PP&E declines in value through normal "wear and tear" and obsolescence, its value is reduced through depreciation, which is a non-cash expense. Accumulated depreciation may be shown as a "contra-account," or deduction, to the PP&E accounts.
- Intangibles: all assets that cannot be physically seen or touched, but which add value to the firm. This includes items such as trademarks, patents, and intellectual property, as well as goodwill, which is excess value paid when acquiring another firm.

Cash, securities, accounts receivable, prepayments, and inventories are regarded collectively as current assets and form one half of the working capital equation. We'll discuss working capital at several points later in the chapter.

Liability accounts generally include:

- Accounts payable: a form of credit accepted by the company from its suppliers. For instance, the company may receive raw materials/services from its suppliers and choose to pay its bills immediately and gain the benefit of "cash" discounts, or it can forgo the discounts and defer payments for 30–180 days; the latter choice is equivalent to accepting short-term loans from the suppliers.
- Short-term debt: credit extended to a company through short-term loans or securities, where maturities are generally defined to be less than 1 year.
- Deferred payments: accounts representing payments due from the company (typically taxes and expenses), but which have been deferred until some future period.
- Medium- and long-term debt: credit extended to a company though medium- and long-term loans and securities with maturities ranging from 1 to 30 years.

We shall discuss some of these liability accounts in more detail in Chapter 5. Accounts payable and short-term debt constitute the general category of current liabilities, which forms the second half of the working capital equation. Total working capital is simply current assets less current liabilities and serves as a good proxy for a company's overall liquidity position, as we'll see below.

The capital accounts, which represent the residual balance remaining after all assets have been liquidated and all creditor (or liability) claims have been repaid, may include:

- Preferred stock (or preference shares): a form of non-voting, dividend-paying ownership capital issued by the company to investors.
- Common stock (or ordinary shares): another form of ownership capital issued by the company to investors. Most common shares carry voting rights and may be entitled to dividends.

The common stock account may be divided into several sub-accounts including par value (the nominal amount of shares issued) and paid-in surplus (the difference between the market value of the amount raised and the par value). If a company repurchases its common stock from the market, it reduces the amount outstanding via the treasury stock contra-account.

- Retained earnings: an account representing a company's accumulated profits which are reinvested in new projects/investments.

We shall discuss some of these capital instruments in greater depth in Chapter 4. The actual balance sheet mix of assets, liabilities, and capital is, of course, company-specific. Each industry sector and each individual firm has its own size and proportion of assets, liabilities, and capital, as we shall note in subsequent chapters.

In addition to balance sheet items, companies may also have certain "off balance sheet" accounts that represent contingencies or uncertainties that can ultimately impact the financial position. These accounts can sometimes be quite significant and must not be overlooked. Items that are generally presented off balance sheet include undrawn/unfunded bank loans, financial guarantees, derivative contracts, and leases.

The actual presentation of the balance sheet is specific to a country and the accounting regime it follows. While most accounting systems feature the accounts listed above and adhere to the fundamental accounting equation, presentation can vary. Figures 2.2 and 2.3, for instance, show accounts in terms of US and UK presentation. Despite differences, the end result in terms of assets, liabilities, and capital is always equal.

To show how the accounts are constructed (and that the US and UK versions are, in fact, equivalent), let's examine the key accounts of ABC Co. Assume that ABC Co., which manufactures certain goods, has a factory worth £500 million (that has already been depreciated by 10 percent, or £50 million), accounts receivable of £100 million, accounts payable of £150 million, inventories of goods in various stages of completion valued at £200 million, cash on hand of £100 million, short-term loans of £100 million and medium-term loans of £300 million; the company was initially capitalized through a common stock issue of £150 million

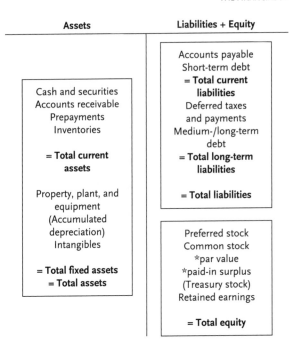

Figure 2.2 Sample US balance sheet

(comprising £10 million of par value and £140 million of paid-in surplus) and over the past few years it has accumulated retained earnings of £150 million.

ABC Co.'s balance sheet position under the US and UK versions is shown in Figures 2.4 and 2.5.

The presentation of the balance sheet created through the financial reporting process is, of course, important, as it provides a snapshot of the firm's position. But the balance sheet becomes even more useful when we examine how it evolves over time and how it compares with the balance sheets of competitors. We'll consider this trend/comparison analysis later in the chapter.

THE INCOME STATEMENT

The income statement (also referred to as the profit and loss account) records the revenues and expenses of the firm throughout

Property, plant, and equipment
(accumulated depreciation)
Intangibles
= Long-term investments
= Total fixed assets

Cash and securities
Accounts receivable
Prepayments
Inventories
= Total current assets

Accounts payable
Short-term debt
= Total current liabilities

Medium- and long-term debt
= Net assets

Preferred stock
Common stock
(treasury stock)
Retained earnings
= Net capital

Figure 2.3 Sample UK balance sheet

the fiscal accounting period. Unlike the balance sheet, which reflects a company's financial position at a single point in time (e.g. each quarter- or year-end), the income statement accumulates

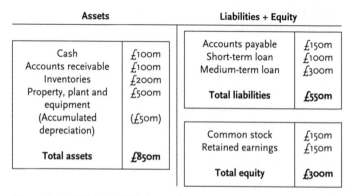

Assets		**Liabilities + Equity**	
Cash	£100m	Accounts payable	£150m
Accounts receivable	£100m	Short-term loan	£100m
Inventories	£200m	Medium-term loan	£300m
Property, plant and equipment	£500m		
		Total liabilities	**£550m**
(Accumulated depreciation)	(£50m)		
		Common stock	£150m
		Retained earnings	£150m
Total assets	**£850m**		
		Total equity	**£300m**

Figure 2.4 ABC Co.'s US balance sheet

Property, plant, and equipment	£500m
(accumulated depreciation)	(£50m)
Total fixed assets	**£450m**
Cash	£100m
Accounts receivable	£100m
Inventories	£200m
Total current assets	**£400m**
Accounts payable	£150m
Short-term loan	£100m
Total current liabilities	**£250m**
Medium-term loan	£300m
Net assets	**£300m**
Common stock	£150m
Retained earnings	£150m
Net capital	**£300m**

Figure 2.5 ABC Co.'s UK balance sheet

all of the revenue and expense information for the reporting period and can therefore be considered cumulative.

Though an income statement may again include a significant number of entries, we focus on several key items:

- Gross revenues: the total amount of goods/services sold by the company to its customers. This is often referred to as gross sales or turnover, and is considered the "top line" reflection of a company's ability to sell goods/services at a particular price.
- Cost of goods sold: the amount that it costs the company to produce or convey the goods/services it sells; this generally includes raw materials and other inputs, as well as labor/production costs. It does not, however, include administrative costs, interest expense, or taxes, which are treated separately.
- Gross profit: the difference between the revenues earned by the company and the cost it incurs in producing those revenues.
- Selling, general, and administrative (SG&A) expenses: the non-production costs that the company incurs in creating its goods/services; this may include marketing, advertising, occupancy, employee health benefits, salaries, and so forth.

- Interest expense: the amount that the company pays its creditors for the use of borrowed funds. Interest expense can relate to any or all of short- and long-term loans and bonds and accounts payable.
- Interest income: the amount the company earns in interest from its investments in short- or long-term securities.
- Other income/expenses: all other inflows and outflows attributable to the company's operations. This can include exceptional items (those which are related to the core business but are unusually large) and extraordinary items (which are non-recurring and out of the normal course of business).
- Operating (or pre-tax) income: the company's gross profit less SG&A expenses, interest expense, and other income/expenses; this figure yields a taxable income equivalent. Note that in some cases interest income/expense is shown below the operating income line.
- Taxes: the amount that the firm has paid in income taxes.
- Net income: the difference between the company's pre-tax income and the taxes paid. This is the "bottom line" result of a company's business and reflects the true profitability of the operation. Net income can be distributed to shareholders in the form of dividends, or it can be reinvested in the business via retained earnings.

Managers and analysts often examine another income statement subtotal – earnings before interest and taxes (EBIT) – which is simply gross profit less SG&A expenses, before any interest or taxes are paid. As indicated above, EBIT can also be defined as operating income (when interest expense is deducted from operating, rather than gross, profit and non-operating income is negligible).

We have again generalized this statement for simplicity. Nevertheless, the structure noted above, and summarized in Figure 2.6, depicts the logic behind income statement construction and is adaptable across industries and countries.

Let's assume that ABC Co. has sold goods that generate revenues of £650 million, and the costs associated with the production of these goods amount to £520 million. The company has also booked £50 million in SG&A expenses, £20 million in interest

Gross revenues	
− Cost of goods sold	
= Gross profit	
− SG&A expenses	
− Interest expense	
+ Interest income	
+ Other income	
− Other expenses	
= Operating income	

Figure 2.6 Sample income statement (before tax effects)

Gross revenues	£650m
− Cost of goods sold	£520m
= Gross profit	£130m
− SG&A expenses	£50m
− Interest expense	£20m
+ Other income	£15m
− Other expenses	£5m
= Pre-tax income	£70m
− Income taxes	£21m
= Net income	£49m

Figure 2.7 ABC Co.'s income statement

expenses, and £5 million in other expenses; these have been partly offset by £15 million in other income. Together, these items produce net income of £70 million. Based on a tax rate of 30 percent, ABC Co.'s net income for the year amounts to £49 million, as illustrated in Figure 2.7.

THE STATEMENT OF CASH FLOWS

The last of the major financial statements intended to convey a picture of a company's financial structure and health is the statement of cash flows, which reveals the nature of the firm's sources and uses of cash, and its net cash position at the end of a reporting period. The basic cash flow statement is generally divided into three segments: operating cash flow, investing cash flow, and financing cash flow.

- Operating cash flow provides information on the actual cash impact (receipts and outflows) of the firm's ongoing core operations. This section begins with the net income generated by the business, adds back depreciation (which is a non-cash operating expense) and then adjusts for changes in working capital. Depreciation is a particularly important item: though it's a non-cash expense, it produces cash flow by reducing taxable income. The net of the operating cash flow section provides information on a firm's ability to generate cash from its core business.

- Investing cash flow yields information on how the company uses its cash in the pursuit of productive ventures or investments. The investing cash flow section examines the purchase of other companies or PP&E (outflows of cash), the purchase of securities and other financial assets (outflow), the sale of existing assets, subsidiaries, or joint venture stakes (inflow), or the sale of securities (inflow). The net of this section provides an indication of whether a company uses its cash to expand into new or existing areas.
- Financing cash flow indicates how much external funding (if any) the firm is using to fund its operating and investing activities. The financing cash flow section focuses on new debt and stock issuance (which represent cash inflows), debt repayment (outflow), dividend payments (outflow), and treasury stock repurchases (outflow). The net of the financing cash flow section indicates whether the firm needs to access external financing to carry on its business activities.

The statement of cash flows helps us understand whether sufficient cash, and access to cash, exists in order for the company to operate as a going concern, how that cash is being used, and whether external financing, such as we discuss in Chapters 4 and 5, is required. Figure 2.8 summarizes the essential cash flow statement; Figure 2.9 provides the same information in slightly different format, focusing on sources of cash and uses of cash.

Let's again extend our example of ABC Co. by examining its statement of cash flows. We know from the income statement presented above that the firm's net income for the year amounted to £49 million. Let's assume that it had annual depreciation expenses of £10 million and decreased its payables by £15 million. From an investing perspective the company sold £25 million of securities from its portfolio and bought new plant and equipment valued at £50 million. Finally, from a financing perspective let's assume that ABC Co. repaid £10 million of debt and borrowed another £50 million, and that it paid £20 million in dividends to its investors. Based on these simple entries, the company's net cash position at the end of the year amounted to £69 million; the results are summarized in Figure 2.10.

Operating cash flow
Net income
\+ Depreciation
− Increase in working capital
\+ Decrease in working capital
= Net operating cash flow

Investing cash flow
Sale of securities
\+ Sale of PP&E
− Purchase of securities
− Purchase of PP&E
= Net investing cash flow

Financing cash flow
Issuance of debt, stock
− Repayment of debt
− Repurchase of stock
− Payment of dividends
= Net financing cash flow

= Net cash surplus/deficit

Figure 2.8 Sample statement of cash flows

Sources of cash (inflows)
Net income
Depreciation
Medium- and long-term debt issuance
Common and preferred stock issuance
Decreases in assets (e.g. receivables, investments)
Increases in liabilities (e.g. payables, deferrals)

Uses of cash (outflows)
Net losses
Capital expenditures
Investment purchases
Medium- and long-term debt repayment
Common stock repurchase
Dividend payments
Increases in assets (e.g. receivables, inventory)
Decrease in liabilities (e.g. payables, deferrals)

Figure 2.9 Common sources and uses of cash

Operating cash flow	
Net income	£49m
+ Depreciation	£10m
− Increase in working capital	
+ Decrease in working capital	£15m
= Net operating cash flow	£74m

Investing cash flow	
Sale of securities	£25m
+ Sale of PP&E	
− Purchase of securities	
− Purchase of PP&E	£50m
= Net investing cash flow	−£25m

Financing cash flow	
Issuance of debt, stock	£50m
− Repayment of debt	£10m
− Repurchase of stock	
− Payment of dividends	£20m
= Net financing cash flow	£20m

| **= Net cash surplus/deficit** | **£69m** |

Figure 2.10 ABC Co.'s statement of cash flows

Adding the £69 million cash surplus to the firm's existing cash holdings on the balance sheet reveals its net cash position at the end of the reporting period. Once again, examining ABC Co.'s cash performance over time is critical.

FINANCIAL RATIOS

Financial ratios are used to supplement the analysis and decision-making process by allowing easy measurement and interpretation of important indicators within, and across, the key statements. Though can compute and analyze literally hundreds of different ratios for any given company, let's focus on measures that a financial manager is most likely to be concerned about, including those related to profitability, liquidity, and solvency (or leverage/capitalization).

PROFITABILITY RATIOS

Profitability ratios quantify how much money a firm makes based on its assets or capital, and how much of its revenues it is able to translate into net income.

- Return on assets describes how much profit the firm's asset base is able to produce and is computed as:

$$\text{return on assets (ROA)} = \frac{\text{net income}}{\text{total assets}} \qquad [2.3]$$

The higher the ROA, the more efficient the company is in using its assets to generate profits. In our example, ABC Co.'s ROA is equal to 5.76 percent (£49 million/£850 million). Naturally, in order to be meaningful this ratio needs to be compared against ABC Co.'s ROA over previous periods and against its competitors and industry peers – this will reveal whether the company is doing better or worse. For instance, if ABC Co.'s ROA over the previous 2 years has amounted to 4.50 percent and 5.25 percent, then the measure suggests the firm's profitability is improving.

- Return on equity measures how much profit the firm's equity base is able to produce. It is computed via:

$$\text{return on equity (ROE)} = \frac{\text{net income}}{\text{total equity}} \qquad [2.4]$$

In this example ABC Co.'s ROE is equal to 16.3 percent (£49 million/£300 million). As with ROA, the higher the figure, the more effective the company is in using its equity base to generate profits. Again, the result must be compared against prior periods and industry peers in order to be meaningful.

- Gross margin indicates how much of each dollar, pound, or euro of revenue (from sales of goods/services) remains after removing the costs of producing the goods/services; it is calculated as:

$$\text{gross margin} = \frac{\text{gross profit}}{\text{revenues}} \qquad [2.5]$$

In ABC Co.'s case the gross margin is 20 percent (£130 million/ £650 million), meaning that, for every pound of sales it generates, 80 pence are used to cover the cost of producing the goods/services. It is easy to see that, if the gross margin rises to 30 percent, then only 70 pence of every pound would be used to cover production costs. In other words, the result becomes more favorable as the margin increases; the same is true of all profit margin computations.

- Operating margin is similar to the gross margin computation, except that it focuses on operating income (profit). It is computed as:

$$\text{operating margin} = \frac{\text{operating profit}}{\text{revenues}} \qquad [2.6]$$

ABC Co.'s operating margin amounts to 10.76 percent (£70 million/£650 million), meaning that costs of production and associated expenses consume nearly 90 pence of each pound of sales. We can also consider the associated measure of operating leverage, or the degree to which a company relies on fixed investments and associated costs to produce revenues (and do so through Finance in action 2.1).

- Net margin is again similar to the gross and operating margins, except that it is based on a firm's "bottom line" profitability – after all expenses, including income taxes, have been met, but before income has been paid in dividends or allocated to retained earnings. It is computed as:

$$\text{net margin} = \frac{\text{net income}}{\text{revenues}} \qquad [2.7]$$

Not surprisingly, the higher the net margin, the more efficient is the firm in managing its total costs. In ABC Co.'s case its net margin is 7.54 percent (£49 millon/£650 million). That is, for every £1 of sales, 7.5 pence flow to the bottom line for onward distribution to investors (as dividends) or for reinvestment (as retained earnings).

Many other profitability ratios can be computed, but these tend to be variations on the theme, or specific adaptations for a given industry.

FINANCE IN ACTION 2.1:   THE BENEFIT AND CURSE OF OPERATING LEVERAGE

In finance, leverage is the name given to a balance sheet or off balance sheet structure or mechanism that magnifies profits and losses. While considerable focus is rightly placed on financial leverage, or the degree to which debt is used to fund the balance sheet (through measures discussed later in this chapter) it is sometimes easy to lose sight of operating leverage – which is no less important in dictating a company's fortunes.

Operating leverage is a simple measure that reflects the degree to which a company relies on fixed investment (with its attendant fixed costs) to create revenues and, ultimately, profits. In general, we can say that a company with a significant fixed asset investment has high operating leverage, while one with low fixed assets has low operating leverage. Thus, industries such as auto manufacturing, computer manufacturing, and energy exploration, extraction, and refining all have high fixed investments, high fixed costs, and high operating leverage. Others, such as retailing, consulting, and financial services, have low fixed investments, low fixed costs, and low operating leverage. Perhaps the easiest way to think about this is by comparing two different kinds of companies, say an auto manufacturer like Daimler, and a retailer such as Sainsbury's. Even before looking at their balance sheets, we know intuitively that Daimler, which produces and sells cars, must have lots of factories to produce those cars, while Sainsbury's, which retails but doesn't generally produce goods, must have lots of merchandise inventory to service its customers. In other words, Daimler's fixed investments as a percentage of its total assets must be relatively high, while Sainsbury's must be quite low; similarly, Daimler's fixed costs must be higher than Sainsbury's. More specifically, Daimler, in building its autos, has very significant investment in its plant and equipment. Each Mercedes that it produces has to go through an extensive factory-line process, powered by the latest technological equipment, computerized processes, robotics, and so forth. In fact, Daimler's plant and equipment represents a significant fixed investment which generates significant fixed costs. This means that the company has to cover its fixed costs – whether it produces one car or 10,000 cars. However, once it covers its fixed costs, each additional car that it produces and sells represents almost pure profit; to be sure, there is some variable cost associated with the steel, glass, and leather going into each individual car, but this cost is relatively small in relation to the sales price of the car. Daimler's operating leverage is thus very high. Sainsbury's, in contrast, has almost no investment in fixed assets. It may certainly own a few flagship stores and lease the rest, but its primary balance sheet assets are inventories – food, clothing, small appliances, cosmetics – which are not fixed assets. This means that Sainsbury's has no significant fixed costs to cover, but has very significant variable costs – the cost of inventory. As demand for Sainsbury's retail items increases, the variable costs that the retailer faces increase as well, as the company has to make sure that it has sufficient goods on hand to meet demand. Sainsbury's operating leverage is thus relatively low, certainly as compared with Daimler's.

So what does this all mean, and how can we measure it?

In the first instance, a company with high operating leverage can magnify its profit contributions once the fixed costs are covered – when demand for Mercedes vehicles is very strong, each incremental car sold creates profits that largely drop to the bottom line once the fixed costs are covered. Unfortunately, the reverse is also true: when demand is very sluggish, Daimler will encounter more difficulties – it may be unable to cover its fixed costs, meaning it will have to generate capital elsewhere (e.g. through borrowing, for example). Companies with high operating leverage are thus more volatile on the upside and downside, and cannot easily change course – Daimler, cannot, for instance, simply dispose of its auto factories when the going gets a bit rough. A company with low operating leverage, in contrast, is more stable and nimble: Sainsbury's will not enjoy the big increase in profitability when demand for retail goods is strong (as it will face growing variable costs via its inventory), but it will be able to quickly reduce its inventory when demand falls off and thus avoid a large drop in profits.

Measuring operating leverage is sometimes a bit tricky, as detailed product line information may not be available to those outside the company. But one operating leverage proxy that analysts often use is given by:

$$\text{operating leverage} = \frac{\Delta \text{EBIT}}{\Delta \text{revenue}} \qquad [2.8]$$

where ΔEBIT is the change in earnings before interest and taxes over a given period and Δrevenue is the change in revenues; note that, rather than EBIT, we may also use operating profit.

Let's take the hypothetical example of three companies – X, Y, and Z – where each one experiences a €100 million increase in revenues over some reporting period. In the case of Company X, its EBIT changes by €50 million, in the case of Company Y the change is €100 million, and in the case of Company Z the change is €200 million. Based on the change in EBIT, we may note the results in Table 2.1. Company Z clearly has higher leverage than Y or X, meaning it will gain more and lose more depending on its ability to generate revenues.

Table 2.1 Operating leverage example

Company	$\Delta EBIT/\Delta revenue$	Operating leverage
X	€50m/€100m = 0.5	Low
Y	€100m/€100m = 1.0	Neutral
Z	€200m/€100m = 2.0	High

LIQUIDITY RATIOS

We have already noted the importance of liquidity: the lack of sufficient liquidity is the single most common reason why companies fail. Employing appropriate ratios to understand the current state of the liquidity position is thus essential.

- The current ratio is a version of the working capital measure that compares current assets to current liabilities. It is computed via:

$$\text{current ratio} = \frac{\text{current assets}}{\text{current liabilities}} \qquad [2.9]$$

ABC Co.'s current ratio is equal to 1.6 (£400 million/£250 million), meaning that the firm has £1.60 of current assets that can be liquidated to meet each £1 of short-term liabilities coming due. Though the trend of the current ratio over time and its relation to peer results are again important in interpreting the result, any ratio over 1.0 is favorable as it means that liabilities coming due can be properly met.

- The quick ratio is a more stringent version of the current ratio that focuses only on the most liquid of a firm's current asset accounts. This means that true liquidity available to meet maturing liabilities is based on cash, securities, and receivables, while inventories, which may not be as readily saleable in an emergency, are excluded. The ratio is calculated as:

$$\text{quick ratio} = \frac{\text{current assets} - \text{inventories}}{\text{current liabilities}} \quad [2.10]$$

ABC Co.'s quick ratio of 0.80 (£200 million/£250 million) reveals that it has 80 pence of cash, securities, and receivables available to cover accounts payable and short-term loans coming due. It is not unusual for firms to post quick ratios below 1.0, but the closer the result is to 1.0, the greater the liquidity buffer.

SOLVENCY (LEVERAGE/CAPITALIZATION) RATIOS

We've noted in the fundamental accounting equation that solvency is one of the most critical factors that companies must focus on – failure to manage the capital position properly can lead to financial distress and even insolvency, so measuring solvency through appropriate ratios is extremely important.

Financial leverage reflects the amount of debt contained within the capital structure and serves as a key measure of solvency. Note that this concept of leverage is distinct from, but still related to, the concept of operating leverage described above. Its impact on a firm's operations can be measured through various ratios:

- Debt to equity, as the name suggests, compares the amount of debt to the amount of equity in the company's capital structure, and can be computed as:

$$\text{debt to equity} = \frac{\text{total debt}}{\text{total equity}} \quad [2.11]$$

Comparing ABC Co.'s payables, short-term debt, and long-term debt to its equity leads to a ratio of 1.83 (£550 million/£300 million), meaning that ABC Co. has £1.83 of debt for every £1 of equity, which is likely to be considered reasonable for an industrial firm. As we shall discover in Chapter 5, debt is a cheaper form of funding than equity and can help maximize corporate value, but too much debt can threaten financial stability – so, the costs and benefits of leverage have to be carefully considered during the financial planning process.

- Debt to assets is similar to the ratio immediately above, except that the measure focuses on the amount of debt in relation to the entire asset base. It can be computed as:

$$\text{debt to assets} = \frac{\text{total debt}}{\text{total assets}} \qquad [2.12]$$

ABC Co.'s debt to assets ratio amounts to 0.647 (£550 million/£850 million), meaning that nearly 2/3 of its asset base is funded through debt, with the remaining 1/3 coming from equity.

- Interest coverage is an income statement measure of a firm's ability to pay its interest expense. Any use of debt creates an obligation to pay periodic interest, meaning that a firm must have enough earnings on hand to meet the expense. One common way of measuring interest coverage is via:

$$\text{interest coverage} = \frac{\text{EBIT}}{\text{interest expense}} \qquad [2.13]$$

ABC Co.'s interest coverage amounts to 4.5 (£90 million/£20 million), suggesting that the firm has more than four times the level of pre-tax profit needed to meet its obligations. The interest cover measure is often used in conjunction with the measures in [2.11] and [2.12] to indicate how much debt a firm can comfortably support.

Not surprisingly, hundreds of other ratios can be computed, such as those that measure the cash payment cycle, inventory turnover, payables and receivables turnover, asset utilization, and so forth. The central point is that financial ratios provide an important metric by which company managers can track performance and make decisions. They also allow outside stakeholders, including potential investors and lenders, to compare current and past performance, and the overall position versus other competitors in order to make proper capital allocation decisions.

Table 2.2 ABC Co.'s historical, current, and industry ratio data

Ratio	Year t–3	Year t–2	Year t–1	Current year	Industry average
Return on assets	4.40%	4.50%	5.25%	5.76%	6.25%
Return on equity	15.50%	15.87%	16.05%	16.20%	18.20%
Gross margin	20.05%	17.62%	18.75%	19.00%	23.50%
Operating margin	11.12%	9.62%	10.08%	10.76%	11.00%
Net margin	7.79%	7.35%	7.40%	7.54%	8.20%
Current ratio	1.62×	1.68×	1.63×	1.60×	1.20×
Quick ratio	0.79×	0.90×	0.87×	0.80×	0.75×
Debt to equity	1.75×	1.90×	1.87×	1.83×	1.75×
Debt to assets	0.69×	0.68×	0.70×	0.65×	0.58×
Interest coverage	3.75×	3.90×	4.21×	4.50×	3.75×

Let's expand our example across time and against industry peer averages to consider the firm's financial position more closely. Table 2.2 contains the current year ratios (as computed above) along with 3 years of historical data; it also includes the current year industry average ratios for all of the companies operating in ABC Co.'s sector.

These results tell us that ABC Co.'s overall ROA and ROE performance has started to improve, but that it still lags behind the industry average. While ABC Co.'s operating and net margins have improved steadily – to the point where they are coming close to the industry average – its gross margins are still weak. This may indicate that ABC Co. is not charging enough for the goods it sells, or is paying too much for its product inputs (e.g. cost of goods sold). The firm's ROA and ROE underperformance can also be traced back to its very strong liquidity position, which is well above the industry average.

Indeed, the very high current and quick ratios mean that ABC Co. may be holding too much in liquid assets that do not generate much of a return (e.g. £100 million of cash on the balance sheet). However, the firm may be recognizing the problem, as both measures have started to move closer to industry norms. From a capitalization perspective the company's overall debt levels are only slightly above industry averages and have been declining for the past 2 years. Interest coverage is extremely strong, indicating that ABC Co. has managed to secure favorable borrowing levels over time and continues to generate sufficient profits to manage the interest expense.

We can summarize several key points from this simple analysis:

- Profitability is improving but remains below industry averages; difficulties establishing proper pricing of goods being sold and managing cost inputs appear to be the primary problem, along with an excess of non-earning liquid (e.g. cash) assets.
- Liquidity is well above industry norms and can safely be reduced in order to boost earnings.
- Leverage is close to industry norms and has been in a moderate downtrend; the current level of debt is acceptable given the firm's ability to comfortably cover its interest costs.

FINANCIAL STATEMENTS AND DECISION-MAKING

Financial statements are the cornerstone of analysis and decision-making. Examination must take account not only of the statements described above, but of detailed information contained in the "management discussion and analysis" section of the accounts, which can provide vital clues about a company's performance, strategies, and future goals. Footnotes to the financial statements, which form part of the company accounts, must also be reviewed as they provide a much greater level of detail than the high-level accounts.

Decisions taken by a company's financial managers over the short or long term will have an impact on the balance sheet, income statement, and cash flow statement. Let's consider a simple example to illustrate the linkages between statements and the decisions that a financial manager might face. Assume that ABC Co. expects its sales to increase (which we know will have an impact on the income statement). In order to support this increase it must make sure that its cash and inventory are properly synchronized and that it knows how much it may need to borrow to fund the increased amount of sales (both of which are balance sheet items). How might it do so?

Assume that ABC Co. forecasts that sales will increase by £1 million. To support this increase it will need to boost its assets by

60 percent of this amount, or £600,000; this represents the additional inventory needed to produce the greater amount of goods to be sold. Let's further assume that ABC Co. finances 40 percent of the sales increase through accounts payable; this amounts to a £400,000 increase in liabilities. ABC Co.'s net working capital to support £1 million of increased sales is therefore £200,000 (£600,000 – £400,000). If management has a net profit margin requirement equal to 5 percent of sales (i.e. each £1 of sales must generate a minimum profit after expenses and taxes of 5 pence), the company must therefore be prepared to borrow £150,000 (e.g. £200,000 of available net assets less £50,000 of net profit requirement).

Let's consider another simple example based on liquidity management. From a corporate perspective, the process can be monitored and managed through cash budgeting, which involves comparing future cash receipts against cash payments (income statement/cash flow statement items) over specific daily, weekly, or monthly time intervals. The cash budget allows a firm's financial managers to detect any surplus or deficits in a given maturity bucket. Any surpluses can be invested in short-term securities (balance sheet item), while deficits must be funded from the firm's cash account or by drawing down on a credit facility (balance sheet items). Note that the cash budgeting process involves both known receipts/payments and potential "what-if" receipts/payments; the latter act as a form of stress-testing to ensure that the company has enough flexibility to meet unexpected payments. Table 2.3 illustrates a simplified example of ABC Co.'s cash budgeting for the coming year, which links together all three financial statements in a single framework.

There are, of course, other tools that companies can use to help estimate how much cash they should keep on hand to cover an average level of deficits. For instance, the cash turnover method divides annual operating expenses by cash turnover; cash turnover is itself a simple computation of 360 days divided by the number of days between the purchase of raw materials and the collection of cash from sales (i.e. the entire life cycle of a product). For instance, if ABC Co.'s annual operating expenses amount to £200,000 and its cash cycle is estimated at six times (e.g. 360 days/60 days between production and sales receipt), then the

Table 2.3 Cash budgeting framework

	Jan	Feb	Mar	Apr	May	Jun	Jul (...)
Receipts	150	125	140	150	160	170	180
Payments	140	140	140	145	165	175	170
Net	10	–15	0	5	–5	–5	10

Invest in short-term securities

Draw down from cash account or credit line

minimum amount of cash that the company needs to keep on hand to cover deficits is £33,333 (e.g. £200,000/6). In order for ABC Co. to manage its working capital properly, it must be sensitive to the minimum level of cash that it needs to keep and the maximum seasonal cash it may require; accordingly, it can supplement computation of the average annual operating figures with maximum and minimum figures, which will provide a range of sensitivities. The difference between the two can be factored into seasonal short-term financial planning.

Financial statements are clearly vitally important for all stakeholders. But financial managers, investors, and lenders who rely on them to make decisions must remember that the statements are "backward looking." Past trends are obviously important, but the past is history and the future is unknown. Accordingly, to be truly effective the analysis and decision-making process has to factor in forward-looking, "what if" assumptions about what might occur in the future.

CHAPTER SUMMARY

Financial reporting is the process by which a company prepares and presents its accounts. It leads ultimately to the creation of financial statements that allow managers, lenders, investors, and other stakeholders to evaluate a company's financial strength or weakness. Financial reporting is based on the accumulation of all daily transactions that impact a firm's operations, which are posted to ledger accounts. Ledger accounts are used to produce trial statements, and trial statements are eventually converted into externally audited financial statements that are released to the public. Financial reporting is based on accepted accounting principles that add a degree of uniformity; however, various accounting principles allow for some amount of interpretation. The central financial statements include the balance sheet (a "point-in-time" representation of assets, liabilities, and capital), the income statement (a cumulative record of the firm's profits and losses), and the statement of cash flows (a cumulative record of the firm's cash inflows and outflows). These are supplemented by management discussion and analysis and detailed financial footnotes. Various important ratio measures can be drawn from the financial statements, which allow for further analysis and interpretation of a company's financial position, its trend, and its standing versus the competition. Ratios can be computed to determine a firm's profitability, liquidity, and solvency. Financial statements and accompanying ratios are ultimately used by internal parties to help make financial decisions and by external parties to determine the acceptability of committing capital. However, the "backward-looking" nature of the statements must always be recognized.

FURTHER READING

Bragg, S., 2012, *Business Ratios and Formulas*, 3rd edn., Chichester: John Wiley & Sons.

Fridson, M. and Alvarez, F., 2011, *Financial Statement Analysis*, 4th edn., New York: John Wiley & Sons.

Graham, B. and Meredith, S., 1998, *The Interpretation of Financial Statements*, New York: Harper Business.

Horngren, C., Harrison, W., and Oliver, S., 2011, *Accounting*, 9th edn., Upper Saddle River, NJ: Prentice Hall.

Robinson, T. R., van Greuning, H., Henry, E., and Broihahn, M. A., 2012, *International Financial Statement Analysis*, 2nd edn., New York: John Wiley & Sons.

Saudagaran, S. and Smith, M., 2013, *International Accounting: A Users Perspective*, 4th edn., Riverwoods, IL: CCH.

Subramanyam, K. R. and Wild, J., 2013, *Financial Statement Analysis*, 11th edn., New York: McGraw-Hill.

3

FINANCIAL CONCEPTS AND TOOLS

CHAPTER OVERVIEW

In this chapter we consider essential financial concepts and tools that financial managers use to make decisions. We begin with a discussion of risk considerations, including the risk/return trade-off, risk diversification, and the impact of risk on enterprise value maximization. We then describe the general structure of interest rates and stock prices and the determination of cost of capital. We then examine time value of money, including present value and future value, and consider how the time value framework can be used to develop investment decisions rules. The chapter concludes with a brief overview of behavioral finance.

RISK CONSIDERATIONS

As we've noted in Chapter 1, a company operating in a free market environment seeks to deliver goods and services to its customers in a timely, cost-effective, and prudent manner so that it can increase its net income and, ultimately, its enterprise value. However, a company will only be able to do so if it can balance its risks properly. If it takes too much risk, it stands a chance of reducing revenues and/or posting losses. If it takes too little risk, it won't be able to generate sufficient revenues or offer investors a suitable return.

Risk, a reflection of the uncertainty of a future event, comes in many forms, including financial risk, operating risk, and legal risk, among others. Return is the amount that a risk-taker requires in order to accept a particular type and quantity of risk. Both elements are intimately related: the greater the risk, the greater the return that the risk-taker will demand, and the lower the risk, the lower the return that the risk-taker can expect to receive. This is a fundamental tenet of finance that we will revisit throughout the book.

Risk can be measured in various ways. One common method is standard deviation, or the degree to which an outcome deviates from the norm, average, or expectation of a probability distribution (which is simply a graphical representation of the likelihood of occurrence of all possible outcomes across a sample or population). Standard deviation (often denoted by the Greek letter σ) can be computed by adding up the probability-weighted outcomes of the squared differences between expected and actual outcomes and then taking the square root; this is shown by:

$$\text{std dev} = \sqrt{\begin{array}{l}[\text{sum across all observations} \\ (\text{actual observation} - \text{expected observation})^2 \\ \times \text{ probability}]\end{array}} \qquad [3.1]$$

In qualitative terms, we may say that a higher standard deviation means a greater chance that some future outcome will deviate from the average and a lower chance that the expected result will occur. A lower standard deviation, in contrast, means a smaller chance of deviating from the norm and a greater chance that the expected result will occur.

Let us consider a simple example of high and low standard deviations. Table 3.1 illustrates the calculations involved in computing the standard deviations of Project 1 (low risk) and Project 2 (high risk).

Project 2 (with a standard deviation of 7.71), is clearly riskier than Project 1 (which has a standard deviation of only 2.34); this provides very useful information for financial managers considering capital projects or investments with risky characteristics. There are, of course, other ways to measure risk, including variance, covariance, coefficient of variation, and a host of risk-specific models such as value-at-risk, the capital asset pricing model, the factor model, and so forth. We shall discuss a few of these later in the book.

Return is often measured as percentage of the capital invested in, or allocated to, a project or asset; this puts results on an equal footing for comparative purposes. For instance, a 10 percent return means that a company will receive a gain of 10 percent on the amount invested in the risky project. Returns are often computed against a common time horizon to ensure comparability.

Figure 3.1 brings these concepts together: return, as a percentage of capital invested, is depicted on the y-axis, while risk, as the standard deviation of returns, is shown on the x-axis. The upward-sloping line suggests that lower risk projects/investments earn a

Table 3.1 Standard deviations of Projects 1 and 2

Project 1

Actual	Expected	(Actual–expected)	(Actual–expected)^2	Probability	(Actual–expected)^2 × probability
35	40	–5	25	10%	2.5
38	40	–2	4	70%	2.8
41	40	1	1	20%	0.2
					Sum = 5.5
					Std dev = $\sqrt{5.5}$ = 2.34

Project 2

Actual	Expected	(Actual–expected)	(Actual–expected)^2	Probability	(Actual–expected)^2 × probability
30	40	–10	100	20%	20
48	40	8	64	50%	32
45	40	5	25	30%	7.5
					Sum = 59.5
					Std dev = $\sqrt{59.5}$ = 7.71

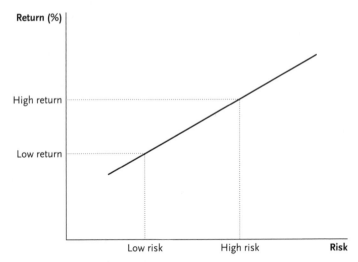

Figure 3.1 Risk and return

lower return, and higher risk projects/investments earn a higher return. This is consistent with the risk/return trade-off mentioned earlier.

It can also be useful to examine expected returns versus risk over time to illustrate how two different projects that provide the same expected return might actually expose a firm to very different risks. These profiles are illustrated in Figure 3.2. While Projects 1 and 2 generate the same average expected return, the standard deviation of the return varies significantly: Project 2 exposes the firm to much greater risk, as the realized return might be much higher, or much lower, than expected. A financial manager facing an investment decision will logically select Project 1: both yield the same returns, but Project 1 does so with less uncertainty. Only when the expected return is higher will the financial manager consider investing in Project 2.

We can also examine the likelihood that the return on a project will approximate the expected return and can do so by focusing on the normal distribution (i.e. the familiar bell-shaped curve), which represents the distribution of all possible outcomes in a population. Given the shape of the curve, we would expect most observations to occur around the average, and a smaller amount

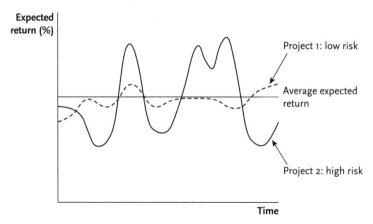

Figure 3.2 High- and low-risk projects

to be above and below; this means that the average has the greatest probability of occurrence. Figure 3.3 illustrates Projects 1 and 2 in terms of statistical distributions. As before, Project 2 features a wider dispersion from the average and is therefore riskier than Project 1. It is important to note that some projects or investments don't follow a normal distribution at all – they may

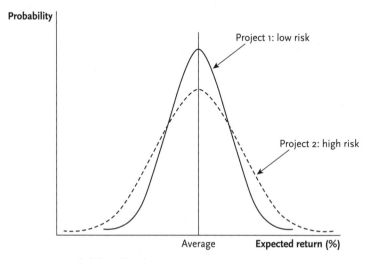

Figure 3.3 Probability distributions

be more properly described by distributions that are skewed or peaked, meaning that assumptions about the likelihood of occurrence necessarily change.

We've already noted that risk/return is a balancing act – a risky project must always provide a greater return than a less risky one if capital is to be allocated optimally. The actual trade-off between risk and return can be measured by the coefficient of variation, which is the standard deviation divided by the expected return. So, if Project 1 and Project 2 each feature an expected return of 10 percent, but Project 2 has a standard deviation of 10 percent and Project 1 has a standard deviation of 5 percent, the coefficient of variation on Project 2 is twice as large as that of Project 1. This, again, makes Project 2 appear less attractive from a risk/return perspective.

We can also use the probability distribution and the concept of expected value to measure the relative appeal of different projects. The future return that ABC Co. can expect to receive on a project or investment is a product of the estimated return and the likelihood that the return will be achieved. Multiplying these two yields the expected value of a project/investment. Consider the hypothetical investments listed in Table 3.2.

Based on these combinations, a company can select investment 1 and, after adjusting for risk, expect to earn 5 percent. Since the probability of the expected return is 100 percent, the investment is essentially risk free. If ABC Co. wants to take more risk, it can choose investment 3, which offers a greater estimated return (9 percent) but injects more uncertainty (e.g. a 30 percent chance that the return won't be realized). The expected value, however, is greater than the expected value of investment 1, meaning the risk/return trade-off is consistent with the relationship illustrated in Figure 3.1. Investment 2, which is also risky, provides an

Table 3.2 Risk/return trade-offs 1

Investment	Estimated return	Probability	Expected value
1 – low risk	5%	100%	5%
2 – middle risk	7%	80%	5.6%
3 – high risk	9%	70%	6.3%

Table 3.3 Risk/return trade-offs 2

Investment	Estimated return	Probability	Expected value
1 – low risk	5%	100%	5%
2 – middle risk	7%	80%	5.6%
3 – high risk	9%	50%	4.5%

"intermediate" opportunity: more risk and return than investment 1, but less risk and return than investment 3.

We are most concerned about a scenario where risk and return appear misbalanced: let's assume that the risk on investment 3 is higher, meaning the probability of obtaining the estimated result is now lower (50 percent). The results, summarized in Table 3.3, show that the risk/return is no longer balanced – a company can invest in risk-free investment 1 and obtain an expected value of 5 percent or invest in risky investment 3 and generate expected value of 4.5 percent. Clearly investment 3 is suboptimal.

RISK DIVERSIFICATION

It is quite common for a company to invest in multiple projects/investments simultaneously. Understanding how each individual project/investment interacts with all others is an important part of the financial evaluation process and can lead to the creation of a properly diversified portfolio of projects/investments. Evaluating the relationship is critical because sometimes risks can increase when two or more projects/investments are combined and sometimes risks can actually decrease.

Let's begin by noting that risks can be classed as diversifiable (sometimes also known as idiosyncratic or specific) and non-diversifiable (systematic or non-specific). A diversifiable risk is a risk that is unique to a project/investment and which can therefore be changed by adding other projects/investments. Importantly, by creating the right mix of projects/investments, the overall risk of the company's portfolio can be reduced – without necessarily reducing the overall expected return. A non-diversifiable risk is a risk common to all projects/investments, meaning it cannot be reduced through diversification.

Projects/investments that are uncorrelated or negatively correlated can help boost returns and/or reduce risk. This happens because, when one project/investment is performing in a certain manner, the other is either remaining neutral (uncorrelated) or performing in the opposite direction (negatively correlated). These relationships can be measured through correlation, a statistical measure that is computed from the covariances and standard deviations of variables a and b (i.e. where a and b are individual projects/investments):

$$\text{correlation} = \frac{\text{cov}(a, b)}{\text{std dev}(a) \times \text{std dev}(b)} \qquad [3.2]$$

Correlation measures the variance of variable a relative to variable b, and reflects the degree to which the two move together: correlation of +1.0 means that the two projects/investments move in lockstep, suggesting that the risk of the two individual projects/investments is additive; correlation of –1.0 means that the two projects/investments move in opposite directions, indicating that the risks offset one another; and, a correlation of 0 means that the two are independent – whatever happens to one project/investment has no bearing on what happens to the other one.

Let's consider a diversifiable risk: if a firm invests in a project that becomes riskier as interest rates rise and another that becomes less risky under the same scenario (i.e. negative correlation), the combination of the two produces a mini-portfolio that is indifferent to the movement of interest rates. By eliminating the risk, more stable returns can be achieved. Conversely, if both react in the same way (i.e. positive correlation), then the firm will either generate a very large return or a very small one – implying a greater degree of variability.

As we might suspect, a non-diversifiable risk is a risk factor that affects all projects/investments equally and thus cannot be reduced or eliminated by adding additional projects/investments. For instance, if all projects/investments are negatively affected if the economy falls into recession, no amount of new projects can be added to reduce the overall risk of a firm's project portfolio.

We can summarize the risk diversification framework by noting that, as more uncorrelated/negatively correlated projects/investments are added to a firm's portfolio, diversifiable risk

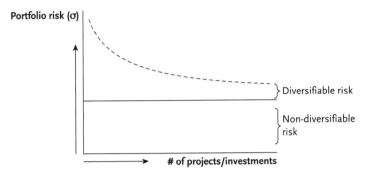

Figure 3.4 Diversifiable and non-diversifiable risks

declines; non-diversifiable risk, in contrast, holds steady, as noted in Figure 3.4.

A key financial concept known as the capital asset pricing model (CAPM) is a logical and important extension of the diversification concept. CAPM is a framework that attempts to relate non-diversifiable risk to the expected return of a security, project, or investment. While CAPM is used primarily with stocks and certain other securities, it can also be applied to projects (though care must be taken in defining an appropriate market benchmark).

The first step in the CAPM framework is to divide risk into diversifiable and non-diversifiable components and assume that there is some relationship between the return of individual assets and the return of the market as a whole (in practice broad market indexes are often used). The next step is to calculate the degree of risk by determining how sensitive asset returns are to market (or index) returns. A stock that moves more than the whole market is riskier than one that moves by less than the market.

This risk sensitivity can be determined by dividing the volatility of a stock's return by the volatility of the market return, which is then multiplied by the correlation between the stock and the market; this yields a result known as the beta of a stock (i.e. the slope of the line between the stock return and market return). A beta greater than 1.0 means the stock is riskier than the market; a beta below 1.0 means the stock is less risky than the market. So, if stock A has a beta of 1.2, we might expect it to rise or fall by 20 percent more than the market; if it has a beta of 0.8 we expect

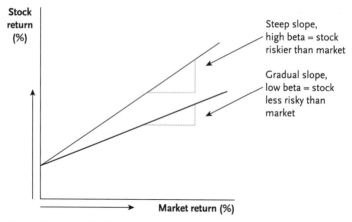

Figure 3.5 A stock's beta

that it would rise or fall by only 80 percent of the market's move. Beta can therefore be viewed as a relative measure of the non-diversifiable risk associated with the returns of a stock, relative to the return of the market index. Figure 3.5 illustrates high- and low-beta stocks.

CAPM states that the actual risk of a stock is equal to a constant (the base risk-free interest rate, which we discuss in the next chapter) plus a market return that is adjusted by beta, along with a minor residual error term:

$$\text{stock return} = {}^{\text{constant} + (\text{beta} \times \text{market return}) +}_{\text{error term}} \qquad [3.3]$$

This is a useful relationship that allows a firm to compare the risk of individual stocks or investment projects against the market as a whole. By doing so, a company can move in the direction of creating an optimal portfolio – one that provides a maximum amount of return for a given level of risk, or a minimum amount of risk for a given level of return.

ENTERPRISE VALUE MAXIMIZATION

Enterprise value maximization is closely related to risk and return. We've outlined the concept of value maximization in Chapter 1 and indicated that, in a free market economy, a company seeks to maximize wealth while complying with various social, legal, and regulatory constraints. This seems like a logical aim. But how does a firm actually accomplish this goal?

The primary way is by using corporate resources as efficiently and effectively as possible. The financial value of a firm is based on its ability to generate net income (or earnings) – the more income the firm produces with a particular base of assets, the greater its worth. Assume that Company X and Company Y have the same base of productive assets: Company X, which can only generate $1 million of earnings every year is worth less than Company Y, which can generate $10 million of earnings every year. So, actions taken to maximize the amount of earnings produced will help maximize the value of the firm – the enterprise value.

The volatility of earnings also plays a role in value determination: the greater the volatility of earnings, the lower the worth of the company, as a strong year might be followed by a weak one. A company with a strong record of stable to steadily growing earnings can be regarded as stronger, and more valuable, than one with an erratic pattern of earnings.

Let's refer back to the income statement described in the last chapter to see how a firm might be able to boost its net income. A company can:

- Increase its revenues while keeping cost of goods sold under control.
- Reduce its selling general and administrative (SG&A) expenses.
- Reduce its interest expense.
- Boost its other operating income and/or reduce its other operating expenses.
- Lower its tax bill.

Each one of these will lead to higher net income, and higher levels of (stable) net income mean greater enterprise value.

Let's also remember that active management of the balance sheet can help achieve similar goals. A company can:

- Lower the amount of debt on its balance sheet.
- Reduce the amount of non-earning assets on the balance sheet (e.g. cash/equivalents).

- Minimize the amount of inventory on hand.
- Invest in project/investments that reduce risk (i.e. are negatively correlated and thus reduce earnings volatility).

Earnings can also be protected through a proper risk management program that ensures that operating inputs and financial risks, as well as productive assets, are not subject to loss or cash flow interruption. Risks can unexpectedly detract from income, which reduces enterprise value. We'll discuss this concept in Chapter 7.

ESSENTIAL TOOLS OF FINANCE

Financial managers use many different tools to make decisions. In this section we consider several of the most important, including the general cost of capital, time value of money, and the investment decision framework.

THE GENERAL COST OF CAPITAL

Every company needs some amount of capital in order to operate. This capital is not, of course, free – a firm must pay to acquire the capital it needs. The actual cost depends on the nature of the funds being raised. Since different forms of capital have different benefits and risks, they each feature a specific cost. This means that a firm must weigh the relative costs and benefits before deciding on the best possible mix.

We begin our discussion with a brief overview of interest rates and stock prices and how they impact a firm's weighted cost of capital – or the average cost of the liabilities and equity that companies need to finance productive assets. We'll expand on the topic when we consider capital-raising instruments in Chapters 4 and 5.

An interest rate can be viewed as the cost of borrowing money, or the amount that can be earned by lending money or depositing funds. The financial markets feature many types of interest rates: government interest rates, private sector (corporate) interest rates, short-term interest rates, long-term interest rates, fixed interest rates, floating interest rates, and so forth. Interest rates are important because they help establish a key part of a company's cost of capital and aid in computing the effect of future cash flows on corporate or investment operations. We'll consider both of these points later in the chapter.

Government interest rates represent a national cost of borrowing via a government treasury or central bank. Highly developed and financially strong nations, such as the USA, the UK, Germany, Switzerland, Japan, Canada, and Australia, among others, borrow money at the lowest possible interest rates since they are considered good credit risks with essentially no likelihood of defaulting (i.e. not paying) on their obligations. We refer to these as risk-free interest rates (r_f). Government rates of less creditworthy nations, such as emerging market nations in Latin America, Eastern Europe, and parts of Asia, are not considered risk free as the likelihood of default is higher; in fact, some emerging nations have a significant history of financial distress and often lack the financial resources needed to avoid debt restructuring or default (see Finance in action 3.1). Lenders providing funds to less creditworthy nations will add a risk premium (r_p) to the risk-free rate to compensate for the additional probability of default. The same applies to corporate borrowing rates: since all companies feature at least some chance of default, they must also pay a risk premium related to their expected probability of default.

FINANCE IN ACTION 3.1:   DEFAULTING SOVEREIGNS

When a country or company can't repay funds that it has borrowed from banks (in the form of loans) or investors (in the form of bonds), it enters a stage of financial distress that can lead to a restructuring or renegotiation of the debt, or to default and bankruptcy filing. We know that companies enter financial distress and default regularly – it is not a particularly unusual event, and can happen to both small, private companies as well as large, public companies (we need only peruse the financial newspapers to note the large number of corporate defaults that have occurred over the years, to wit Marconi, Parmalat, Enron, Tyco, WorldCom, Lehman Brothers, Charter Communications, Dana Corporation, General Motors, Chrysler, British Energy, CIT, Japan Airlines, and a host of others).

We might, however, be surprised to find that countries default with some frequency as well. This might seem curious, as we assume that countries have significant resources – they can generate revenues through taxes and they have the "power of the printing press" and can thus coin money. However, even these solutions have limits: a country cannot tax its citizens and businesses to the extreme without eventually causing an economic slowdown, nor can it print money without creating inflation. Ultimately, some sovereign nations fall victim to excessive debt-financed spending, economic and financial mismanagement, and/or corruption. When this occurs, a country might work with its international bankers to try and restructure outstanding debts. This technically avoids a default, but generates losses for bank lenders and often places the country under economic austerity measures (which tend not to sit well with the local population). In fact, this occurred with a number of countries in the early 1980s, which nearly collapsed under massive debt burdens but were ultimately "rescued" by debt restructuring via international bank lenders – Mexico, Argentina, Brazil, Venezuela, and a host of others were all part of this "near miss," which cost banks tens of billions of dollars. Similar "near misses" happened in South Korea, Thailand, and the Philippines in the aftermath of the Asian Crisis of 1998.

However, not all countries have been able to successfully restructure or renegotiate their debts, and many have thus been forced to declare selective or total defaults on their liabilities; Table 3.4 lists sovereign defaults that have occurred since 1975 on national external debt (hard currency), domestic debt (local currency), or both. This, in most cases, has constrained their ability to borrow in the international markets for a period of up to several years. Not surprisingly, any subsequent return to the capital markets in the aftermath of default is accompanied by a much higher risk premium.

Table 3.4 Sovereign defaults since 1975

Country	Year of default
Albania	1990
Algeria	1991
Angola	1976, 1985, 1992
Argentina	1982, 1989, 2001, 2007, 2014
Belize	2006
Bolivia	1980, 1982, 1986, 1989
Brazil	1983, 1990
Bulgaria	1990

Country	Year of default
Cameroon	2004
Central African Republic	1983
Chile	1983
Costa Rica	1983
Cote d'Ivoire	1983, 2000
Dominican Republic	1982, 2005
Ecuador	1982, 1999, 2008
Egypt	1984
El Salvador	1981
Gabon	1999
Ghana	1982, 1987
Guatemala	1986, 1989
Honduras	1981
Indonesia	1998, 2002
Iran	1992
Iraq	1990
Kenya	1994, 2000
Kuwait	1990
Liberia	1989
Madagascar	2002
Mexico	1986
Morocco	1984, 1987, 1997
Myanmar	1982, 1986, 1992, 2001, 2004
Nicaragua	1983, 1987
Nigeria	1982, 1986, 1992, 2001, 2004
Panama	1986, 2003
Paraguay	1980, 1984, 1985
Peru	1983
Philippines	1981
Poland	1986
Romania	1991, 1998
Russia	2008
Seychelles	1989, 1993
South Africa	1981
Sri Lanka	1982
Turkey	1987, 1990, 2003
Ukraine	1998
Uruguay	1983, 1990, 1995, 1998, 2004
Venezuela	1983
Vietnam	1985
Zambia	1983
Zimbabwe	2000, 2006

Some interest rates, such as government bond rates, are fixed for a particular maturity (e.g. 3, 5, 10, or 30 years). Others are variable (or floating), changing every 1, 3, 6, or 12 months. The London Interbank Offered Rate (LIBOR), for example, is a very widely used floating interest rate that is used as a reference for many kinds of financial contracts (see Finance in action 3.2). Other common floating interest rates include national government treasury bill rates, bankers' acceptance (BA) rates, Euro Overnight Index (EURONIA) rates, and so forth.

FINANCE IN ACTION 3.2:   FROM BBA LIBOR TO ICE LIBOR

LIBOR, which effectively represents the average rate that a major international bank expects to pay for unsecured funds in the London money markets, is the most widely used short-term interest rate reference in the financial markets, and is involved in the pricing of floating rate loans, floating rate notes and bonds, interest rate swaps, deposits, foreign exchange transactions, and even certain kinds of mortgages. Though other important floating interest rates exist, LIBOR is still the king of the hill – being used as the reference in some $10 trillion in loans and $350 trillion in swaps.

The British Bankers' Association (BBA, an industry trade group) has historically been responsible for the daily LIBOR setting, managing the process between 1985 and 2012 for 10 different currencies across 15 different "time buckets" (or maturities) ranging from overnight to 1 year.

Under the BBA regime, the process began every day just before 11 a.m. London time, when eight to 16 BBA-approved contributing banks indicated how much they "believed" they would have to pay for borrowing unsecured funds in "reasonable size" from other banks in a specific currency (e.g. dollars, pounds, euros, yen), for a specific time bucket (e.g. overnight, 1 week, 1 month). The contributions were strictly hypothetical – that is, they weren't based on real funding deals and were thus rather subjective. In addition, the concept of "reasonable size" was never explicitly defined – it could mean millions, tens of millions, or hundreds of millions of a specific currency deposit. Data provider Thomson Reuters gathered the requested rate information between 11 a.m. and 11.20 a.m. London time from the dealing desks of each contributor, vetted the figures, and then performed the relevant calculations for 150 different rates (i.e. 10 currencies with 15 different maturity points). The computation was (and remains) an arithmetic mean that excludes the top and bottom quartiles of all contributed rates. Let's consider a simple example of how 1-month BBA $ LIBOR was set. Table 3.5 highlights the contributions of 16 banks, including the upper and lower discarded quartiles. After the top and bottom quartiles are discarded (reflecting maximum and minimum offer rates of 3.25 percent and 2.85 percent), the remaining eight data points are combined into an arithmetic mean that leads to a 1-month $ LIBOR quote of 2.99 percent. That reference rate would then be used for the business day on any transaction (such as a loan or swap) using 1-month $ LIBOR as a benchmark.

Table 3.5 LIBOR contributor data

Bank	1 month $ offer (%)	
A	3.25	
B	3.20	Upper quartile
C	3.20	discarded
D	3.15	
E	3.05	
F	3.00	
G	3.00	
H	3.00	Middle two quartiles
I	3.00	yield average rate of 2.99%
J	3.00	
K	2.95	
L	2.92	
M	2.90	
N	2.90	Lower quartile
O	2.90	discarded
P	2.85	

After nearly 30 years, the BBA's role in the setting of LIBOR ended in June 2012 when it came to light that some of the banks submitting quotes acted to manipulate rates to their own particular advantage; the violators were sanctioned and forced to pay heavy fines. The first changes to the LIBOR process were enacted following a 2012 review, with the BBA permanently relinquishing its role to the Intercontinental Exchange (ICE), owner of the NYSE Euronext and LIFFE, which became the new administrator. ICE LIBOR, as the benchmark is now known, serves as the "new" LIBOR. While ICE LIBOR is computed for only 5 currencies (USD, EUR, CHF, JPY, GBP) across 7 maturities (yielding 35 data points instead of 150), the topping and tailing of quotes and the arithmetic processes for "reasonable size transactions" noted in the example remain the same. However, ICE-approved quoting banks are now required to indicate with greater precision their borrowing levels by answering the question: "At what rate could you borrow funds, were you to do so by asking for and then accepting interbank offers in a reasonable market size just prior to 11 am London time?" The intent is to get away from hypothetical transactions (subject to "judgment") and closer to real transactions with a more objective grounding – which will hopefully benefit all direct and indirect participants.

Another useful representation of interest rates is found in the yield curve, which maps the cost of borrowing across different time buckets (maturities), from overnight to 30 years (rates beyond 30 years can be obtained, though these are quite rare). Figure 3.6 illustrates a hypothetical yield curve built from rates extending from 1 to 30 years. In a normal market environment the yield curve is upward sloping (positive), meaning short-term rates are lower than long-term rates; this suggests that it costs less to borrow in the short term than over the long term. Yield curves that are flat (short-term rates equal long-term rates) or inverted (short-term rates exceed long-term rates) are rather less common. These states are depicted in Figure 3.7.

What drives the level of rates and the shape of the yield curve? Academic and empirical research points to several possible forces, including expectations, liquidity, and market segmentation. Expectations embedded in the middle and long maturities of a yield curve are simply an expression of the market's belief of what will happen to rates in the future. An upward-sloping curve suggests that the market expects that rates in the future will be higher than they are today. The expectations theory contains a

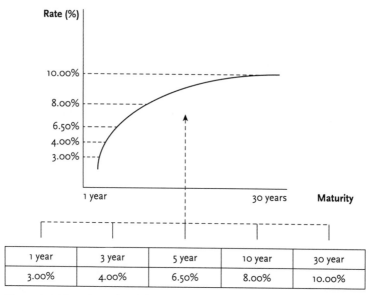

1 year	3 year	5 year	10 year	30 year
3.00%	4.00%	6.50%	8.00%	10.00%

Figure 3.6 Hypothetical yield curve

liquidity preference argument, which indicates that the longer the investment horizon, the greater the chance of default-related losses; accordingly, investors buying long-term securities will require a liquidity premium in order to accept this risk. The market

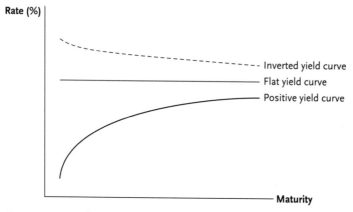

Figure 3.7 Sample yield curves

segmentation theory looks primarily at market structure and the supply/demand forces that exist within different investor groups at different points in the curve.

The second element of capital that we must consider centers on corporate stock. Let's first clarify some terminology: in the USA, Canada, and certain other nations, stock is the name given to equity capital, while in the UK it applies to all manner of securities, particularly bonds and other fixed-income securities; the preferred term in the UK for equity capital is shares. For ease, we shall refer to equity capital as stock.

We recall from our balance sheet discussion that stock is another way to fund a company's assets and, as we might assume, carries an explicit cost. In fact, issuing stock is a cost to the company because investors will only supply capital if they receive a fair return – where the fair return is a function of the perceived risk of the company and its ability to generate value. Since we know that the risk/return trade-off demands proper calibration, we can make two important observations about stock: stock is riskier than debt, and some companies are riskier than others. Let's examine these statements.

In the first instance, stock is riskier than debt, because its function is to absorb losses before debt capital. Consider a situation where ABC Co. has £200 million in stock and £300 million in debt. Assume ABC sustains £150 million in losses as a result of some event. That amount will be subtracted from the firm's stock accounts; in other words, stock investors will absorb the first losses. If the losses are even greater, say £250 million, the capital accounts will be depleted in sequence: the first £200 million will be absorbed by the stock investors, and the remaining £50 million will be borne by the debt holders. Of course, at this stage ABC will be technically insolvent (recalling our accounting equation from Chapter 2), but the point is that creditors will be protected by the stock investors in the first instance. Knowing this, we assume that stock investors will demand a greater return than debt holders – they are, after all, bearing more risk.

Second, companies all have different levels of riskiness. Thus, a well-established, stable, and mature company is generally regarded as less risky than a new, unproven, high-flying company. Since the latter is riskier than the former, stock investors in the high-flyer will demand a greater return on their invested capital than investors in the mature company – they are bearing more risk. In fact, this relationship can be captured via the beta measure described earlier.

All of this leads us to believe that stock, as a form of capital used to fund the balance sheet, will cost more than debt. In addition, stock for a risky company will cost more than stock for a less risky company.

So, how much does equity capital cost? Unfortunately, the answer isn't as tidy as it is for interest rates, and depends on both the nature of the company and the specific valuation technique employed, as we shall see in the next chapter. For now let us note that we have to distinguish between new companies that have never issued stock before, for which a "comparables" analysis is often used (e.g. benchmarking to other competitors) and those that have already issued stock and want to issue more – and for whom the existing stock price is obviously a good indication of cost. In the latter case we may note that the fair price of a stock represents expectations related to the future worth of the firm. In other words, it reflects the discounted amount of earnings that the company is expected to make over a period of time. Investors purchase stock in a company in expectation of receiving a return – either a rise in the stock price (capital gain), a periodic payment (dividend), or both. The value assigned to the stock is therefore the market's collective assessment of such return opportunities. We can therefore use the stock price, as well as information about dividends and growth rates, to come up with the cost of equity capital.

Capital can be raised internally and externally. We recall from the last chapter that a firm's net income, if not paid out as dividends, can be reinvested in productive operations. This is internal capital, reflected in the retained earnings (or retained profits) account, meaning it is a form of equity. External capital comes from outside sources: either lenders or credit investors (in the case of debt – i.e. loans and bonds – which is our topic in Chapter 5), or equity investors (for common and preferred stock, which we cover in Chapter 4). For purposes of our discussion in the rest of this chapter we shall consider the cost of capital to be a generic weighted "average" of a firm's internal and external costs based on equity and debt (computed on an after-tax basis for reasons that we will consider in Chapter 5); we shall separate retained earnings from equity to reinforce the point that this capital is internally generated – though we know in practice that total equity equals retained earnings and common and preferred stock. This weighted average cost of capital (WACC), which includes total capital as the sum of debt, equity, and retained earnings, can be computed as:

$$
\begin{aligned}
\text{WACC} = &\text{ after-tax cost of debt} \times \left(\frac{\text{debt}}{\text{total capital}} \right) \\
&+ \text{cost of equity} \times \left(\frac{\text{equity}}{\text{total capital}} \right) \\
&+ \text{cost of retained earnings} \times \left(\frac{\text{retained earnings}}{\text{total capital}} \right)
\end{aligned}
\qquad [3.4]
$$

Based on this equation, a firm's WACC is a function of both the amount of a particular type of capital in the total capital structure, and the specific cost assigned to that class of capital. It can be used to consider the advisability of investing in one or more projects and of raising an incremental amount of funding for future expansion (i.e. the next dollar, pound, or euro of financing).

Consider a situation where ABC Co. has £100 million in total capital, including £50 million of equity, £25 million of retained earnings, and £25 million of debt. Its cost of equity is 10 percent, its cost of retained earnings is also 10 percent, and its after-tax cost of debt is 5 percent. Based on this information, ABC Co.'s WACC is 8.75 percent. ABC's manager can use this figure to objectively evaluate a series of financing and investing decisions, as noted below.

TIME VALUE OF MONEY

Time value of money is a central tool of financial analysis and decision-making, and in this section we consider its two pillars, present value and future value.

Let us first review some general tenets of money and time as related to inflation and interest. On one side, inflation erodes the purchasing power of money over time: as prices rise, each dollar, pound, or euro buys less. Since most national economies have some persistent amount of core inflation, idle money gradually erodes in value. On the other hand, if an institution puts such money to work in an earning environment for a period of time, it can create value: when interest rates are positive (as they virtually always are), a sum of money invested today will be worth more in the future. By extension, the value of a future sum of money will be lower today than in the future.

Determining a present value (PV, which is today's value) or a future value (FV, which is the value at some future point) requires three inputs:

- The cash flow that is to be paid or received today or in the future.
- The relevant time horizon.
- The proper interest rate, discount rate, or cost of capital – we may consider the terms as interchangeable. We will use the generic cost of debt from our discussion above as the discount rate in the formulas that follow. For a risky company or nation this is, of course, equal to the risk-free rate and risk premium described earlier.

Let's begin with PV. If a company is to receive some cash flow in the future, we know that it will be worth less today than tomorrow because it can always place the cash into an account today that pays interest; when the company withdraws the cash at a future time, it will be worth more. This simple relationship can be captured by the following:

$$PV = \left[\frac{\text{cash flow}}{\left(1 + \text{discount rate}\right)^{\text{time horizon}}} \right] \qquad [3.5]$$

This formula is straightforward and powerful: it reduces the value of a cash flow expected in the future by the discount rate, meaning financial managers can make decisions today using today's discounted cash flows. For instance, the PV of a $1 million cash flow to be received in 1 year when the discount rate is 5 percent is simply:

$$PV = \left[\frac{\$1m}{\left(1 + 0.05\right)^{1}} \right]$$

or $952,380.

We can expand this basic equation in two ways: by adding additional cash flows and by changing the discounting frequency. Each of these is useful in evaluating investments or projects with multiple cash flows over time.

To add more cash flows, we simply sum across the individual cash flows and their relevant time periods via:

$$PV = \text{sum across each time period}$$
$$\left[\frac{\text{cash flow}}{(1 + \text{discount rate})^{\text{time horizon}}} \right] \quad [3.6]$$

So, if we expect to receive $1 million in periods 1 and 2, then the PV (using the same 5 percent discount rate is):

$$PV = \left[\frac{\$1m}{(1 + 0.05)^1} \right] + \left[\frac{\$1m}{(1 + 0.05)^2} \right]$$

or $1,859,409 ($952,380 + $907,029). In other words, $2 million expected in equal $1 million installments over the next two periods is worth approximately $1.86 million today when discounted at a 5 percent rate. Note that a contract that pays equal cash installments over an extended period of time is known as an annuity.

So, what happens if the discount rate is greater than 5 percent? We would intuitively expect the result to be smaller, because dividing by a larger figure yields a smaller result. For instance, if the discount rate is 10 percent instead of 5 percent, the two-period cash flows are now:

$$PV = \left[\frac{\$1m}{(1 + 0.10)^1} \right] + \left[\frac{\$1m}{(1 + 0.10)^2} \right]$$

or $1,735,536 ($909,090 + $826,446); this is $124,000 less than the cash flows discounted at 5 percent. Accordingly, we may say that the larger the discount rate the greater the discounted cash flows, and the lower the resulting PVs. This is an important fact that we will revisit when we discuss risky debt in Chapter 5; we will see that risky cash flows have a higher discount rate, leading to smaller PVs.

What if the cash flows occur twice in a single period (e.g. every 6 months instead of every year)? We can make the formula above more generic by including a factor that takes account of the frequency of payments, as follows:

PV = sum across each time period

$$\left[\frac{\left(\dfrac{\text{cash flow}}{\text{fractional period}} \right)}{\left(1 + \dfrac{\text{discount rate}}{\text{fractional period}} \right)^{\frac{\text{time horizon}}{\text{fractional period}}}} \right] \qquad [3.7]$$

If we assume from the example above that the $1 million of cash flows for each of two periods is actually paid as $500,000 over four periods (e.g. semi-annual instead of annual), and the annual discount rate is 5 percent, the PV is:

$$PV = \left[\frac{\$500,000}{(1 + 0.025)^{\frac{1}{2}}} \right] + \left[\frac{\$500,000}{(1 + 0.025)^{\frac{2}{2}}} \right]$$
$$+ \left[\frac{\$500,000}{(1 + 0.025)^{\frac{3}{2}}} \right] + \left[\frac{\$500,000}{(1 + 0.025)^{\frac{4}{2}}} \right]$$

or $1,939,394 ($493,864 + $487,804 + $481,819 + $475,907). Note that this PV result is greater than the one in the single-period payment immediately above ($1,859,409) because it assumes that, as the $500,000 payments are received each period, they are reinvested at the same discount rate.

As the fractional period gets smaller and smaller (e.g. quarterly, monthly, weekly, daily) we can condense the process by deriving the continuously compounded cash flow as an exponential function (exp, which we take as the natural exponent constant 2.718); this is equal to instantaneous discounting, and can be computed via:

PV = cash flow x exp (–discount rate x time horizon)   [3.8]

For instance, a single $1 million payment to be received in 2 years is worth $904,837 today when discounted continuously at 5 percent. We can, of course, add multiple cash flows together, as in the examples above.

We can also consider the special case of the perpetuity, which is simply a fixed cash flow that is paid forever (e.g. as in an endowment fund or perpetual bond). Its value can be estimated through a simplification of the PV formula above:

$$PV = \left[\frac{\text{cash flow}}{\text{discount rate}} \right] \qquad [3.9]$$

For instance, a perpetuity might pay $100,000 per annum. If the discount rate is 5 percent, the PV of the perpetual stream is:

$$PV = \frac{\$100,000}{0.05}$$

or $2 million. If the discount rate is 10 percent, the PV is $1 million. It is important to remember that, while a perpetuity exists forever, the most distant cash flows reduce the present value to a very small amount.

The reverse of the PV calculation is, of course, the FV calculation, which tells a company how much a series of cash flows will be worth in the future. If a company invests some amount of cash today, it will be worth more in the future. This means that it must now multiply, or compound, the current cash flow by some appropriate rate over the relevant time horizon, and can do so via:

$$FV = \text{cash flow} \left(1 + \text{discount rate}\right)^{\text{time horizon}} \qquad [3.10]$$

For example, a $1 million sum invested today, for 1 year, at an annual discount rate of 5 percent is equal to:

$$FV = \$1m(1 + 0.05)^1$$

or $1,050,000. Similarly, if the discount rate is increased to 10 percent, the FV rises to $1,100,000. This makes intuitive, as well as mathematical, sense, since the higher the return on a cash flow invested today, the greater will be the future value of that cash flow.

The FV of multiple cash flows received over time again requires summation:

$$FV = \text{sum across each time period}$$
$$\left[\text{cash flow} \left(1 + \text{discount rate}\right)^{\text{time horizon}} \right] \qquad [3.11]$$

Thus, $1 million of cash flows to be received in periods 1 and 2 when the discount rate is 5 percent yields an FV of:

$$FV = \$1m(1 + 0.05)^1 + \$1m(1 + 0.05)^2$$

or $2,1525,000 ($1,050,000 + $1,1025,000).

When cash flows are invested in fractional periods we can again introduce a fractional multiplier process, as in [3.12]:

FV = sum across each time period

$$
\left[\frac{\text{cash flow}}{\text{fractional period}} \left(1 + \frac{\text{discount rate}}{\text{fractional period}} \right)^{\frac{\text{time horizon}}{\text{fractional period}}} \right] \qquad [3.12]
$$

So, $1 million received over two semi-annual periods (i.e. cash flow of $500,000 per period) rather than a single annual period, with an annual rate of 5 percent, yields an FV of:

$$
FV = \$500,000 \left(1 + \frac{0.05}{2} \right)^{\frac{1}{2}} + \$500,000 \left(1 + \frac{0.05}{2} \right)^{\frac{2}{2}}
$$

or $1,018,711 ($506,211 + $512,500).

Using the logic above, we can summarize the generalized future value of a continuously compounded cash flow as:

FV = cash flow x exp (discount rate x time horizon)   [3.13]

Again, $1 million compounded continuously at 5 percent for 2 years yields an FV of $1,105,170.

Understanding the logic and intuition of time value of money is very important, as the framework is fundamental to many financial decisions.

INVESTMENT DECISIONS

Financial managers seeking to optimally allocate scarce resources must be able to make rational financial decisions during the financial planning phase. Net present value (NPV) gives managers a measure by which to evaluate multiple projects or investments. The NPV equation, which builds on the time value concepts we have just mentioned, takes an extra step by including initial costs or capital investment.

We know from the section above that a productive project (investment) will yield cash flows over its life, and these can be discounted to provide a PV estimate. In order to receive the benefit of such future cash flows, a company must typically invest some amount of capital. This initial investment is a cost to the firm and leads to the creation of a simple NPV equation which embeds both costs and benefits. We may express this through:

NPV = – investment + sum across each time period

$$\left[\frac{\text{cash flow}}{(1 + \text{discount rate})^{\text{time horizon}}}\right] \qquad [3.14]$$

The initial investment is not discounted by the discount rate because it is made today. Of course, if the project requires interim investment or maintenance costs, these can be subtracted from the positive cash flows directly (i.e. the periodic cash flow is net of additional costs paid). Consider, for instance, a firm that has an opportunity to invest in a simple three-period project that costs $5 million and yields equal annual cash flows of $3.5 million. If the firm's cost of capital is 10 percent, the NPV of the project is:

$$NPV = -\$5m + \left(\frac{\$3.5m}{(1.10)^1} + \frac{\$3.5m}{(1.10)^2} + \frac{\$3.5m}{(1.10)^3}\right)$$

or $3,704,000 (e.g. $8,704,000–$5,000,000). Let's now assume that the firm can also decide to invest in another project, which costs $7.5 million but generates $3.75 million per year for 4 years. Which project is better? The NPV approach allows an examination of the two on an equal basis:

$$NPV = -\$7.5m + \left(\frac{\$3.75m}{(1.10)^1} + \frac{\$3.75m}{(1.10)^2} + \frac{\$3.75m}{(1.10)^3} + \frac{\$3.75m}{(1.10)^4}\right)$$

This yields an NPV of $4,386,000, suggesting that the second project is the preferred investment. Alternatively, a company can use the NPV framework to identify projects that meet some minimum rate of return, or hurdle rate. This can be done by computing an internal rate of return (IRR), which is simply the cost of capital that forces the NPV to zero. Converting the example immediately above into the IRR framework yields the following equation:

$$0 = -\$7.5m + \left(\frac{\$3.75m}{(1+x)^1} + \frac{\$3.75m}{(1+x)^2} + \frac{\$3.75m}{(1+x)^3} + \frac{\$3.75m}{(1+x)^4}\right)$$

Table 3.6 Sample projects, NPVs, and IRRs

Project	Horizon (years)	NPV	IRR
1	3	$5m	8.50%
2	3	$6.5m	8.75%
3	5	$5.5m	4.50%
4	4	$6m	9.75%
5	5	$7.25m	9.00%
6	5	$7m	8.75%
7	3	$6.5m	8.80%

In this case the firm solves for x, or IRR, to find whether the minimum return meets an internal hurdle rate set by management. In this example the IRR is 10 percent. This framework is particularly useful for comparing among several competing projects, all of which demand an investment of the firm's capital. Even though all feature positive NPVs, the IRR rule lets a company make an objective decision. For instance, if a company is presented with the projects noted in Table 3.6, Project 4 appears to be the superior alternative.

When a project's IRR is greater than the cost of capital, the company achieves a higher return than it is paying for its capital, meaning that investment in the project is sensible and value-creating. When IRR is less than the cost of capital, the company does better not to invest its capital in the project, as doing so would be value-destroying. By defining a master IRR curve, such as the one illustrated in Figure 3.8, a company can create an entire relationship of NPVs and acceptance/rejection decisions.

A firm may assign a different cost of capital to each one of its investment projects, or it may use a blended cost of capital (i.e. the WACC). Individual cost of capital may be selected when projects have unique characteristics, such as long maturities, special risks, and so forth; this approach can lead to more accurate decisions as project profitability won't be overstated or understated. A blended WACC approach may be suitable when a firm's investments are largely uniform and no individual project features unusual risks or characteristics.

We can refine the process described above to make it even more realistic. Every time a company raises funds to invest or expand,

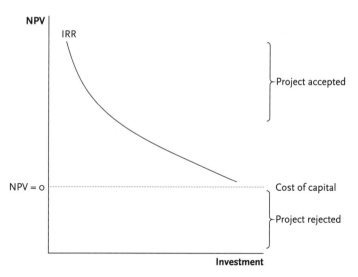

Figure 3.8 IRR, NPV, and decision rules

its marginal cost of capital rises; capital is scarce and the limited supply leads to a higher cost for each increment raised. Therefore, if we are considering each incremental dollar, pound, or euro of investment, we shouldn't look only at the WACC. We must examine decisions in light of the weighted marginal cost of capital (WMCC), which is an upward-sloping function (i.e. marginal cost increases with each incremental amount of capital raised). Figure 3.9 replicates Figure 3.8 with a WMCC curve (rather than a constant cost of capital or WACC curve); we notice in this illustration that the acceptance region for projects becomes smaller, meaning that a firm will have to find projects with a higher IRR in order to satisfy an increasing cost of capital.

EXTERNAL FORCES AND FINANCIAL DECISIONS

While our discussion above focuses on internal issues, we must not forget our comments from Chapter 1: a firm doesn't operate in isolation, meaning it is impacted by external market forces that must be considered when applying financial concepts and tools to decision-making. It's easy to imagine that the current and

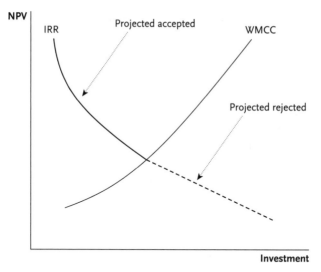

Figure 3.9 IRR, NPV, and WMCC

anticipated state of the economy, the level of interest rates and inflation, the size and direction of essential capital flows, and the nature of competition and regulation can all play a part in shaping a company's fortunes. The decision-making process must therefore take account of these external variables.

Consider one very simple example: ABC Co. wants to invest in a new project that will expand capacity. Its initial decision on whether to invest will be based on various internal concepts (motivations, optimal financial structure) and its quantitative evaluation of the opportunity (WACC, NPV decision rules). However, if ABC Co. is acting prudently, it must also consider how the expansion will affect, and be affected by, the outside environment. If the economy is in recession and expected to stay that way for several more quarters, it may be prudent to delay the project. If inflation is accelerating and ABC Co.'s costs of production are set to rise in tandem, the profit margins on the new production may be squeezed to the point where the investment is no longer compelling. Or, if the economy is strong and interest rates are at a low point in the cycle it may be sensible to proceed to lock in a low cost of capital for future capital investment. These forces may have a bearing on ABC Co.'s ultimate success/failure with the project and need to be considered during the decision-making phase.

BEHAVIORAL FINANCE

Much of finance, and much of what we discuss in this book, is based on financial theory and some of the rules, methods, and tools we have described. This approach is well established and, though it relies on certain assumptions, has proven to be quite useful over time. However, it is also important to consider the important subclass of behavioral finance, which moves from a framework of standardized measurement based on rational and optimal behaviors to one that is infused with psychology and the realities of human "emotion" and market "irrationality."

More specifically, behavioral finance deals with the actions and psychology of investors and companies when they must deal with the realities of a real-world environment – abandoning the safety of "rational" actions, efficient markets, and optimal decision-making. The subclass attempts to overlay emotions and cognitive biases (i.e. any deviation from normal behavior) onto the actions that drive financial decisions and determine how such decisions may then affect the financial markets. While standard financial (and economic) theories focus on efficient markets and rational behavior, behavioral finance explores the fact that markets may not be efficient and that the behaviors of individuals and companies are often "irrational." A small sampling of some key areas of study includes:

- Excessive discounting, or the desire by investors and companies to prefer immediate payoffs to those appearing in the future (which appears to grow stronger, the closer the payoffs are to the present time).
- Overconfidence/undue pessimism, or the excessive response by investors and companies to positive or negative news (e.g. euphoric buying, panic selling).
- Loss aversion, or the reluctance by investors and companies to sell losing investments or abandon money-losing capital projects.

- Herding, or the influence of group feedback, euphoric buying and panic selling on financial activities and markets.
- Money illusion, or the tendency of investors and companies to make decisions on the basis of the nominal value, rather than the purchasing power value, of money.
- Selective perception, or the tendency for expectations to influence or affect perception and, thus, decision-making of investors and companies.

Many other cognitive biases exist. While studies in behavioral finance are relatively recent (with some academic work appearing in the 1980s but more serious attention, including mathematical models, arriving in the new millennium), the field appears to have much to add to the overall financial framework.

CHAPTER SUMMARY

Financial decision-makers require a set of concepts and tools in order to make reasoned decisions. Risk is central to any discussion of financial decision-making. Risk must always be weighed against potential return in order to strike a proper balance. An investment or project that carries a greater degree of risk, as measured by standard deviation (or the variation of actual outcomes from an expected value), must feature a greater return than a similar project with a lower degree of risk. In order to properly manage overall risks, the effects of adding multiple investments or projects to a portfolio must be considered; this process is known as risk diversification. Positively correlated investments/projects can create incremental risk, while those that are negatively correlated can reduce risk. Enterprise value can be managed by understanding the impact of risk, inputs, and outputs on corporate operations. Firms that feature either low absolute earnings or high earnings volatility are likely to be worth less than those with high absolute earnings or low earnings volatility. The cost of capital is an essential element of the financial decision process, reflecting the cost to the firm of raising capital to fund the asset side of the balance sheet. Cost of capital can be segregated broadly into cost of debt and cost of equity. Combining the proper proportions of each component in the firm's capital structure yields a weighted average cost of capital. The time value of money is another central building block of finance. Present value reflects the value today of cash flows to be generated in the future; such cash flows are discounted back to the present by a company's cost of capital (or discount rate). Future value reflects the value, at some point in the future, of a stream of cash flows; the cash flows compound at a rate determined by the cost of capital (discount rate). Net present value is an associated decision rule that allows evaluation of cash investment (outflows) and receipts (inflows) on a project or investment; internal rate of return is the cost of capital that forces the NPV computation to zero. Behavioral finance, a blend of finance and cognitive biases, focuses on the fact that not all financial decisions occur under optimal conditions and that financial participants are influenced by a range of factors that may lead to seemingly "irrational" behaviors.

FURTHER READING

Brigham, E. and Ehrhardt, M., 2008, *Financial Management: Theory and Practice*, 12th edn., Mason, OH: Thomson Higher Education.

Emery, D., Finnerty, J., and Stowe, J., 2012, *Corporate Financial Management*, 4th edn., Upper Saddle River, NJ: Prentice Hall.

Forbes, W., 2009, *Behavioural Finance*, London: John Wiley & Sons.

Higgins, R., 2011, *Analysis for Financial Management*, 10th edn., New York: McGraw Hill.

P A R T

INSTRUMENTS
AND TRANSACTIONS

4

COMMON AND PREFERRED STOCK

CHAPTER OVERVIEW

In this chapter we consider common and preferred stock (alternatively, ordinary and preference shares), which together constitute equity capital, the first of two major classes of external corporate financing. We commence with a review of why and how stock is used, the relative costs and benefits of borrowing through the equity markets, and the trade-offs that exist between using too much and too little equity financing. We then analyze dividend policy and the forces that determine equity costs and share values. We conclude the chapter by describing the characteristics of major classes of stock and how the instruments are issued and traded. The material in this chapter should be compared and contrasted with the debt financing discussed in the next chapter.

USES OF COMMON AND PREFERRED STOCK

As we've seen in Part I, a company exists to provide its customers with goods and services while simultaneously creating a profitable business that builds wealth for the proprietors (owners). The actual ownership structure of a firm can take various forms. For instance, a firm can be founded as a sole proprietorship (single owner), a partnership (several partners serving as owners), or a corporation (many investors serving as owners). The corporate structure provides the greatest amount of flexibility, because it allows a firm to raise a much larger amount of capital, it provides for continuity over time, and it shields the owners from unlimited liability. Let's explore each of these characteristics before considering the particulars of common and preferred stock.

First, a firm constituted as a corporation can raise a greater amount of capital as it will have access to the public capital markets, where the pool of investment capital is substantial. Proprietorships and partnerships tend to rely on informal sources of funding (e.g. bank loans, revolving credit lines, government grants, personal resources), meaning that capital access is quite restricted. This capital restriction invariably constrains growth. Second, a corporation is not identified with a single individual or group since it features large and diffuse ownership. In fact, it is intended to exist as a perpetual entity. Proprietorships and partnerships do not necessarily provide the same continuity: they often rely on a few individuals to guide the business, and their outlook may be threatened if one or more of the key individuals departs. This can ultimately lead to an unwinding of the structure. Third, corporations convey the right of limited liability, meaning that owners of a corporation's shares are not liable for more than the amount they have invested. Partnerships and proprietorships, in contrast, follow the tenet of unlimited liability: owners and partners are responsible and liable for debts that they incur on behalf of their organizations and must repay claims from personal assets if insufficient funds exist within the business.

The initial issuance of shares by a company to investors occurs once all approvals have been obtained and the board of directors (external professionals charged with independently representing investor interests) and an executive management team are in place. This issuance, which we discuss later in the chapter, is the essential capital-raising effort that allows a corporation to sell to investors transferable interests representing pro-rata ownership of its operations. This equity capital becomes a permanent form of financing on the company's balance sheet, providing a continuous source of funds. Subsequent share issuance can also be arranged, providing the company with additional equity capital.

Each share issued to investors represents an ownership interest in the company, conveying legal and rent rights. The legal rights entitle the investor to vote on issues that are important to the continuing success of the company (e.g. selection of board directors) and to receive periodic audited financial statements. The rent rights (or economic rights) entitle the investor to a share in the profits of the company. These profits can be conveyed via dividends (i.e. a periodic fixed or discretionary payment), or capital appreciation (i.e. a rise in the share price), or both. Shares can be issued as common (ordinary) stock or preferred (preference) stock: common stock investors have the right to vote and a right to a share in the earnings, but must bear the first losses; preferred stock investors receive first right to dividends but cannot vote, though they are protected from losses by common stock investors. We will focus our discussion on common stock in the section below, which is the most widely used form of external equity financing.

Let's assume that ABC Co., currently a partnership, wants to increase the scope of its operations, and can only do so by expanding beyond the partnership stage. It decides to incorporate and sell shares to investors through a public stock offering of £200 million. In doing so, the firm specifies a par value for its shares, which becomes part of the accounting treatment of the stock after flotation. So, if ABC Co. selects £1 of par value for each share, it can issue up to 200 million of shares. After the initial public offering (IPO) is completed, ABC Co., as an enduring corporation with limited liability, will have a capital base of £200 million, which it can use to meet all of the objectives cited above.

As ABC Co. conducts its operations over the coming years, it will (hopefully) begin to generate profits. These profits can be used in two ways (once expenses and taxes have been paid). First, after-tax income can be used to pay equity investors – the new owners of the company – a dividend. Corporations regularly pay dividends, which represent a disbursable profit, to common (and preferred) stock investors. But common stock dividend payments are discretionary, rather than mandatory, meaning that a company's board of directors can choose not to pay them if it believes that the funds can be put to better use. Second, after-tax income can be reinvested in the company, so that additional productive resources can be acquired to produce more goods and services.

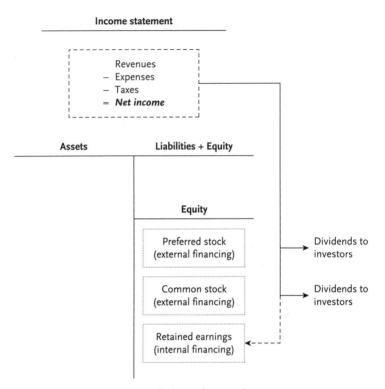

Figure 4.1 Income statement, balance sheet, and net income

This happens by leaving a portion of the profits undistributed – preserving them in an account that is aptly named retained earnings (or retained profits). As we've noted in Chapter 2, retained earnings form part of the equity account on the corporate balance sheet. Importantly, retained earnings represent an internally generated source of financing (unlike the issuance of equity, which is an external source of financing).

The decision on what to do with after-tax profits is based on achieving the highest possible return for the owners of ABC Co. shares. If ABC Co.'s management can invest in additional productive endeavors that generate an internal rate of return equal to, or better than, some benchmark, then it may choose to retain most of its earnings and pay only a modest amount (if any) in the form of dividends. Figure 4.1 highlights a simple income statement and balance sheet that reflect the flow of net income on the external and internal equity financing accounts.

DIVIDEND POLICY

Investors buying stock often expect to receive dividends as part of their risk compensation. Some prefer investing in the stocks of companies that pay very high dividends, while others are content to buy those that pay lower dividends, under the assumption that income not paid in the form of dividends will be profitably reinvested in the firm, which will lead ultimately to a higher share price. Since dividends are, in some sense, a representation of a company's ability to generate earnings, they impact the value of a company's shares. Dividends also affect a company's investing and financing plans. For instance, a company that insists on paying very high dividends will have less internal funds available to pay for new projects or corporate expansion, and may require external financing – which can alter its capital structure and cost of capital, as we'll see in the next chapter.

Financial managers must craft a sensible dividend policy during the financial planning stage. Finance features competing theories on optimal dividend policies. One theory (put forth by economists Modigliani and Miller) suggests that the value of a firm isn't actually impacted by dividend policy. The reasoning is as follows: since dividends are residual payments, they don't form part of the investment decision of a firm and generate no earnings. The cost of capital and the level of earnings therefore don't change when dividend policy changes. A rational firm will reinvest all of its retained earnings as long as the return on investments is greater than the return that can be obtained in the market. However, this theory is put forth under a series of rather restrictive assumptions (e.g. no taxes, or a regime where capital gains taxes are less than ordinary income taxes, no friction costs, perfect capital markets).

Another theory indicates that the value of the firm is, indeed, affected by its selection of a dividend policy. This approach doesn't rely on any specific assumptions apart from the fact that investors assign greater value to current cash dividends than future cash flows obtained from reinvested retained earnings. Payment of cash dividends can thus lead to lower investor uncertainty, which lowers risk and the cost of capital. Importantly, dividend payments can also serve as a signaling device: if investors believe a company intends to pay dividends at a constant or gradually increasing rate over time, they will have greater comfort that future earnings will be strong; the reverse is also true, of course. Either path will have an impact on share price.

In practice, a company that has predictable earnings growth is more likely to pay a higher portion of its earnings out in the form of dividends. But a high payout doesn't imply earnings stability. A company may pay a large amount of its current earnings in dividends in order to attract investors, but may also suffer from volatile earnings that can jeopardize its ability to deliver future dividends. In fact, investors view companies that cut their dividends in an unfavorable light, and may sell their shares. A prudent dividend policy therefore requires directors and executives of a firm to determine future earnings growth and analyze sensitivity to changing market circumstances and economic cycles.

EQUITY CAPITAL COSTS AND SHARE VALUATION

We've already noted that risk/return is the fundamental trade-off of the financial world. Investors who seek a greater return must be willing to accept a greater amount of risk; those preferring a smaller amount of risk can expect a smaller return. A company arranging financing faces the same trade-off: if it is funding through an instrument that generates more risk for investors, it will have to pay them a greater return than if it uses a less risky instrument. This relationship is central in determining a firm's capital costs and optimal financing mix.

Below we'll see how these trade-offs relate to a company's funding. First, however, let's consider the position that investors in ABC Co.'s new shares have in the company's capital structure. The capital provided by equity investors and the retained earnings which are rightly theirs as owners of the company are used as a buffer to protect all other forms of financing that rank above it, including the preferred stock issues that we discuss below, as well as bond and loan financing that we consider in the next chapter. In effect, equity investors are the first to bear losses should the worst come to pass – though only to the extent of their original investment. We recall that the equity accounts of the balance sheet comprise paid-in capital and retained earnings. If ABC Co. experiences financial difficulties that generate large losses, it begins to deplete these accounts. If ABC Co.'s losses are so large that it completely drains these equity accounts, it will file for bankruptcy and investors with claims that rank higher than the equity claims will be repaid first. When all of ABC Co.'s assets of value are liquidated and outstanding claims are repaid, the residual amount left for the common equity investors may only amount to a fraction of the original invested value – if anything at all.

Why would an investor be interested in bearing this first loss risk? Why not sit "higher up" in the capital structure where there is more protection against losses and a greater chance of a larger recovery if the worst happens? The answer, of course, is the desire to earn a higher return. In order to entice investors to supply capital through shares, the company will have to offer a return that compensates for the risk of bearing the first losses. Some investors are willing to accept the increased level of risk associated with stock if they believe they are being appropriately compensated. We can therefore view the common stock buyer as a limited liability investor, with voting power, who receives a higher return than other capital suppliers in order to compensate for any "first losses" that might occur. We must also bear in mind that the higher cost of equity capital – what we might call the equity risk premium – must also compensate for time: an equity security is a perpetual instrument that never matures. Accordingly, the probability that an investor may one day bear some degree of loss is higher than it is on a security with a finite maturity. Finally, we must note that in many jurisdictions investors are taxed on their dividend income. In order to entice investors to commit equity capital, a company must make the after-tax return sufficiently attractive, generally through a "gross-up" of the dividend payment – which adds to the cost of equity.

So, how much does equity capital cost? How much will ABC Co. have to offer investors in order to raise the type of permanent financing that it needs to fund its operations? The answer depends on various external and internal factors. It also depends on whether ABC Co. is raising equity for the first time (via an IPO) or tapping the market for additional equity (via a secondary offering or rights issue). We'll focus our discussion on the latter scenario for the time being.

Let's start with external factors. Market supply of, and demand for, equity capital influences the cost of equity for all firms. When investors believe that the market provides a proper equity risk/return, they will be inclined to participate. This means that liquidity flows into the market and the overall cost of equity declines (but bearing in mind that costs for individual firms may still be higher or lower than the overall market, depending on the internal factors noted below). The opposite scenario also holds true. If investors don't believe that equity prices correctly reflect risk, they will withhold their capital, causing a supply shortage that leads ultimately to a rise in overall equity financing costs. Companies that want to issue stock will have to entice investors to supply funds and will only be able to do so by offering them greater returns (i.e. selling stock at a cheaper price, which means a higher cost of financing).

Internal company-specific factors play an equally important role in establishing equity costs. Once market forces establish the minimum expected equity return, the ability of a company to generate earnings that create value (via dividends and capital appreciation) helps define the actual cost of accessing equity capital. A risky company that has uncertain earnings-generation power will have to pay more for its capital than one that has a stable, gradually expanding, earnings stream. If a company regularly misses its earnings targets because it cannot properly control its revenues or costs, then investors will view this as an extra risk that demands compensation; this additional compensation is obviously a cost to the company, which will be reflected in the premium over the market return paid to attract investor capital. Naturally, other financial variables can impact the stability of the company and negatively affect the perceived riskiness of the firm. The opposite is also true: a firm that is able to manage its business and financial position properly will enjoy a lower equity risk premium.

Though exogenous and endogenous forces clearly impact costs, actually estimating the cost of equity capital can be a complicated endeavor. One method is to use a form of the capital asset pricing model (CAPM) that we described in the last chapter as a risk value proxy. Remember, we are attempting to estimate the cost of equity capital for a single company, and this will be influenced by the external and internal variables described above. We know that beta is a measure of a company's riskiness versus the market at large. Accordingly, the cost of equity can be set as a function of beta, the risk-free rate and the market return:

cost of equity = risk – free rate +

$$\text{beta}(\text{market return} - \text{risk-free rate}) \qquad [4.1]$$

For instance, if ABC Co.'s beta is 1.25, the market return is 10 percent, and the risk-free rate is 4 percent, ABC Co.'s estimated cost of equity capital – the return that investors will demand for holding ABC Co.'s equity – is 11.50 percent. While this approach is widely used and perfectly valid, it obviously requires comfort with the assumptions underlying CAPM.

Our discussion has centered on the cost of equity for a company that has issued stock in the past. Such a company has a track record of performance in the market so that its stock price, beta, and dividend record are all known and can figure as the necessary inputs. For companies embarking on an IPO, that track record is clearly not available, meaning that alternate measures must be used to provide a stock valuation and, by extension, a cost of equity. One common approach is comparables analysis (or relative valuation), where the target company and its bankers identify a group of peer companies already trading in the market, take key indicators from each one of these peers as a multiple to current stock prices (net earnings, earnings before interest and taxes, sales, and so forth), compute the average of those peer multiples, and then apply the multiples to the base of the ratio of the target company; the end result is an estimate of the pre-IPO company's stock price, which can be used to obtain the cost of equity. Though not perfect, it can serve as a useful proxy measure.

While most of the cost of equity financing is covered by the external and internal variables noted above, a company still needs to pay its bankers for arranging a transaction. Bankers arranging new or secondary issues are responsible for coordinating the entire process and charge fees for doing so. In fact, the fees payable by a company for an equity issue can be significant, ranging in most markets from 1 to 5 percent. This, as we'll see in the next chapter, is relatively expensive and adds considerably to an issuer's total funding expense. Fees must always be factored in to obtain a true cost of equity.

We have intentionally focused on externally generated equity in our discussion. However, we must not forget that retained earnings are a form of equity and also involve a cost. Though there are no fees associated with retained earnings since they are generated by post-tax/post-dividend income, they attract a cost of capital that is generally set equal to the cost of common stock. Naturally, a firm does not face a single cost of equity capital: common and preferred stock, for instance, draw different costs because they have different risk and return characteristics. We can generalize overall costs by noting that a company faces a cost hierarchy defined as follows:

cost of common stock, cost of retained earnings >
cost of preferred stock > cost of debt   [4.2]

This relationship holds true because of claims seniority in the capital structure and the order in which losses are allocated.

Once a company has issued equity, it is useful to consider its current and projected theoretical value. This provides an indication of whether a stock is undervalued ("cheap"), overvalued ("rich") or fairly valued. Various models are available to help determine share value. We can refer to at least two major (and somewhat related) approaches: dividend-based models and cash flow-based models.

Dividend-based models require information on dividends in order to produce a valuation. As we've noted, dividends are paid from after-tax earnings, meaning that they generate no tax advantage, which we'll discuss in more detail in the next chapter. The dividend yield of a security, computed by dividing the current dividend by the current stock price, is an important measure of the current return of an equity security, allowing investors to compare returns across companies and industry sectors. Similarly, the dividend payout ratio, computed by dividing dividends per share by earnings per share, indicates how much of a company's net earnings are going to investors rather than the retained earnings account. Of course, estimating dividends is not a precise science, since the exercise involves unknown future cash flows and subjective decision-making by directors. Nevertheless, some estimates have to be made in order to produce a fair value. One convenient measure, commonly used in the models discussed below, is the dividend growth rate, computed via:

$$\text{growth} = \frac{\text{net income}}{\text{equity}} \left[1 - \left(\frac{\text{dividends per share}}{\text{earnings per share}} \right) \right] \qquad [4.3]$$

We may note that the growth rate is a function of both return on equity (net income/equity) and the dividend payout ratio (dividends/earnings).

Let's begin our dividend share valuation analysis with preferred stock, the simplest of the equity claims. Preferred stock is an equity-like security that gives the investor a fixed dividend payment stream in perpetuity; this means valuation of the security is quite simple: the future dividend cash flows are contractually fixed, and there is no need to take account of the redemption value of the principal, as the security is never redeemed. So, if we assume that a share of preferred stock pays a periodic dividend (quarterly, semi-annually, or annually), the value of a share of stock is simply the present value of the dividend stream in perpetuity, discounted by the firm's cost of preferred equity:

$$
\begin{aligned}
\text{price of preferred stock} = {} & \frac{\text{dividends}}{\left(1 + \text{cost of preferred}\right)^{\text{time 1}}} \\
& + \frac{\text{dividends}}{\left(1 + \text{cost of preferred}\right)^{\text{time 2}}} \qquad [4.4] \\
& + \frac{\text{dividends n}}{\left(1 + \text{cost of preferred}\right)^{\text{time n}}} \\
\Rightarrow {} & \frac{\text{dividends}}{\text{cost of preferred}}
\end{aligned}
$$

For instance, if we assume that ABC Co.'s cost of preferred equity has been estimated at 15 percent and a share of its preferred stock pays an annual dividend of £2.50/share, the fair price of the preferred is £16.67/share. This formula also suggests that, as the dividend rises, the value of the preferred increases, and vice versa – a perfectly logical relationship. Thus, if the annual dividend is amended to £3.50/share, the price of the preferred rises to £23.33/share; if it declines to £1.50/share, the price of the preferred falls to £10/share.

We can adapt the same general approach in valuing a share of common stock. Common stock, like preferred stock, will never be redeemed, so there is no need to account for the present value of the redemption amount. Unlike preferreds, however, a company's common stock may not always pay dividends. And, if a company does pay dividends, those payments are likely to change over time. To take account of these unique characteristics, we can use one of several approaches, including the discrete dividend model, the constant growth dividend model, and the growing dividend model, some of which rely on the growth computation in [4.3]. Regardless of the method used, we recall that the cost of common equity used to discount common dividend cash flows is higher than the cost of preferred equity used to discount preferred dividend cash flows, since common stock is riskier than preferred stock.

Valuing a share of stock based on discrete dividends, or individual dividend payments that can vary from period to period, requires a precise estimate of how much a company will pay in each period. Once the estimate for each future period is determined, the dividend flows are simply discounted back using the cost of common equity and summed up to create an estimate of the value:

$$
\text{price of common stock} = \frac{\text{dividends 1}}{\left(1 + \text{cost of common}\right)^{\text{time 1}}}
$$
$$
+ \frac{\text{dividends 2}}{\left(1 + \text{cost of common}\right)^{\text{time 2}}} \qquad [4.5]
$$
$$
+ \ldots + \frac{\text{dividends n}}{\left(1 + \text{cost of common}\right)^{\text{time n}}}
$$

For instance, an analyst might estimate ABC Co.'s annual dividends over the next 5 years at £1, £1.50, £1.50, £2, and £2.25 per share. If ABC Co.'s cost of common equity is 20 percent, then the estimated price of common stock is equal to £4.60. Of course this is a simplified example, because we only include five periods, when we know that a company is intended to exist in perpetuity. We can easily imagine that, as we add more periods to the computation, the present value of the dividend flows will translate into a higher stock price, even though estimates of more distant dividend payments are necessarily less precise (and discount to a smaller figure). To overcome this, we can make use of terminal value, a concept we discuss below.

When the dividend on a common stock is assumed to be constant, with no growth, we can adjust the formula slightly:

$$\text{price of common stock} = \frac{\text{dividends}}{\text{cost of common}} \qquad [4.6]$$

This is much simpler, as it makes no assumption about potential dividends in each individual period. Thus, if ABC Co. is expected to pay £2 per share in dividends forever and its cost of common equity is 20 percent, the fair price of each share is £10. Similarly, if we assume that a dividend will be paid based on a defined growth rate (as exemplified in [4.3]), we can use the following:

$$\text{price of common stock} = \frac{\text{dividends}}{(\text{cost of common} - \text{growth rate})} \qquad [4.7]$$

Let's assume that ABC Co.'s cost of common equity is 20 percent, its current dividend is £2/share, and the expected dividend growth rate is 3 percent. The fair value of ABC Co.'s common stock under the constant dividend growth model is £11.76. Under this scheme it is relatively easy to deduce that, if earnings increase and dividends expand in tandem, the cost of equity capital will decline. This finding is consistent with our earlier statement: companies with a stronger base of earnings and growth are perceived as less risky than those with weak and/or volatile earnings, meaning that the returns payable to investors are lower.

The second major stream of valuation focuses on cash flow models. Of course, this suite of techniques is also related to the dividend framework above, since dividends are paid from cash flows (as described in Chapter 2). As above, stock valuation can be computed on the basis of both discrete cash flows and constantly growing cash flows (CF). For instance, the price of common stock can be estimated through a forward estimate of a company's cash flows over time:

$$\text{price of common stock} = \frac{\text{CF1}}{\left(1 + \text{cost of common}\right)^{\text{time 1}}}$$
$$+ \frac{\text{CF2}}{\left(1 + \text{cost of common}\right)^{\text{time 2}}} \qquad [4.8]$$
$$+ \dots \Rightarrow \frac{\text{CFn}}{\left(\text{cost of common}\right)^{\text{time}}}$$

Naturally, putting together reliable estimates is difficult after a certain number of periods (e.g. several years). Accordingly, a slight refinement adds to the periodic cash flow estimates a "lump sum" estimate of terminal value, which can itself be determined via a liquidation value (e.g. an estimate of the proceeds generated through the disposal of a company's assets) or multiple value (e.g. an estimate based on applying a multiple to earnings or revenues based on market comparables). Note that the same process can be applied in the dividend model above.

A further alternative that we can consider is similar to [4.7] above, where we assume a constant growth rate. This is shown as:

$$\text{price of common stock} = \frac{\text{cash flows}}{\left(\text{cost of common} - \text{growth}\right)} \qquad [4.9]$$

A hybrid model combines [4.8] and [4.9], with estimates of discrete cash flows for the first 3–5 years, followed by a constant cash flow growth rate thereafter. Finally, we may note that a variation on the two frameworks described above, known as an earnings-based model, can also be used to obtain stock values. Such an approach is consistent with what we have already described, except that earnings, rather than dividends or cash flows, feature as the central valuation variable.

INSTRUMENT CHARACTERISTICS

As we've noted, equity comes in various forms, each with unique characteristics. In this section we consider essential features of the main types of external equity instruments, which are summarized in Figure 4.2.

KEY CHARACTERISTICS

Common and preferred stock issues are defined by a number of characteristics, each negotiated in advance of flotation. These include size, dividend, maturity, placement mechanism, market, and seniority.

- Size: the amount of stock being placed with investors. This can range from less than $1 million (or equivalent in sterling,

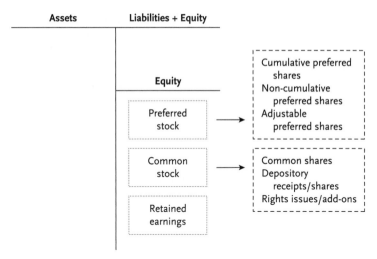

Figure 4.2 Equity accounts on the corporate balance sheet

euros, yen, and so forth) to well over $1 billion, depending on the issuing company, its needs, investor appetite, and market conditions. ABC Co., for example, may wish to issue £200 million in common stock and £100 million in preferred stock as part of its overall financing plan.

- Dividend: the specific dividend being paid for a given series of shares. This applies primarily to preferred stock issues, which may feature a fixed or variable dividend payable on a cumulative or non-cumulative basis; as we've noted, common stock features no contractual dividend payment. ABC Co., for instance, may pay an annualized dividend of 7 percent every quarter on its preferred stock issue, which becomes a contractual characteristic of the security.
- Maturity: the specific term of the issue. This is quite an exceptional characteristic, and relates only to a small number of preferred stock issues with redemption features. In all other cases, i.e. common stock issues and conventional preferred stock issues, the securities are perpetual and can only be retired or redeemed through a specific repurchase mechanism.
- Placement mechanism: the manner in which securities are placed with investors. Inaugural issues of stock form part of

the IPO mechanism, meaning that the securities are registered and can be offered to a broad range of investors. Any subsequent issues (e.g. secondary placements) may be offered as rights issues (to existing investors) or add-on issues (to all investors). ABC Co., in floating its initial common stock offering, arranges the transaction as an IPO; any subsequent share offering that it may arrange can be done as a rights offering or an add-on issue.

- Market: the specific marketplace being accessed. This applies primarily to common stock, which may be issued in the domestic (onshore or home) market, where funds are raised from resident investors, or the international (offshore) market, where funds are raised from non-resident investors. Non-resident offerings can be arranged through euro-equity issues and global depository receipts (which we discuss in the next section). The selection of a market depends on various factors, including cost (i.e. where a company can issue stock on the best terms), availability (i.e. which pools of investors are willing to supply capital), and overall market conditions (i.e. where market stability (or volatility) may attract (or repel) capital). Since ABC Co. is UK-based and is well known to UK investors, it may choose to float sterling-denominated common and preferred shares in the domestic market.

- Seniority: the priority of the stock regarding claims on the issuing company's assets. The seniority of shares dictates the priority of payments to equity holders, should a company declare bankruptcy. While all forms of debt rank senior to equity (as we shall discuss in more detail in Chapter 5), we have already noted that preferred stock ranks above common stock.

KEY INSTRUMENTS

The key instruments of the equity sector include:

- Common stock: this can be issued in the local market to meet the demand of local investors or it can be floated in the offshore markets in order to attract a base of international investors. Common stock is typically issued as a scripless (dematerialized) ownership interest with a stated par value; it is a perpetual security that can pay dividends, though is not contractually obliged to do so. Non-resident issues can be made in various forms. Euro-equity issues are securities issued in multiple markets simultaneously, in relevant currencies (e.g. a sterling tranche for the UK, a dollar tranche for the US, a euro tranche for the Continent). Depository receipts (global or American) are securities that are issued by a depository on behalf of the issuing company; the company lodges shares with the depository, which then issues tradable receipts to investors (with each receipt typically representing a single share). Subsequent issues offered to the market at large are known as add-ons.

- Rights issues: these are secondary placements of stock that are offered initially to existing shareholders, giving them the right of first refusal to invest in the new shares; the rights allow existing investors to control dilution, or the diminishing of legal and rent rights through the addition of new investors, by exercising the rights to take up new shares (generally at some discount to the prevailing market price); existing investors can retain the same proportion of ownership and control, meaning that they are not specifically diluted.

- Preferred stock: this is a security that pays investors a periodic dividend and does not generally permit any participation in capital gains (i.e. its price is quoted in a relatively narrow range). The dividends established for a preferred stock can be structured in various ways. Cumulative preferred stock, for instance, accumulates dividends that are due to preferred investors in cases where the company is unable to make a current dividend payment; no other dividends can be paid to other equity investors until these dividend arrears have been settled. The non-cumulative structure, in contrast, does not provide for dividend accrual; if a dividend is skipped, non-cumulative investors have no continuing claim on that dividend.

ISSUING AND TRADING
ISSUING

Before any stock issue can be launched in the market, it must receive the approval of the relevant national securities commissioner or regulator. Once this occurs, the stock issue becomes known as "authorized." When a company decides to issue a certain amount of stock, the actual shares that are floated are known as "authorized and issued"; these become part of a company's permanent capital base. In practice, a company generally only issues a portion of its shares initially so that it can preserve additional capacity for future issues. Any additional capacity is shown as a note on the financial statements as stock that is "authorized but not issued." The equity account is not impacted, as shares that have not been floated obviously raise no funds; still, investors are alerted to the fact that future issuance may occur. For example, the national regulator may approve up to £1 billion of shares, but ABC Co. may elect to float only £200 million, leaving an "authorized but not issued" balance of £800 million. In some cases a company may decide to repurchase some of its outstanding stock issue because it believes that it is overcapitalized and cannot find profitable opportunities to use the capital; repurchased shares are known as treasury stock. It can do so by buying them in the open market for cash; when this happens, the treasury stock contra-account is adjusted by the amount of the repurchase. Shares in this account are known as "issued and not outstanding." For instance, ABC Co. may decide to repurchase £50 million of its shares, causing its common stock base to decline by that amount. We summarize these states of the common stock account in Figure 4.3.

Raising equity capital begins when the issuing company and its bank establish necessary equity financing requirements, prepare detailed preliminary disclosure (known as a "red herring" or "pathfinder prospectus") and register the proposed issue with the national securities regulator. Once the regulator approves the disclosure, the bank begins a pre-marketing phase to determine investor appetite and potential pricing levels; this process involves a detailed analysis of where the stock prices of comparable companies are trading and ultimately dictates the company's cost of equity capital. The final price of the shares is established on launch date, and securities are placed with investors based on an allocation method determined by the lead bank.

In most instances a bank arranging a stock issue is not required to deliver a specific amount of funds to the issuing company. Thus, if ABC Co. seeks £200 million of common stock but

Paid-in capital account	
Authorized and not issued (1 billion shares at £1 par value)	—
Authorized and issued (200 million shares at £1 par value)	£200 million
Issued and not outstanding (50 million shares)	−£50 million
Total paid-in capital account	£150 million

Figure 4.3 Impact of shares on paid-in capital

investors are only interested in purchasing £150 million at the quoted price, the company only receives £150 million. However, in some instances (mainly add-ons or rights issues), a bank may agree to purchase the entire block of £200 million at a fixed price, and then distribute the shares to investors. These "block trades" ensure that companies like ABC Co. receive the full amount of equity they are seeking – but are relatively risky for the arranging bank, because the price may fall before the bank can place all of the shares. In order to protect itself from any possible losses, the bank generally purchases the block at a discount to the prevailing market price.

SECONDARY TRADING

Major banks and securities dealers actively quote prices on a range of small and large capitalization stocks on a continuous basis. Dealers provide bids and offers on individual issues, allowing investors to enter or exit the market once an issue has been launched. An investor can buy a stock ("go long") to take advantage of an increase in stock prices, or it can borrow the stock and sell it ("go short" or "short sell") to try and profit from a fall in stock prices (to close the short, the investor will buy the stock back and return it to the lender). The prices that dealers are willing to quote are based on the macro and micro variables that we've discussed. If these factors are favorable or benign, dealers will be willing to quote tighter bid–offer spreads than if they are unfavorable or volatile. For instance, if the market environment is positive and the outlook for ABC Co.'s earning is strong, a dealer may quote shares at £10.00–10.02, meaning that it stands ready to buy a share at £10 and sell the same share at £10.02, making a profit of £0.02 in the process. Conversely, if the markets are volatile, investors are nervous, or ABC Co.'s earnings prospects are weakening, the dealer may widen the spread to £10.00–10.07; the wider spread is intended to compensate the dealer for the additional risk taken in owning the shares.

A significant amount of secondary equity trading still occurs through conventional exchanges, such as the London Stock Exchange, New York Stock Exchange Euronext (NYSE, owned by the Intercontinental Exchange), Deutsche Boerse, Tokyo Stock Exchange, and National Association of Securities Dealers Automated Quotations (NASDAQ), among many others. Most conduct trading electronically rather than physically; in fact, among major exchanges, the NYSE is the only one that still features a physical trading floor – though it also supports electronic trading and makes full use of advanced technologies. The advent of computing power and advanced networking, along with changing regulations, has led to the creation of many electronic trading platforms, some of which have taken market share from traditional exchanges and forced them to change their own business models (see Finance in action 4.1).

FINANCE IN ACTION 4.1:   EVOLUTION OF ELECTRONIC TRADING

The world of stock trading has changed dramatically over the years: gone are the days when brokers and specialists would meet physically on the floor of an exchange to buy and sell stocks on behalf of clients or for their own accounts. Today's markets are driven almost exclusively by electronic, off-exchange trading platforms. Many of these are still constituted as exchanges, but they lack the physical trading floors that we are used to seeing on television – all buying and selling occurs through electronic input and routing of orders, which are matched through centralized engines.

Electronic stock trading in the USA dates back to 1969, when Instinet (then known as the Institutional Network) was created as an electronic platform to automatically match large buy and sell orders.

NASDAQ was created in 1971, as an all-electronic, quote-driven marketplace based on a system of market-makers; NASDAQ rose to power by listing stocks of many high technology companies, such as Microsoft, Apple, Google, and EBay. Even the "granddaddy" of the US exchanges, the NYSE, which was originally founded as a physical, order-driven, auction-based market composed of specialists, entered the electronic sphere in the early 1970s with its DOT computerized order router, which allowed it to pass orders electronically from members down to the trading post for execution by specialists. In the late 1970s Instinet introduced the first electronic trading "montage" screen, showing quotes on NYSE stocks. ITG's POSIT (Portfolio System for Institutional Trading) emerged as another pioneering platform in the late 1970s, matching block trades electronically away from the exchanges on a scheduled basis.

Further electronic development followed in the 1980s. Large broker/dealers like Merrill Lynch, Goldman Sachs, and Morgan Stanley began trading stocks internally, matching orders from their clients against each other, or against positions from their own trading books – all of this was done electronically, away from traditional exchange floors. After-hours trading through electronic platforms emerged in 1986 via Instinet's pioneering platform, which made it possible for investors to trade large capitalization stocks after official market close (4 p.m.).

Naturally, electronic efforts of this period were not confined to the US markets, but were also emerging in other markets. For instance, Paris Bourse (now part of the combined NYSE Euronext), developed a leading-edge electronic trading platform for the French stock market as early as 1989, which they eventually licensed to various other global exchanges. Most other major European exchanges, such as the London Stock Exchange, Swiss Stock Exchange, and Deutsche Boerse, converted their trading operations into pure electronic open order books during the 1990s. Much the same happened in Asia, with exchanges such as the Tokyo Stock Exchange, Osaka Stock Exchange, Hong Kong Stock Exchange, and Singapore Exchange conducting dealing through computerized networks.

Though advances were clearly occurring in electronic trading during the late 1980s and early 1990s, it was not until the late 1990s and the early part of the millennium – as technology, communications, and networking took a quantum leap forward – that so-called alternative trading systems (ATSs) emerged as a viable force. This was especially evident in the US markets, which embraced new electronic trading platforms like Island, Archipelago, Brut, Tradebook, and RediBook. The rising stock global stock market (built largely on the dot-com/Internet wave), lower execution costs, and the popularization of electronic day trading helped fuel interest and growth. The expansion process continued throughout the decade, with new venues such as BATS, DirectEdge, and a host of other "dark pools" (which we consider separately) taking significant market shares from NYSE and NASDAQ. In response, the big exchanges started to create more sophisticated electronic ventures, in part by purchasing some of the upstarts. The same phenomenon appeared in Europe through so-called electronic multilateral trading facilities (MTFs), which were created in the second half of the first decade. It is safe to say that the days of physical trading are now well behind us – technology has created a new business model for trading of stocks.

While most secondary trading in stocks occurs in a visible manner through the exchanges and platforms we have described, more than 20 percent of all volume now takes place "in the dark," through so-called "dark pools" (see Finance in action 4.2). Dark pools are an increasingly important factor in the trading world, as they permit a great deal of confidentiality, which helps large buyers and sellers of stock improve their execution prices. The flip side, of course, means that there is less certainty surrounding the price discovery process.

FINANCE IN ACTION 4.2:   DARK POOLS

The "dark pool" is quickly becoming an integral part of the traded financial markets of the twenty-first century. So, what is the mysterious sounding dark pool?

Quite simply, a dark pool is a venue or mechanism that contains anonymous, non-displayed trading liquidity that is available for execution.

Anonymous, non-displayed trading liquidity is order flow that is submitted by an investor or trader confidentially and is not visible to the market at large; that is, it does not appear in public order books, like those operated by exchanges. The fact that the flow is not visible has given rise to the term "dark" liquidity.

A venue is any electronic platform that is either solely or partly involved in housing non-displayed liquidity.

A mechanism is any structure within an exchange, or any participant in the market, that houses non-displayed liquidity.

Execution is the ability to buy or sell a security through the submission of an order.

So, we may summarize by saying that a dark pool is an amalgam of orders to buy or sell securities, but whose existence is not publicly known or advertised. In practice, dark trading occurs through dedicated platforms called crossing networks (or price reference systems), which use prices set by exchanges to confidentially match buyers and sellers, and via hidden orders (totally dark orders) and reserve orders (partly dark, partly visible orders) that are embedded in exchanges or in electronic platforms. So, why is dark-pool trading so important? Costs savings and potential price improvement are important factors, but confidentiality, which leads to reduced market impact, is the real driving force.

Let us consider the case of an institutional investor that is thinking about buying a large block (100,000 shares) of ABC Co. It seems reasonable to assume that, if this buying interest is generally known in the marketplace, other investors might try and jump ahead of the investor to buy the same stock – effectively pushing up the price of the stock in the process, and creating a market impact – or unfavorable price movement – for the investor. If, however, the investor can confidentially purchase the stock before anyone is aware of the action, it is likely to be able to do so without moving the price of the stock – thus avoiding a market impact. Dark pools allow shares to be traded confidentially, meaning that sensitive information doesn't fall into the hands of competitors or others who might have an interest in such details.

Consensus research appears to indicate that more than 40 percent of all trades in the USA are executed through dark pools. While volume in Europe and Asia trails the USA, with some 10 percent and 5 percent, respectively, the same growth trends exist. Various research estimates predict that further migration to dark trading will occur globally in the coming years.

CHAPTER SUMMARY

Every firm established as a corporation must have some amount of stock on its balance sheet, suggesting that equity finance via preferred and common stock is an essential component of corporate financing. The cost of equity capital is higher than that of debt capital for three reasons: first, equity investors accept greater risk than debt holders, bearing the first losses if a firm becomes insolvent; second, equity does not generate the same tax-shield as debt, because dividends are paid from after-tax, rather than pre-tax, income; and, third, investors are often taxed on the dividends they receive, meaning that they will need to be enticed through a higher dividend return in order to be willing to invest in the stock. Determining the proper amount of equity to use in funding the balance sheet is important: too little equity means too much debt, which can lead to financial distress. However, too much equity can prove expensive and may result in the rejection of investment projects that might otherwise be appropriate when financed through cheaper forms of capital. The cost of a company's equity is based on market and company factors; the overall level of market returns, the risk-free rate, and the specific characteristics of the company itself all influence cost. Valuation models exist to estimate the value of a company's stock – these are based on estimates of current and future dividends or cash flows. Common and preferred stock can be issued in various forms and are defined by key characteristics that include deal size, placement mechanism, dividend, market, and, for certain classes of preferred, maturity. An active secondary market exists for many forms of equity. A significant amount of equity trading now occurs electronically, away from traditional exchanges, and some is conducted "in the dark" rather than in a visible manner.

FURTHER READING

Damodaran, A., 1996, *Damodaran on Valuation*, 2nd edn., New York: John Wiley & Sons.

Edwards, R. and Magee, J., 2012, *Technical Analysis of Stock Trends*, 10th edn., Boca Raton, FL: CRC Press.

Graham, B. and Dodd, D., 2008, *Security Analysis*, 6th edn., New York: McGraw-Hill.

Harris, L., 2002, *Trading and Exchanges*, Oxford: Oxford University Press.

Koller, T., Goedhart, M., and Wessels, D., 2010, *Valuation*, 5th edn., New York: John Wiley & Sons.

Malkiel, B., 2015, *A Random Walk Down Wall Street*, 11th edn., New York: W.W. Norton.

Stimes, P., 2008, *Equity Valuation, Risk and Investment*, London: John Wiley & Sons.

5

LOANS AND BONDS

CHAPTER OVERVIEW

In this chapter we examine loans and bonds, which together constitute debt capital, the second major class of external corporate financing. We commence with a review of why and how loans and bonds are used, the relative costs and benefits of borrowing through the debt markets, and the trade-offs that exist between using too much and too little debt financing. We then consider the macro and micro forces that drive borrowing costs, and describe the characteristics of loans and bonds, and how they are created and traded; we conclude by introducing an example of the popular, and somewhat more complex, securitization structure. The concepts of debt financing covered in this chapter should be compared and contrasted with the equity financing material discussed in Chapter 4.

USES OF LOANS AND BONDS

In our last chapter we noted how equity can be used to fund the corporate balance sheet. While equity is obviously essential to any financial plan, it is not the sole source of funding. In fact, the availability of debt capital is critically important to companies attempting to maximize enterprise value, as we shall discover.

We've already seen that ABC Co. can use the equity markets to meet its financing requirements. But we also know that equity can be expensive. Since investors in ABC Co.'s common shares bear the risk of first losses, they will demand a higher return on their invested capital. The higher return to investors is, of course, reflected in a higher overall cost of capital for ABC Co. We have also indicated that in some markets equity dividends aren't tax deductible, meaning that they are paid from after-tax, rather than pre-tax, income. This also adds to the company's cost of capital, because in order to persuade an investor to buy the dividend-paying shares, the pre-tax cost of funding has to be increased to reflect the additional tax burden.

What ABC Co. really needs is another financing alternative so that it can lower its capital costs and allocate more of its income to retained earnings or dividends. Fortunately, the company can turn to the loan and bond markets to finance a significant portion of its operations, generally at a much lower cost; in fact, debt can be up to several percentage points cheaper than equity, and cost savings can lead ultimately to an increase in enterprise value.

We recall that ABC Co. can issue equity in the market for the equivalent of 11.5 percent, so that each £100 million that it has to raise for its operations costs £11.5 million. If ABC Co.'s total assets amount to £1 billion, total financing costs through equity add up to £115 million. But, what if ABC Co.'s treasurer found that the company could raise debt at a cost of only 5 percent? Ignoring present value calculations, that's a saving of £6.5 million for every £100 million raised. If ABC Co. decided to do the majority of its funding (i.e., 99.9 percent) in the form of debt rather than equity, its total financing cost would amount to just under £50 million – a compelling saving versus the cost of equity financing. In fact, this saving is one of the key reasons why companies used loans and bonds so actively.

Such big savings might bring to mind two questions: why is debt so much cheaper than equity? And, if it is so cheap, doesn't this mean that the financing decision is relatively easy – all debt and no equity?

Let's start with the first question. Debt financing is cheaper than equity financing for two reasons. First, debt is an "IOU," or corporate promise to repay a lender or investor any amount borrowed, plus interest, in the future; debt may take the form of a payable or loan, or it may be issued in standard tradable form as a security. Debt holders are therefore creditors, while equity investors are owners. In fact, unsecured debt holders have no ownership claim on a firm's assets because they are not owners. In order to protect against this lack of ownership claim and ensure equitable treatment in the event of default and bankruptcy, most legal systems give debt holders payment priority over equity investors. This means that, if a company files for bankruptcy, assets with value are used to repay debt holders first (the actual order of claims priorities within the debt capital structure varies, as we'll discuss later). Because of this bankruptcy claim priority, debt holders bear less risk than equity investors, and we already know that lower-risk investments command lower returns. This translates into a lower cost of financing for the company.

Second is the fact that interest expense used to pay debt holders for the use of their capital is tax deductible. That is, interest expense is paid from operating revenues, before taxable income is computed. This deductibility generates what is commonly known as a tax shield. Equity dividends generally aren't tax deductible and therefore don't create the same shield. Let's consider the simplified income statements in Table 5.1 to demonstrate the tax effect of debt and equity financing. The debt-financed income statement carries £10,000 of interest expense, while the equity-financed income statement features £10,000 of dividend expense.

Table 5.1 Debt- and equity-financed income statements

Debt-financed income statement, 000s		Equity-financed income statement, 000s	
Revenues	£200	Revenues	£200
Cost of goods sold	−£100	Cost of goods sold	−£100
Gross profit	= £100	Gross profit	= £100
Interest expense	−£10	Interest expense	−£0
Pre-tax profit	= £90	Pre-tax profit	= £100
Tax at 20%	−£18	Tax at 20%	−£20
After-tax profit	= £72	After-tax profit	= £80
Dividends	−0	Dividends	−£10
Net profit to retained earnings	= £72	Net profit to retained earnings	= £70

We immediately note that the equity-financed income statement features a higher tax bill since no interest expense is incurred and no tax shield is generated; the debt-financed income statement, in contrast, creates an extra £2,000 of retained earnings through the shield.

We see, then, that the cost of debt must be adjusted to reflect the tax benefit, helping generate an after-tax cost that is lower than the cost of equity. This can be calculated as:

$$\text{after-tax cost of debt} = (1 - \text{tax rate}) \times \text{cost of debt} \qquad [5.1]$$

Thus, if ABC Co.'s borrowing rate on a loan is 7 percent and its tax rate is 27.5 percent, its effective after-tax cost of debt is just over 5 percent. Again, this is a significant saving compared to the 11.5 percent that it is paying for its equity capital.

This brings us back to our second question. If debt is relatively inexpensive compared to equity, it seems that ABC Co.'s treasurer has a simple decision: issue as much debt as possible so that financing costs are as small as possible. Unfortunately, the answer is not this easy. While too much equity can be extremely expensive, too much debt can create significant financial burdens. A company that borrows creates a fixed charge (or debt service), because the borrowing commits it contractually to paying interest and principal on a pre-set schedule. The company must make these agreed payments if it wants to avoid default. This means a portion of every dollar, pound, or euro earned has to be earmarked for this fixed charge, which reduces the company's financial and operating flexibility (i.e., no longer can it do precisely what it wishes to do with its revenues and income). The same obligation doesn't exist with equity, since common stock dividends are discretionary.

Too much debt can therefore lead to an excessive burden on operating revenues and reduce corporate flexibility; it can also lead to more volatile earnings, as noted below. In fact, the burden can become so large that a company can enter into a state of financial distress, where the likelihood of bankruptcy rises dramatically. Knowing this, we can conclude that there must be some point where too much debt and too little equity becomes suboptimal. In practice the best mix of debt and equity on a company's balance sheet depends on its business, expansion plans, investment opportunities, relative debt and equity financing costs, and tax rates. Debt/equity levels also vary by industry. Credit rating agencies, which independently analyze and rate companies, and bank lenders monitor the debt levels of companies and industries, and tend to penalize those that stray too far from industry norms or those that cannot handle the financial burden.

FINANCIAL LEVERAGE

As we've noted, leverage is the magnification of a profit or loss based on the structure of a company's operations and financials. We have considered the concept of operating leverage in Chapter 2 and now turn to its cousin, financial leverage, to describe the magnification of profit or loss created through the use of debt. During the financial planning process a company can determine the proper amount of debt to use by examining the degree to which debt can be safely employed to finance investment and operations. We know that interest cost generates a tax shield as well as an interest burden, so a company attempting to optimize debt capital must consider earnings before interest and taxes (EBIT) and earnings per share (EPS). Let's examine a very simplified example based on ABC Co.'s capital structure in two forms – unleveraged and leveraged. Table 5.2 contains sample data.

The degree of financial leverage can be computed via a simple formula:

$$\text{financial leverage} = \text{EBIT}/(\text{EBIT} - \text{interest expense}) \qquad [5.2]$$

The unleveraged ABC Co. has financial leverage equal to 1.0, while a leveraged ABC Co. has financial leverage of 1.087. This means that, for every unit increase in EBIT, unleveraged ABC Co.'s net income increases by 1 unit, while leveraged ABC Co.'s net income increases by 1.087 units. Unfortunately, the reverse holds true for every unit decline: the leveraged ABC Co.'s net income falls by 1.087 instead of just 1.0. The magnification on the upside and downside is thus clear.

We notice through these results that a leveraged ABC Co. features higher EPS as a result of the tax shield and the smaller

Table 5.2 ABC Co: leveraged and unleveraged results

	ABC Co. unleveraged	ABC Co. leveraged
Total capitalization	£200m of equity (10m shares outstanding), £0 debt	£100m of equity (5m shares outstanding), £100m of debt
EBIT	£100m	£100m
Interest expense (at 8%)	£0	£8m
Operating profit	£100m	£92m
Tax expense (at 20%)	£20m	£18.4m
Net income	£80m	£73.6m
EPS	£8/share	£14.7/share

number of shares included in the total capital base. This means that, as the business environment strengthens and ABC Co. sells more goods and generates more profits, it delivers greater EPS to its shareholders than if it were unleveraged. But the downside is also obvious: if the economy weakens, ABC Co.'s revenues and profits may decline but its interest burden will remain the same, squeezing profits and reducing EPS. This increases financial pressures, raises the cost of capital, and lowers the firm's stock price.

We can summarize by saying that, if too little debt is used, the benefits derived from financial leverage are not being fully exploited, meaning that more debt can be added; in doing so, the likelihood of higher earnings and EPS also rises. Conversely, if too much debt is used, the interest burden rises, earnings and EPS may decline, investors will demand a higher return, the cost of capital rises, and the stock price declines. In the extreme, excessive debt can lead to financial distress.

So, how is the optimal degree of leverage determined? In practice, we may point to at least three forces. In the first instance it will be determined by the nature of the company's operations and its short- and long-term strategies. In the second instance it will relate to the relative costs/benefits that can be obtained in the marketplace (and in practice will be adjusted or "fine-tuned" over time). And, in the final instance, it will be associated in some way with peer and industry norms that are prescribed by rating agencies and lenders.

BORROWING COSTS

Borrowing costs are a function of several variables. Like equity financing, some of these are external, or market-related, while others are internal, or company-specific. The two ultimately dictate how much a company will pay for its debt financing and how it can optimize its capital structure.

Let's begin with the external factors. The level of market interest rates is the base variable that impacts every company's debt funding. We know from Chapter 2 that interest rates represent the general cost of borrowing, or the level at which debt capital can be attracted from investors/lenders. Since interest rates represent some minimum cost of accessing debt capital, it follows that they have a bearing on what ABC Co. can expect to pay for funds. If market interest rates are low, overall corporate borrowing costs will be low, and if rates are high, costs will be high. Of course, this is just a benchmark level, because when we refer to interest rate levels generically we refer to the risk-free market rates accorded to high-quality government borrowers. Since individual companies are riskier than government borrowers – certainly in the case of industrialized markets – they will have to supplement the base interest cost with some premium related to their own level of riskiness; we'll defer this point until later since it is an internal factor.

We have previously noted that the maturity of borrowing has an impact on costs. In a "normal" upward-sloping yield curve environment, rates are lower in the short term than in the medium or long term, meaning that those wanting to borrow short term will pay less, and those wanting to borrow long term will pay more. The opposite is true when the yield curve is in the less common downward-sloping state. Figure 5.1 highlights sample high-, mid-, and low-interest-rate environments and associated upward-sloping yield curves; these are key macro drivers in determining borrowing costs.

This point raises another question: if short-term rates are lower in an upward-sloping yield curve environment – the most common market scenario – shouldn't a company always borrow short-term funds? Not necessarily. Short-term funding (which ranges from overnight to 12 months) requires a company to

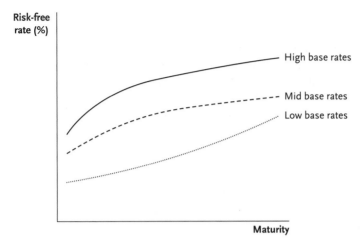

Figure 5.1 Base yield curve scenarios

continuously renew, or "roll over," its obligations in order to maintain the same level of funding. If rollovers are not possible as a result of market disruptions (i.e., investors or lenders don't want to provide short-term capital) a company risks getting caught in a liquidity-funding squeeze, which can have dangerous financial consequences – including, in the most severe cases, bankruptcy. In addition, short-term rates can always rise, leading to what is commonly termed refunding risk. A company that borrows medium- or long-term funds locks in its interest costs for an extended period of time and therefore isn't susceptible either to funding withdrawal or a rising-rate scenario.

Overall market supply and demand of capital is another external factor that can influence borrowing levels. When lenders and bond investors feel that the market properly compensates them for providing risk capital, they will participate. This means that liquidity flows into the market and overall credit borrowing levels can decline – again, with a cautionary note that individual borrowing costs may be different, depending on company-specific factors. A system that features a larger amount of liquidity in search of a fair return leads systematically to lower debt financing costs. The opposite scenario also holds true. If investors and lenders feel that rate levels do not provide fair compensation they will invest capital elsewhere, causing a supply shortage and a rise in overall borrowing costs. Companies seeking funding will have to entice investors/lenders to supply funds by offering greater returns – in other words, a higher cost of financing.

Internal factors also play a vital role in setting borrowing costs. Once market forces establish the minimum base borrowing rate, a company's financial condition crystallizes the actual cost of accessing debt capital. As we've said, the greater the risk, the greater the return that capital suppliers will require, so a risky company that is in poor financial condition will have to pay more for its capital than one that is in strong financial shape. This idiosyncratic feature is reflected in the debt risk premium (or credit spread), which is simply a company's percentage or basis point (bp: 1/100th of 1 percent) spread above the base risk-free rate prevailing in the market. We can summarize this total cost of debt as:

$$\text{cost of debt} = \underline{\text{risk-free rate}} + \underline{\text{risk premium}} \qquad [5.3]$$

Internal (idiosyncratic) influence

External (systematic) influence

Credit spreads, as a debt risk premium, reflect creditworthiness. As we've noted, rating agencies evaluate and rate companies prior to the issuance of debt and bank lenders perform a similar exercise before extending loans. These analyses and ratings, which reflect financial standing, have a real impact on borrowing levels; the lower the rating, the greater the risk of default and the larger the credit spread (risk premium) that investors/lenders will demand.

Still, we have to bear in mind that credit spreads are dynamic, just like other financial indicators, and can be partially influenced by market forces. Short-term supply and demand levels can move spreads, meaning that borrowing levels can change. Although ABC Co. might be able to borrow at 50 bps above the risk-free government rate today, it may only be able to do so at 60 bps in 1 month if supply/demand conditions become unbalanced – even though ABC Co.'s credit might be unchanged.

Factors driving credit spreads are based on financial actions that are within a company's control. For instance, if ABC Co.

decides to increase its debt load by a significant amount, its financial standing will necessarily change. The same can occur if it enters a new line of business that triples sales, or divests a loss-making subsidiary. Changes may therefore be positive or negative, and they may have a small or large impact on a company's financial condition and, ultimately, its credit spread.

Recalling our discussion in Chapter 2, financial strength and stability are analyzed by looking at a company's liquidity, leverage, capital base, revenue and income generation, and cash flow stability – at a point in time, as a trend over time, and versus peers. These factors are supplemented by examining less tangible, but highly important, variables, such as management quality, company strategy, product/service innovation, and industry competition. During a period of economic growth, a strong and financially stable company is regarded as being of the highest quality (AA- or AAA-rated) and may only pay a few basis points above the base risk-free rate. One that is of middle quality (BBB-rated) may pay 50 to 150 basis points above the base rate, while one that is of weak quality (BB-rated and lower), may pay several hundred basis points above the base rate. The market thus distinguishes between high-grade companies (AAA to BBB–) and high-yield companies (BB+ and lower), and any actions taken to strengthen or weaken financial standing will change market perception and, by extension, borrowing costs.

We now know that total borrowing costs on a bond or loan are a function of the level of the base yield curve rate, certain capital supply/demand forces, and company-specific financial standing or creditworthiness. Let's assume that ABC Co., rated AA, is interested in borrowing 5-year funds (via a loan or bond) when the middle interest rate scenario is in force. This means that its borrowing costs will be a function of 5-year risk-free rates dictated by the sterling government bond (or gilt) yield curve, as well as the credit spread accorded to AA-rated companies – which we assume, for purposes of this example, is 10 bps over the gilt curve. If 5-year gilts are quoted at 4 percent, ABC Co.'s 5-year borrowing rate is 4.10 percent. But we needn't stop at the 5-year point. Let's also assume that ABC Co. might be interested in borrowing for 3 years or 7 years, and the market quotes AA-rated 3-year credit spreads at 5 bps and 7-year spreads at 15 bps. If the

Table 5.3 ABC Co.'s borrowing costs

	Gilt base rate	AA spreads	AA borrowing costs	BBB spreads	BBB borrowing costs
3 years	3.75%	0.05%	3.80%	0.30%	4.05%
5 years	4.00%	0.10%	4.10%	0.40%	4.40%
7 years	4.25%	0.15%	4.40%	0.50%	4.75%

3-year gilt is 3.75 percent and the 7-year gilt is 4.25 percent, ABC Co.'s total financing costs would amount to 3.80 percent for 3 years and 4.40 percent for 7 years.

Let's now assume that ABC Co. is a BBB-rated company, meaning that it faces larger (or wider) credit spreads. If 3-, 5-, and 7-year BBB credit spreads are 30, 40, and 50 bps above the gilt curve, then ABC Co.'s borrowing costs will amount to 4.05 percent, 4.40 percent, and 4.75 percent, respectively. We summarize these results in Table 5.3 and Figure 5.2.

While most of the cost of funding is incorporated in the base rate and the credit spread, we know that banks arranging loans and bonds don't work for free. As such, certain fees need to be added to the equation. Loans to high-quality borrowers command

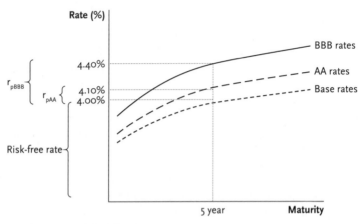

Figure 5.2 ABC Co.'s borrowing costs

rather small fees, perhaps as little as 5–10 bps upfront; those to lower quality borrowers can rise to 25–50 bps. Loan fees can be explicit (part of deal costs) or implicit (placing funds at the bank on an interest-free, or compensating balance, basis), and they may be paid upfront or over time. In general, bonds carry fees that can range from 2 to 10 bps for high-grade credits, to over 50 bps for lower-rated credits.

We can extend equation [5.3] by incorporating fees into total borrowing costs; to remain consistent with per annum interest rate costs, upfront fees can be amortized annually over the life of the financing:

$$\text{cost of debt} = \text{risk-free rate} + \text{risk premium} + \text{fees} \qquad [5.4]$$

To summarize our example, if ABC Co., rated AA, is borrowing £100 million via 5-year bonds in the middle interest scenario (and paying a 5 bp upfront fee for doing so), its total annual pre-tax borrowing costs are £4.1 million, plus an additional £50,000 in upfront fees (or £10,000 per year, if amortized over the 5-year horizon and ignoring time value of money for simplicity). The after-tax equivalent can be computed using equation [5.1].

INSTRUMENT CHARACTERISTICS

Debt comes in many varieties, each with unique characteristics. In this section we describe the features of the main types of loans and bonds, with a caveat that many other subtle variations exist.

We can classify debt instruments by focusing on the liability portion of a typical corporate balance sheet. In many accounting regimes, liabilities are segregated by maturity, ranging from short term (sub-1 year), to medium term (generally 1–10 years) and long term (generally over 10 years); each maturity sector features its own types of instruments, as highlighted in Figure 5.3.

Short-term liabilities include debt obligations that provide a company with short-term credit or cash to meet liquidity needs, seasonal cash flow aberrations, or emergency payments, or to serve as a temporary "bridge" until longer-term financing can be arranged. Short-term financing needs are a function of a company's liquidity position, seasonal supply and demand forces, expected

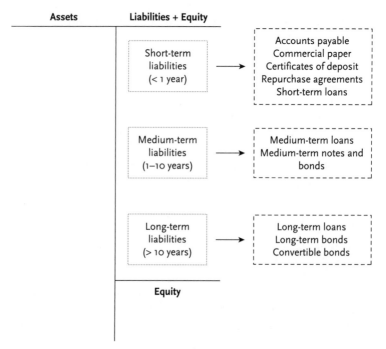

Figure 5.3 Loans and bonds on the corporate balance sheet

short-term cash inflows and outflows, and perceived need to maintain a buffer for emergency purposes.

Medium- and long-term liabilities include obligations that provide funding for semi-permanent expansion and investment requirements, such as purchase/upgrade of factories or financing of long-term research and development projects. Since this medium-/long-term funding covers a multi-year period, it isn't intended to be drawn and repaid repeatedly. Accordingly, it is best suited for capital projects/investments, rather than seasonal or emergency financing.

KEY CHARACTERISTICS

Bonds and loans are characterized by a number of key features, all of which are negotiated in advance of borrowing. These include deal size, coupon/rate, maturity, repayment schedule, placement/ borrowing mechanism, optionality, market, and seniority.

- Size: the amount being placed with investors or borrowed from banks or other creditors. This can range from less than $1 million (or equivalent in other currencies) to well over $1 billion, depending on the borrower, its needs, investor appetite, and market circumstances. For instance, ABC Co. may decide to borrow up to £100 million to fund its operations.
- Coupon/rate: the specific interest rate being paid for the funds, which is a reflection of the borrowing costs discussed above. The coupon may be set in fixed- or floating-rate terms: fixed rates remain unchanged for the life of the financing; floating rates reset periodically, generally every 3, 6, or 12 months, meaning that a borrower's funding cost will change. A company may also issue a zero coupon bond, selling the security at a deep discount but paying no interest; the bond redeems at par value (100 percent) at maturity, meaning that the investor earns an "implied" interest rate. In our example ABC Co. may borrow its £100 million for a fixed rate of 5 percent or, if it prefers floating-rate funds, sterling London Interbank Offered Rate (LIBOR) + 50 bp.
- Maturity: the specific term of the liability. As noted above, the maturity may be short, medium, or long term. The decision on optimal maturity depends on a company's goals (i.e., whether it is attempting to manage liquidity or fund a capital investment program) and overall market conditions (i.e., whether the yield curve is relatively flat, suggesting an opportunity to lock-in cheaper long-term funding, or very steep, indicating a short-term rollover strategy may be preferable). In our example, ABC Co. opts to borrow intermediate 5-year funds through its bond issue.
- Repayment schedule: the manner in which the principal amount of the bond or loan is to be repaid. Common mechanisms include amortizing repayment (where the borrower repays a portion of the principal on every interest payment date, so that there is no large principal payment due at maturity), bullet repayment (where the borrower makes no principal payment until the final maturity), and balloon repayment (where the

borrower makes small principal payments for the first few years of the borrowing, followed by a large payment at maturity). In borrowing £100 million via its bond issue, ABC Co. may select a bullet structure, repaying the entire principal in 5 years. Bullets are, in fact, very common in bond financings.

- Placement/borrowing mechanism: the manner in which funds are placed with investors or drawn from banks. Bonds can be placed on a public or private placement basis. Public bonds are securities registered with regulators that are accompanied by detailed information on the issuer (i.e., financial statements and projections) and the deal (i.e., terms and conditions). They are often listed on a national exchange, though secondary trading tends to occur in the over-the-counter (OTC) market. Private placements, in contrast, are exempt from regulatory registration and are designed for sophisticated institutional investors that can bear more risk than the average individual investor. Within the loan market, a borrower can arrange to access the entire amount of funds at once, or it may do so in tranches over time, or it may use a revolving credit mechanism, where a drawdown is followed by repayment and future drawdowns/repayments, much like a consumer might use a credit card. In our example, ABC Co. may choose a standard public bond deal in order to increase the universe of investors and add to market liquidity.
- Optionality: the inclusion of issuer or investor options in bonds that enhance yield or lower funding costs. During some market cycles it can be attractive to float a callable bond, which is a bond that grants the issuer the right to call (buy back) the bond from investors; this option gives investors an enhanced yield. Alternatively, it may be wise for a firm to issue a puttable bond, or a bond that gives investors the right to put (sell) the bond back to the issuer; this gives the issuer a lower funding cost. In arranging its bond, ABC Co. could consider including put options to lower its funding cost by several basis points.
- Market: the specific marketplace being accessed. Bonds may be issued in the domestic (onshore) market, where funds are raised from resident investors, or the international (offshore, or Euro) market, where funds are raised from non-resident investors. Loans can also be raised in a domestic or offshore setting. The selection of a market depends on various factors,

including cost (i.e., where a company can borrow on the best terms), availability (i.e., where investors are willing to supply capital), overall market conditions (i.e., where market stability (or volatility) may attract (or repel) capital), and regulatory restrictions (i.e., where barriers may impede domestic or offshore access). Since ABC Co. is UK based and is well known to UK investors, it may choose to float a sterling-denominated bond in the domestic market.

- Seniority: the priority of the liability regarding claims on the borrower's assets in the event of default. Recalling our discussion from Chapter 3, we know that the seniority of claims dictates the priority of payments to creditors and equity investors, should a debtor company declare bankruptcy. Equity investors, bearing the first loss, are the most junior in the capital structure, ranking below all forms of debt capital. Loans or bonds that are secured by a company's assets (such as receivables, cash/securities, or hard assets, like plant and equipment) receive first repayment priority; in fact, the source of repayment for such secured creditors in the event of distress is typically the very asset being held as collateral. Within the general class of unsecured creditors, loans or bonds that are accorded senior status are repaid before those with a junior ranking. When considering the seniority of a transaction and the creation of payment priority in default, we can look to historical statistics on recovery rates to see that senior, secured creditors may receive 60–100 percent of their capital upon default, senior, unsecured creditors can receive 30–60 percent, and the broad class of junior creditors as little as 10–30 percent. In our continuing example, ABC Co.'s 5-year bond may be issued as a standard senior, unsecured instrument. If the company were rated sub-investment grade, it might choose to secure its bond with specific assets rather than face the high interest costs of an unsecured issue; this would make bond investors senior, secured creditors.

KEY INSTRUMENTS

The key short-term debt facilities and instruments (< 1 year) include:

- Accounts payable: these accounts constitute the general class of trade credit described in Chapter 2. Trade credit serves as a *de facto* short-term loan because, if a company borrows from its suppliers and chooses not to take advantage of a discount by paying within an allotted time frame, it essentially accrues a finance charge – just as it might under a revolving loan facility. Accounts payable can extend to 360 days, though maturities in the 30- to 180-day sector are more common.
- Commercial paper (CP) and Euro commercial paper (ECP): these instruments are senior, unsecured, discount instruments issued almost exclusively by the very best companies. CP/ECP facilities must typically be rated by one or more of the independent credit rating agencies and may be supported by bank lines that allow the issuer to replace its funding if notes cannot be rolled over at maturity. In the US market, CP has a maximum maturity of 270 days (to avoid registration requirements), while in the non-US domestic markets and the Euro markets, maturities can extend to 360 days. CP and ECP are generally issued with minimum denominations of 100,000 dollars, pounds, or euros.
- Certificates of deposit (CDs): these are unsecured, discount or coupon instruments issued exclusively by banks; coupon-bearing CDs may have fixed or floating coupons. CDs can be issued in various currencies in the domestic or offshore markets and traded on a secondary basis. The instruments have maturities ranging from 1 week to 1 year (though certain 1- to 5-year instruments are also available, and would thus form part of the medium-term funding noted below) and are available, in both small and large denominations. In some national systems, depositors investing in CDs benefit from deposit insurance, a scheme which protects against default by the bank issuer (up to certain maximum amounts).
- Repurchase agreements (repos): these are a popular form of secured financing for securities firms and other financial institutions that deal actively in portfolios of government and corporate bonds. Repos are collateralized borrowings, where the financial institution sells securities (the collateral) to another party for cash (the borrowing), agreeing simultaneously to repurchase them at a future time, which can range

from overnight to 1 year; the securities sold serve as collateral against the cash loan.

- Short-term loans: these loans, with maturities ranging from 3 to 12 months, are interest-bearing liabilities used by companies requiring additional liquidity. The facilities may be secured or unsecured, fixed or floating rate, and are typically of large size (e.g. millions of dollars, pounds, or euros). They may be arranged as straight term loans or as revolving credit facilities that can be drawn down and repaid during a particular horizon.

The primary medium-term (1–10 years) and long-term (10 years+) debt instruments include:

- Medium-term notes (MTNs) and Euro medium-term notes (EMTNs): these securities, which can be likened to long-term versions of the CP and ECP described above, have become a popular form of financing as they can be launched very quickly, from shelf-registered programs that require only a minimum amount of documentation. MTNs and EMTNs feature maturities ranging from 1 to 30 years (though most issuance activity is in the sub-10-year sector) and can be structured with fixed or floating rate coupons and callable or puttable features. Issues are generally unsecured and can be floated in a variety of currencies.

- Bonds and Eurobonds: standard fixed and floating rate bonds and Eurobonds are similar to MTNs and EMTNs – featuring 1- to 30-year maturities, fixed or floating rate coupons, and callable/puttable options – except that the issues are floated on a "one time" basis rather than through a shelf program. This means that relatively extensive registration and disclosure procedures are required for each new issue. Bonds issued by the best-quality companies are considered high-grade securities; those issued by sub-investment-grade companies form part of the high-yield (or junk) bond market. Secondary trading in many issues is extremely active.

- Convertible bonds: convertibles are hybrid debt/equity instruments that can be considered debt or equity, depending on the dominant characteristics of the security at any point in time.

Convertibles pay a minimum coupon, generally on a fixed rate basis, and allow investors the option of converting the bond into common shares if a conversion level is reached. If converted, the bond is extinguished and bondholders become equity investors. Convertibles carry maturities of 1 to 30 years, and can be issued in the domestic or offshore markets.

- Medium- and long-term loans: these loans, with maturities ranging from 1 to 30 years, represent borrowings by companies from banks and other financial institutions. The facilities may be secured or unsecured and feature a fixed or floating rate. Loans can be structured as conventional term loans or revolving credit facilities with multiple drawdown/repayment opportunities.

- Leases: these are liability financing contracts, which, depending on accounting convention and product type, may appear on or off the balance sheet. However, even when a lease appears off balance sheet it acts as a form of debt, and any reasonable analysis of a company's liabilities must incorporate its effects. A lease is a private transaction between the lessor, which owns an underlying asset (e.g. computer, factory, airplane), and the lessee, which wishes to use/rent the asset in exchange for lease payments. At the end of the lease contract the lessee returns the leased asset (though it may be given the option to purchase the asset at a pre-defined residual value); the asset's ownership is never transferred from lessor to lessee. The lessee thus obtains *de facto* "financing" from the lessor in exchange for periodic payments that are similar to interest payments on a loan. The lessee benefits from not having to borrow and make an investment to buy the underlying asset being used; the lessor benefits from the tax advantages that accrue from depreciating the asset. A lease can be structured as an operating lease or capital lease. The operating lease typically has a maturity of less than 5 years and is generally cancelable by the lessee; maintenance and repairs are the responsibility of the lessor and the contract is generally shown off balance sheet. The capital lease, in contrast, is a long-term, non-cancelable, contract, where the lessee is responsible for maintenance and repairs; in many jurisdictions the capital lease must be shown directly on the balance sheet.

In addition to the liabilities described above, there exists a thriving market for securitized bonds that are created by combining pools of assets and issuing securities to finance the pools (see Finance in action 5.1).

FINANCE IN ACTION 5.1: THE COMPLEX WORLD OF SECURITIZATION

While bonds issued by individual companies (and sovereigns) constitute a very significant portion of the overall bond market, more complex alternatives exist, including the securitization structure – which dates back to the 1970s but gained true popularity in the 1990s and new millennium. Growth in the securitization markets has been phenomenal, being slowed only temporarily by the 2007 financial crisis.

A securitized bond is simply a bond or note that is secured by, and which receives cash flows from, a pool of assets. Companies – and especially financial institutions – often wish to securitize portfolios of assets because it allows them to remove risk from their balance sheets, thereby giving them capacity to do more business. Certain types of investors are also attracted to these securities as it gives them risk/return characteristics related to a diversified pool of assets. The underlying assets in a pool may be mortgages (mortgage-backed securities), credit card receivables, auto loans, or leases (asset-backed securities), and even other bonds and loans (collateralized debt obligations). The trick is to put together a large and well-diversified pool of assets – this helps ensure that investors will receive their principal and interest under all but the most dire of financial crises.

Let's take a quick look at a generic financial securitization. An issuing trust is established on behalf of an arranging bank as an independent, bankruptcy-remote entity, responsible for managing cash flows, administering receivables and payables, arranging swap hedges, and so forth. In order to generate the desired risk and return profiles for each tranche, the trust redirects cash flows from the underlying assets, repaying investors principal and interest (P&I) in order of priority. Thus, the most senior (i.e., lowest return, lowest risk) investors are repaid first, and the most junior (i.e., highest return, highest risk)

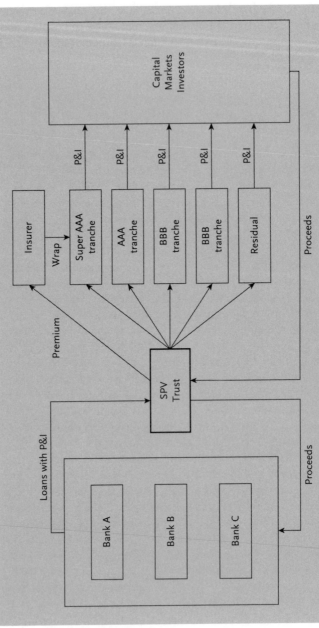

Figure 5.4 Structural cash flows of a CDO

investors last. In most cases the issues are supported by a highly subordinated "equity-like" tranche, known as the residual, which carries very high returns (e.g. 20+ percent) and risks (i.e., it bears the first losses from any assets in the pool that default).

Periodic "tests" are performed throughout the life of a deal to ensure that there is enough cash on hand to pay investors – if there is any shortfall (as a result of a large number of defaults in the asset pool), available cash flows are redirected to the most senior investors, meaning that the most junior investors may not receive any cash flows at all. In some cases, the arrangers also credit-enhance (or "wrap") certain tranches through letters of credit, overcollateralization, financial guarantees or insurance policies, thus creating securities with a very high rating (including so-called "super AAA" tranches, where the risk of default is infinitesimal). Figure 5.4 depicts basic cash flows related to the pooling of corporate loans from various banks to create a collateralized debt obligation (CDO) (the same process applies to all other asset securitizations). It is also worth noting that the same can be accomplished using credit derivatives rather than actual assets, leading to a so-called synthetic securitization.

BORROWING, ISSUING, AND SECONDARY TRADING

BORROWING AND ISSUING

The process of creating the liabilities described above varies according to instrument type.

Borrowing via the loan markets is based on a well-established procedure where a bank, working closely with a company, arranges a loan facility that suits the company's funding needs, drafts and executes a loan agreement (with details on terms, conditions, collateral requirements, and any financial ratios to which the borrower must adhere), and then provides funds based on the terms contained in the documentation. The bank may then retain the entire loan in its portfolio until maturity, or sell a portion to other banks or loan investors in the secondary markets. A large loan, generally in excess of several hundred million dollars, pounds, or euros, may be syndicated (divided), among a larger group of banks during the primary market phase. The arranging bank creates a syndicate of banks, each of which commits to funding a portion of the loan; this mechanism allows risk to be more prudently distributed.

Raising debt capital via the securities markets is based on a slightly different process. In a public deal a bank, again working closely with the borrowing company, confirms funding requirements, prepares detailed preliminary disclosure (which ultimately becomes the prospectus), and registers the issue with the national securities regulator. The bank then begins a pre-marketing phase to determine investor appetite and potential pricing levels (e.g. a coupon/yield that will prove attractive to investors). If a deal is particularly large, the bank may again decide to assemble a syndicate to help in the distribution efforts. The final bond price/yield is established on launch date and the syndicate places securities with investors.

If a bond deal has been arranged as a "best efforts" transaction, the bank places as many bonds as it can, but is not required to deliver the full amount that the company needs if investor appetite is limited. So, if ABC Co. wants £100 million of 5-year funds but investors are only interested in purchasing £75 million at the quoted yield, the company only receives £75 million. However, if the bank agrees to a "firm underwriting" or "bought deal," it must deliver the full amount to the company and then try to place the securities with investors.

The issuance process is quite similar for private placements, except that the pool of investors to which banks can pre-market is much smaller. The process for other "exempt securities," such as CDs, CP, and ECP, also follows the same path: securities are issued with a minimum of disclosure through a shelf or tap mechanism that allows for quick distribution. Unlike private placements, however, a broader range and number of investors can purchase these exempt instruments.

In some cases companies can eliminate the role of the bank by placing securities directly with end investors, saving themselves a few basis points in fees. This process of direct placement (a form of disintermediation, as we shall discuss in Part III), is increasingly common, though still reserved for large, creditworthy borrowers that have strong global name recognition.

SECONDARY TRADING

Most debt trading occurs in bonds and other securities rather than loans. Though a secondary market has developed for loans in recent years, total turnover is still small compared to the largest domestic bond markets and the Eurobond market. As such, we'll focus our discussion on secondary trading of bonds.

Major banks and securities dealers actively quote prices on a range of bonds on a continuous basis. This market-making role, providing a bid and offer price on individual securities, allows other investors to enter or exit the market once a particular issue has been launched – that is, once the primary market phase of a deal has been concluded. The prices that dealers quote are a function of the variables we've already discussed, including external factors (i.e., overall interest rate levels, market conditions/outlook, supply of investment capital) and internal factors (i.e., specific creditworthiness of a company and/or its sector).

The secondary marketplace often quotes in price terms rather than yields. Thus, ABC Co.'s £100 million 5-year bonds, launched 12 months ago at par (100), may now be quoted at 101.79–101.89. This means that a market maker will buy bonds from existing investors at 101.79 and will sell them to new investors at 101.89. The 0.10 points is the market maker's compensation for assuming credit risk (e.g. the risk that ABC Co. will deteriorate or default before the bonds have been resold), and liquidity risk (e.g. risk that investors will suddenly lose interest in the bonds, leaving the market maker with a "stuck" position).

Let's run through several simple scenarios to see how ABC Co.'s secondary prices can change as risk-free rates and credit spreads change. We begin by adapting the basic present value (PV) equation from Chapter 3. Since a bond is simply a series of future cash flows (interest and principal) and we are interested in determining its value today, we need only discount the cash flows by the relevant cost of debt, as follows:

$$PV = \text{sum across all periods} \left[\frac{\text{interest coupon}}{\left(1 + \text{discount rate}\right)^{\text{time horizon}}} \right] + \left[\frac{\text{principal}}{\left(1 + \text{discount rate}\right)^{\text{maturity}}} \right] \qquad [5.5]$$

Assume ABC Co. launched its original 5-year £100 million bond at par 12 months ago with a coupon of 5 percent; for simplicity we also assume that the 5-year gilt rate at that time was 4.50 percent and the company's credit spread was 50 bps, or 0.50 percent. Through the equation above, the price at launch was precisely equal to par:

$$P = \frac{5}{(1.05)^1} + \frac{5}{(1.05)^2} + \frac{5}{(1.05)^3} + \frac{5}{(1.05)^4} + \frac{105}{(1.05)^5}$$

or:

$$100 = 4.7619 + 4.5351 + 4.3192 + 4.1135 + 82.227$$

Let's now assume that gilt rates fall from 4.50 percent to 4.00 percent and ABC Co.'s spread remains unchanged at 0.50 percent. With 4 years left to maturity the new price is:

$$P = \frac{5}{(1.045)^1} + \frac{5}{(1.045)^2} + \frac{5}{(1.045)^3} + \frac{105}{(1.045)^4}$$

or:

$$101.79 = 4.7847 + 4.5786 + 4.3815 + 88.0480$$

Even though only 4 years remain until maturity, the price has risen from 100 to 101.79 because base rates have fallen by 50 bps. A market-maker quoting ABC Co.'s bond in this market may thus be willing to buy at 101.79 and sell at 101.89. This illustrates an important fact between bond prices and rates: there exists an inverse relationship between the two, meaning that, when rates rise, bond prices fall and when rates fall, bond prices rise. This is true because new bonds issued in a higher rate environment with high coupons will appear more attractive than those with lower coupons; investors will sell the old bonds (causing yields to rise) and buy the new ones (causing yields to fall) until an equilibrium point is reached.

What if base rates remain unchanged from the time of issuance (4.50 percent) but ABC Co.'s creditworthiness has deteriorated dramatically? In this case the premium may have risen from 50 bps to 100 bps (1.00 percent), meaning that the cost of debt rises

Table 5.4 Impact of the risk-free rate and risk premium on bond prices

Risk-free rate	Bond price	Risk premium	Bond price
↑	↓	↑	↓
↓	↑	↓	↑

to 5.50 percent. The secondary price of the bond, with 4 years until maturity, is thus:

$$P = \frac{5}{(1.055)^1} + \frac{5}{(1.055)^2} + \frac{5}{(1.055)^3} + \frac{105}{(1.055)^4}$$

which gives us a price of:

$$97.9014 = 4.3933 + 4.4923 + 4.258 + 84.758$$

This makes intuitive, as well as financial, sense: ABC Co.'s credit standing has deteriorated, meaning that its prospect of default has increased; investors will only be willing to pay a lower price (i.e., they will demand a higher yield) to own the bond.

As base rates rise, secondary prices fall, and vice versa; as credit spreads widen, secondary prices fall, and vice versa; these are summarized in Table 5.4. Market makers must therefore remain vigilant to changes in both before quoting prices.

Secondary bond trading can occur via an exchange or OTC. Though the market has long favored voice-based OTC trading, the advent of computing power and advanced networking has led to the creation of new electronic bond trading platforms, and more volumes are gradually being directed through such conduits.

As a final point, it is worth noting that many of the concepts described above also apply to government bills, notes, and bonds. Sovereign nations, through their treasuries or central banks, routinely issue liabilities to investors, which can be held until maturity or traded on a secondary basis.

CHAPTER SUMMARY

Debt financing via loans and bonds is a critical element of overall corporate financing. The cost of debt capital generally compares very favorably to that available via the equity markets, because creditors occupy a more secure position in the capital structure through payment priorities over equity investors, and debt interest deductibility creates a tax shield. The optimal amount of debt that a company should assume is driven by its liquidity and capital investment requirements and industry norms; too little debt implies excessive reliance on more expensive equity financing, while too much debt can create a large fixed charge burden and increase the likelihood of financial distress. Actual borrowing costs are determined through a combination of market-related and internal factors. Favorable markets can lead to lower base rates, while strong financial standing can lead to lower credit spreads; the opposite scenarios also hold true. Bonds and loans can be issued or arranged in a variety of forms and are defined by key characteristics that include deal size, coupon/rate, maturity, repayment schedule, placement/borrowing mechanism, optionality, market, and seniority. More complex debt instruments, including securitized and structured bonds, are also an important part of the marketplace. An active secondary market exists for many forms of debt, especially publicly registered bonds; some of this trading activity is migrating from exchange- and voice-based mechanisms to a purely electronic environment.

FURTHER READING

Fabozzi, F., ed., 2012, *Handbook of Fixed Income Instruments*, 8th edn., New York: McGraw-Hill.

—— 2012, *Bond Markets, Analysis and Strategies*, 8th edn., Upper Saddle River, NJ: Prentice Hall.

Fight, A., 2004, *Syndicated Lending*, London: Butterworth-Heinemann.

Stigum, M. and Crescenzi, A., 2007, *Stigum's Money Market*, 4th edn., New York: McGraw-Hill.

Taylor, A. and Sansone, A., 2006, *The Handbook of Loan Syndications and Trading*, New York: McGraw-Hill.

6

INVESTMENT FUNDS

CHAPTER OVERVIEW

In this chapter we examine investment funds, which are financial products that combine into managed portfolios assets such as the debt and equity securities discussed in the last two chapters. We begin with a review of why and how investment funds are used, the general classes of funds, and the role that diversification plays in the creation of funds. We then consider the main types of investment fund vehicles, including open-end funds, closed-end funds, hedge funds and other alternative funds, and exchange-traded funds, and the strategies that portfolio managers use to create investor returns. We conclude by describing how different classes of investment fund shares are created, traded, and redeemed.

USES AND CLASSES OF INVESTMENT FUNDS

In the last two chapters we've described capital securities that firms issue to fund their balance sheets. We know that an investor buying securities supplies capital in exchange for a return. Each individual stock or bond that an investor buys represents a separate exposure to the stock or bond issuer. The investor holds a concentrated position in the risk of the issuer, and, if something goes wrong – perhaps the issuing company sustains large financial losses or even falls into bankruptcy – some amount of invested capital may be lost. Although the return the investor earns is supposed to compensate for such risks, there are times when it may prove insufficient.

Naturally, many investors are comfortable bearing this "concentrated" risk, especially when they feel that the returns they are receiving are appropriate. Some, however, are less willing to do so – particularly if they lack the knowledge needed to properly evaluate potential risks and returns. In these cases they may prefer allocating capital across many stocks or bonds. This spreads the risk: if one of the issuing companies has trouble while the others remain sound, the investor continues to earn an acceptable return. To facilitate this process, investors can use investment funds, which are simply vehicles that purchase a wide range of securities on behalf of investors. In fact, the market for investment funds has grown rapidly over the past few decades and is now worth several trillion dollars.

The investment fund framework involves various parties. Investors provide capital to a portfolio manager, who then purchases specific securities based on a specific strategy and investment mandate; the returns generated by the underlying securities are paid to investors periodically. In exchange for performing the management function, the portfolio manager charges a fee – either annually, at the time of purchase, or at the time of sale; some managers also charge a performance fee. A separate trustee oversees the process and ensures independent valuation and proper safekeeping of securities. Note that, once an investor gives capital to the portfolio manager, it has no say in the actual purchase/sale of securities in the fund's portfolio; the manager has complete discretion to invest as he or she sees fit (within the confines of the investment mandate, as discussed below). The only recourse available to an investor that disagrees with the investment decisions (or is otherwise dissatisfied with a fund's performance) is to exit by selling the position in the fund.

While diversification is perhaps the most important characteristic of many investment funds, the fund product also features other advantages. Some investors are drawn to funds because they provide for continuous, professional management of capital.

Seasoned portfolio managers constantly monitor the performance of their funds, buying and selling securities based on the strategies that they have developed. Investors therefore needn't depend on their own research skills and monitoring efforts. Funds are also cost efficient. While an investor can create a diversified portfolio by buying a large number of individual stocks or bonds, the process can be tedious, time-consuming, and expensive.

While many funds diversify, some are created primarily to provide investors with the possibility of enhanced returns – and not necessarily to reduce risk through diversification techniques. In fact, these funds thrive on risk: they deliberately assume a great deal of exposure in hopes of creating very large returns for investors. These specialized investment funds, which include hedge funds, private equity funds, and venture capital funds, are intended primarily for the most sophisticated investors.

It has become standard practice in the industry to classify investment products as being either conventional, alternative, or private wealth, which we can apply based on the discussion above:

- Conventional: this sector is based primarily on the first class of diversified, professionally managed, funds described above, including mutual funds and their equivalents. However, it also includes pension funds and insurance funds, which invest assets on behalf of employees or policyholders. While their focus is on a specific clientele, the techniques that they use and the strategies they follow are not unlike those we might find in the mutual fund sector.
- Alternatives: this sector includes the riskier group of funds, including hedge funds, private equity funds, venture capital funds, and, in some instances, so-called sovereign wealth funds (which are large funds managed at a national level by certain government authorities, and which may invest in a broad range of diversified or concentrated risks).
- Private wealth: this sector includes all private wealth which is managed through individual advisors or private bankers and which may be invested in all manner of investment vehicles, such as mutual funds and alternatives, but also in securities, foreign exchange, real estate, and other "hard" assets.

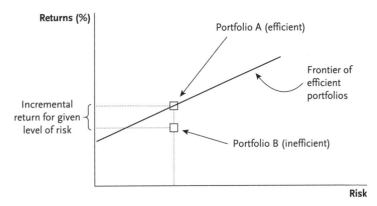

Figure 6.1 Risk, return, and efficient portfolios

PORTFOLIO DIVERSIFICATION

We indicated in Chapter 3 that an investor can reduce or eliminate diversifiable (idiosyncratic) risk of a security by holding other securities that are uncorrelated, or negatively correlated, with the target security. It comes as no surprise that this concept is the linchpin of the investment fund world: combining the right mix of uncorrelated/negatively correlated securities creates diversified, efficient portfolios of securities. An efficient portfolio generates the highest possible returns for a given level of risk, while an inefficient portfolio generates lower returns for the same level of risk, as noted in Figure 6.1. The rational investor will always prefer the efficient portfolio.

Selecting securities with the right correlation characteristics is the key to diversification and the creation of an efficient portfolio.

Empirical studies conducted over the years have focused a great deal of attention on the existence of market efficiency, or the degree to which the market prices of securities absorb and reflect all known (public) and unknown (non-public) information. The existence of this relationship is important in determining whether a portfolio manager can create a diversified portfolio that regularly "beats the market." In the weakest form of the so-called efficient market hypothesis (EMH), information is not regularly or accurately absorbed, suggesting that the market prices of assets may not be accurate. This means that a portfolio manager can actually outperform a market or index with some frequency. In the strongest form of the EMH, asset prices reflect all public and non-public information, meaning that it is very difficult, if not impossible, for a portfolio manager to regularly beat the market. Some practitioners believe that the market features an intermediate form of efficiency, suggesting that it may be difficult for a portfolio manager to create a strategy that regularly outperforms the market. Accordingly, some fund managers choose simply to try and match the market – selecting a benchmark index and creating a replicating portfolio through a process known as indexing:

- Pure index-tracking: target returns of a fund are precisely equal to the benchmark index.
- Enhanced index-tracking: target returns may be up to 1 percent away from a benchmark index.
- Constrained active management: target returns may be 2–4 percent away from the benchmark.
- Unconstrained active management: target returns may be more than 4 percent away from the benchmark.

The farther a portfolio manager moves away from the pure index-tracking strategy, the less passive and more active the management of the portfolio becomes. At the extreme end of the spectrum we encounter alternative funds, which feature no index relationship at all; that is, they seek to generate absolute returns of any magnitude, rather than returns relative to an index. Such absolute returns are known as alpha (as distinct from beta, which we have discussed earlier); consistently producing alpha is a very difficult task.

INSTRUMENT/VEHICLE CHARACTERISTICS

In this section we consider several of the most popular types of investment funds, including investment companies (open-end funds, closed-end funds, and unit investment trusts), hedge funds and other alternative funds, and exchange-traded funds. Open-end funds constitute the largest segment of the investment fund market and are designed for the broadest group of individual and institutional investors. Closed-end funds, which operate in a similar fashion but with greater restrictions, represent a much smaller portion of the market. Hedge funds and other alternative funds, designed for sophisticated investors, often take a great deal of risk and have become a popular alternative investment in recent years. Exchange-traded funds (ETFs) are "hybrids" that combine the structural features of open-end funds with the trading and liquidity features of actively traded corporate securities.

KEY CHARACTERISTICS

The fund balance sheet

We can examine an investment fund in light of the balance sheet presented in Chapter 2 to establish a frame of reference. Though a fund can be legally structured in various ways – such as a registered investment company, a special purpose entity (SPE), a trust, or a limited partnership – it always has assets, liabilities, and capital, which we know are the essential ingredients of any balance sheet. In some cases a fund may also have some off balance sheet items, such as derivatives.

The asset portion of the fund consists of the securities that the portfolio manager has purchased, along with a small cash balance reflecting funds awaiting investment and any extra liquidity needed to meet redemptions (i.e. sales of fund shares by investors). The equity account consists of the capital that investors in the fund have given to the portfolio manager for investment. Depending on the nature of the fund and its specific authorizations, the balance sheet may also feature a certain amount of short- or long-term debt. The general structure of a fund's balance sheet is illustrated in Figure 6.2.

General fund categories

Funds can invest in a wide range of asset classes and employ different types of investment management techniques. But they must always operate under rules specified by their investment

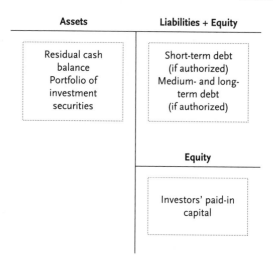

Figure 6.2 General fund balance sheet

mandates. This ensures that investors are actually receiving the type of investment they wish to receive.

Investors can select from among many funds to obtain the desired balance of risk and return. For purposes of our discussion we can divide fund categories into earnings type, geographic focus, asset class, and sub-asset class.

- Earnings type: the earnings dimension relates to the specific source of a fund's income, which may include dividends, interest, and/or capital gains. Funds that rely on dividends and interest (so-called current income) tend to be less risky than those that rely on capital gains, since current income cash flows, such as those derived from bonds and dividend-paying preferred and common stock, are a great deal more certain.
- Geographic focus: the geographic dimension relates to a fund's spatial focus, which may be national (i.e. confined to a specific country), regional (i.e. based on a related group of national markets), or global. Those with a regional or international component may expose investors to currency risks, since some of the assets purchased are likely to be denominated in a currency other than the investor's "home" currency.

- Asset class: the asset class parameter relates to the markets in which a fund invests. These are generally stocks and bonds, but may also include currencies, commodities, and other alternatives. Many funds limit their investments to a single asset class (e.g. equity only, bond only), though most also hold a certain amount of cash equivalents to meet redemptions. Equity funds represent the single largest asset class in the investment sector.
- Sub-asset class: a sub-asset class distinction is relevant in some instances. For instance, an equity fund might invest only in large capitalization stocks (e.g. companies with $5 billion + or equivalent in market capitalization), mid-cap stocks ($1–5 billion), small cap stocks ($500 million–$1 billion), or micro-cap stocks (up to $500 million); each market sector is considered a distinct sub-asset class. Sub-asset classifications can exist with fixed income (e.g. government bonds only, corporate bonds only) and commodity funds (e.g. energy complex only, precious metals only).

These general fund categories, which can be applied to conventional, alternative, or private wealth schemes, are summarized in Figure 6.3.

KEY FUND CLASSES

Open-end funds

Open-end funds – also known as mutual funds in the USA and unit trusts in the UK – are the single most common form of investment fund; most individuals and institutions have some quantity of open-end fund shares in their investment or retirement accounts. Open-end funds are available across asset classes and many are structured to provide some form of indexed returns.

The mechanics of the open-end fund are straightforward: investors give a fund capital in exchange for shares in the fund. With rare exception, open-end funds can create new shares at will – hence the name "open-end." As long as investors continue to contribute capital, a fund continues to create new shares. New

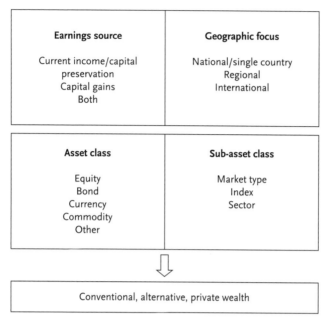

Figure 6.3 General fund categories

capital received from investors is used by the portfolio manager to purchase securities for the portfolio.

Every publicly traded open-end fund is valued at the net asset value (NAV), which is computed via:

total net assets = cash and equivalents + market

value of securities held in the portfolio – current   [6.1]

liabilities (including accruals)

This result can be converted into a per share figure via:

$$\text{NAV per share} = \frac{\text{total net assets}}{\text{shares issued}} \qquad [6.2]$$

An investor wanting to buy or sell shares in the fund will do so at the NAV (plus any applicable fees or commissions, which may be payable upfront, upon exit, or annually); trading generally occurs once a day, at the market closing NAV. Let's assume that Fund

XYZ has a total of €100 million of cash on hand, €1.5 billion of equity securities, €50 million of liabilities, and 100 million shares outstanding. The NAV, per the equations above, is €15.5/share. If the value of the stocks that XYZ holds rises tomorrow so that the worth of the portfolio increases from €1.5 billion to €1.7 billion (and all other account balances remain unchanged), the NAV increases to €17/share.

Since open-end funds are intended for distribution to the public at large (including individual investors who may need extra protection) they must adhere to strict legal and regulatory requirements. Investment companies must generally register their funds with the national securities regulator and comply with minimum standards related to disclosure, reporting, and income distribution.

An open-end fund is often structured in corporate form so that new shares can be created with ease. The investment company acting as sponsor is responsible for organizing the fund, making operating and investment decisions, and marketing the fund to investors. Each fund has its own investment mandate, which outlines permissible investments, strategies, and risks. For instance, some funds can only buy securities with capital on hand, while others can borrow or use derivatives. Similarly, some can invest in very risky securities while others can buy only the safest of assets.

Various other parties are involved in the operation of an open-end fund. An independent custodian typically holds a fund's assets and monitors cash inflows/outflows on behalf of investors. A transfer agent tracks share purchases and sales, maintains shareholder records, computes the daily NAV, and arranges for dividend/interest payments and capital gains disbursements. Many of the largest fund companies also have fund distributors (underwriters), or affiliates, which are responsible for marketing fund shares to investors. Participants involved in creation and management of an open-end fund are summarized in Figure 6.4.

Closed-end funds

Closed-end funds represent a much smaller portion of the investment fund sector. Closed-end funds, like their open-end counterparts, are professionally managed portfolios that are listed and traded on exchanges. But closed-end funds can issue only a limited

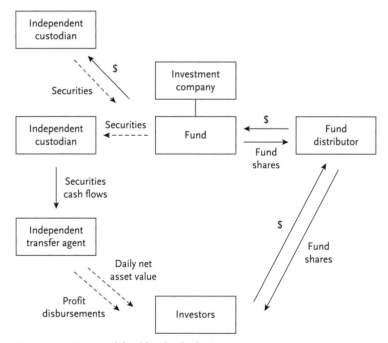

Figure 6.4 Open-end fund legal vehicles/participants

number of shares, meaning they cannot create new ones at will. In some cases the combination of a fund's investments and its limited ability to create new shares leads to illiquidity, or difficulty on the part of investors in selling shares at the quoted price when needed. Accordingly, closed-end funds are considered to be most suitable for investors with a medium- to long-term investment horizon.

The unit investment trust (UIT), a subset of the closed-end fund class, features a specific, rather than indefinite, maturity date. A UIT is a "passive" fund that accepts an initial (and limited) amount of investor capital, purchases a target portfolio of securities, and holds the securities until the maturity of the fund.

Hedge funds and other alternative funds

Hedge funds are flexible investment conduits intended primarily for sophisticated investors that can absorb greater risk than the average individual. In fact, minimum amounts of income and/or net worth are usually required of those seeking to participate. As we've noted, hedge funds attempt to create alpha through active management. In other words, they do not benchmark to indexes or engage in passive investment strategies. Hedge funds may increase their risks (and potential returns) by using borrowed funds to buy securities, taking concentrated positions, short-selling securities, and buying/selling illiquid assets and derivatives.

Hedge funds enjoy considerable flexibility in allocating investors' capital across markets and strategies. Common hedge fund strategies include:

- Directional asset allocation: buying/selling securities in one or more asset classes to take advantage of the direction of the market.
- Arbitrage/relative value: buying/selling securities in one or more asset classes to take advantage of the differential between the assets, rather than the absolute direction of the market.
- Restructuring/event driven: buying/selling securities of companies that are subject to possible corporate "events" such as takeovers, divestments, bankruptcy, or recapitalization.
- Macro: buying/selling securities and/or commodities based on macroeconomic analysis, and often including investments in a range of currencies.

Many hedge funds are exempt from regulations that are applied to open- and closed-end funds. In fact, most hedge fund managers are considered to be unregistered investment advisors and cannot therefore advertise or market their funds directly to the public. But they must still distribute to prospective investors offering memoranda with essential details on the fund, its activities, and its risk factors.

Hedge funds may be structured as private partnerships using a general partner (GP)/limited partner (LP) framework. The fund's management team acts as the GP, managing daily operations and making all investment management decisions. Investors in the fund act as the LPs, holding passive interests in the fund and remaining liable up to the amount of the capital they have invested in the venture. Certain hedge funds may also choose to be established as investment companies. In fact, funds are often set up with multiple entities that cater to domestic and offshore investors. Even though the fund might use multiple partnerships, it invests capital in the same strategies. Figure 6.5 summarizes this process.

Hedge funds generally charge asset-based fees (just as any other fund might), and supplement these with performance fees. For instance, a fund may charge 1–2 percent p.a. on assets under management, and a 20 percent performance fee on any gross earnings generated; this compares to all-in fees of sub-1–2 percent for other types of funds. So, the general partners of a hedge fund with €100 million under management that posts €20 million in returns will receive €6 million (i.e. 2 percent of €100 million and 20 percent of €20 million). The returns paid to investors (limited partners) come from the earnings that remain after all asset and performance fees have been paid.

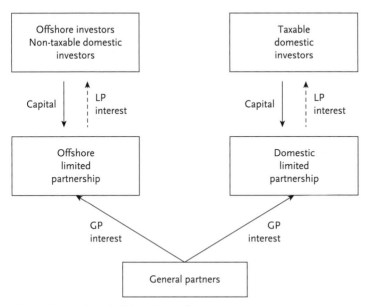

Figure 6.5 Onshore/offshore hedge fund structure

FINANCE IN ACTION 6.1:   THE RISE OF THE HEDGE FUNDS

Hedge funds are not particularly new to the financial world – the first hedge fund was founded in 1949, and others followed during subsequent decades – but they came into greater prominence in the late 1990s and into the new millennium, as financial markets continued extended bull market runs and investors sought to participate in the alpha-generation capabilities of these seemingly astute fund managers.

Despite the near-collapse of Long Term Capital Management in 1998 (a very prominent hedge fund run by ex-Salomon Brothers traders, which was brought to the brink by excessive leverage and asset illiquidity) and the market corrections that followed the bursting of the Internet stock bubble in 2001–2002, investor interest in hedge funds continued to build. In fact, during the first half of the 2000s thousands of new funds were created – with a total of 8,000 in existence by the end of 2008 (and with the 400 largest controlling 80 percent of invested capital). Total capital under management exploded from a rather modest $400 billion in 2001 to $2 trillion at the end of 2006 and a peak of $2.8 trillion during the first quarter of 2008. Of course, the Credit Crisis of 2007–2009 (which we discuss later in the book) took some of the shine off the sector – collapsing financial markets, sector-wide losses of nearly 20 percent and investor withdrawals caused total capital under management to decrease by nearly $1 trillion, to $1.8 trillion, by the end of 2008. That, however, seems only to have been a temporary pause – by early 2010, capital under management rebounded to the $2 trillion mark and by 2014 the figure had expanded to just over $3 trillion. Despite periodic market dislocations that can affect fund performance, the value proposition that hedge funds have been able to offer investors over the past decades suggests that they will continue to be an important part of the investing landscape.

Private equity funds and venture capital funds, which allocate investor capital to the financing of private companies or start-up ventures, rather than securities, commodities, or other tradable assets, join hedge funds in the alternative space. These funds are typically structured in general/limited partner form and every few years they "harvest" their portfolios by privately selling or publicly floating some of their investments, hopefully creating attractive returns for investors. As we might imagine, such funds often have very concentrated positions in ventures that are very illiquid and must therefore be considered risky. Sovereign wealth funds, large national funds that often enjoy a broad investment mandate, often invest in a range of public and private securities, as well as in hedge funds and mutual funds.

Exchange-traded funds

Exchange-traded funds (ETFs) are popular investment funds that combine features of the open-end fund sector with conventional securities trading. ETFs allow new shares to be created and redeemed at will, and permit continuous intra-day trading (just as in stocks and bonds), rather than the typical end-of-day trading characterizing open-end and closed-end funds. The cost structure of ETFs also tends to be lower than that of open-end funds. All of these features have helped the instrument build a critical mass of interest. ETFs are available on baskets, industry sectors, country sectors, and broad market indexes. In recent years a number of structural variations have also been introduced, including those that allow for short (sold) rather than long (purchased) positions and those that incorporate varying degrees of leverage.

ETFs can be created using an investment company structure, where a fund manager is responsible for all coordination and investment allocation decisions. Under this scheme the investment company tracks (but may not precisely replicate) a reference index, and can use derivatives and physical securities to achieve desired investment results. ETFs created as trusts are used primarily for smaller baskets of securities that track specific sectors. All ETFs, regardless of legal structure, must meet certain regulatory requirements, such as disclosure by the trust bank of the next day's creation/redemption baskets, purchase/redemption of ETF receipts with the underlying securities, and use of a central clearing/depository. As noted, ETFs generally feature lower costs than equivalent open-end funds; management fees and annual expenses are generally very modest, and processing fees associated with the creation/redemption of ETF shares are small.

ISSUING, REDEEMING, AND TRADING

ISSUING AND REDEEMING

The creation and redemption of investment fund shares (or partnership interests) depend on the type of fund, which we can analyze in light of the four major classes described above.

An investor wishing to buy shares in an open-end fund transfers a minimum amount of cash to the fund distributor, which forwards the cash to the fund; the fund then buys the securities forming part of the investment strategy. Since the fund is structured as an open-end vehicle it can create new shares at the NAV without limitation. Although open-end funds almost always accept new funds from investors, a small number eventually accumulate too much and may close to further subscriptions, either temporarily or permanently. This is a defensive mechanism that helps ensure portfolio managers do not suffer from "style drift" – investment outside of a given area of expertise that can result in a misbalancing of risk/return. An investor selling (redeeming) shares submits instructions to the fund, which uses its cash reserve or liquidates a pro-rata amount of securities to meet the redemption. Open-end funds generally preserve a cash buffer of 5–10 percent of assets in order to meet redemption orders. Of course, fund managers always attempt to minimize the size of the cash buffer, as holding too much cash reduces fund earnings.

As we've noted, closed-end funds do not issue new shares regularly but nearly always arrange for a single issue of capital, which is preserved over time. While the constant level of capital may be seen as a limiting factor, it can also be regarded as an advantage: fund managers don't have to worry about continuous cash inflows and reinvestment, and are unlikely to suffer from style drift. Closed-end funds do not redeem outstanding shares; all shares issued remain outstanding until a fund is liquidated or restructured. Investors wanting to sell their shares must find other investors willing to buy them, and do so through a standard brokered transaction.

The supply of shares in a hedge fund (or private equity fund) is controlled very strictly. Partnership shares are generally arranged as private placements sold directly to accredited investors through the onshore or offshore entities mentioned above. Once the initial capital has been raised, proceeds are invested in one or more strategies. In some cases a fund may arrange a new issuance of capital to finance another fund strategy. But this is best seen as an independent transaction, rather than a continuous creation of capital. Similarly, redemption of fund shares is very limited. Investors that want to sell their interests may only be able to do so at defined points during the calendar year (e.g. every month or quarter), and may have to provide several months' advance notice. If too many redemptions occur simultaneously, as might happen during a crisis, a fund may impose a "gate," which limits the amount that can be withdrawn. Since hedge funds don't have to worry about providing daily liquidity they can optimize their portfolios by holding very little cash.

The ETF share issuance and redemption process is rather more involved because it is based on unlimited share creation and continuous share trading. In a typical ETF an authorized participant (e.g. a financial institution) purchases a portfolio of securities representing the underlying reference index, which it deposits with a trust bank. The trust bank places the securities in a trust account and issues divisible depository receipts. Once the receipts are issued, they can be subdivided and bought and sold through an exchange, just like any other listed corporate security. If an investor wants to sell ETF shares it has purchased, the shares are not redeemed by the fund (as in a standard open-end fund transaction), but are simply sold to another investor. If overall demand for the ETF declines – that is, no further buying interest exists – the authorized participant can gather up the receipts, reassemble them, submit the single receipt to the trust bank, and receive the underlying portfolio of securities in return. It can then liquidate the securities, thus returning to its original cash position. This process is summarized in Figure 6.6.

SECONDARY TRADING

The degree of secondary trading in investment funds depends again on structure.

ETFs feature the greatest amount of secondary trading. Investors can purchase and sell shares in the fund several times during

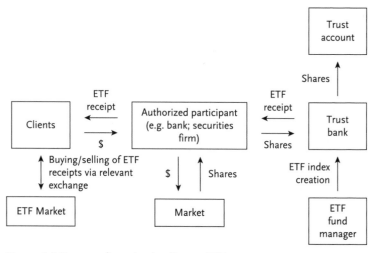

Figure 6.6 Process of creating/trading an ETF

the trading day or they can hold them for the intermediate or long term (note, of course, that each purchase and sale attracts a bid–offer spread and a brokerage commission charge). The existence of continuous pricing and the depth of liquidity in the most popular indexes have led to the creation of derivative contracts on select ETFs. This, in turn, helps promote further activity and liquidity in the ETF, in a self-fulfilling cycle.

The shares of major open-end funds are actively traded as well, but can only be bought or sold at the end-of-day NAV rather than at continuous prices. However, since new shares can be created constantly and existing shares can be redeemed without difficulty, turnover can be reasonably good – particularly for large, well-known, funds with a strong performance record. The

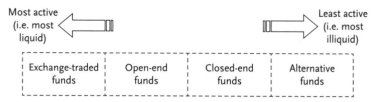

Figure 6.7 Secondary trading activity in funds

same is obviously not true for closed-end funds or hedge funds, which have virtually no turnover. Hedge fund and private equity fund shares can be particularly illiquid: investors may only be able to sell their shares every few weeks or months and must generally give the fund administrator several weeks' (months') advance notice of their intention of doing so.

Figure 6.7 summarizes the spectrum of secondary trading activity, from the most active (or most liquid) to the least active (or most illiquid).

CHAPTER SUMMARY

Investment funds, which combine debt and equity securities into single portfolios, have become popular and important financial conduits. Funds feature several important benefits: they provide investors with exposure to investments through professionally managed portfolios featuring risk and return characteristics that cater to a broad range of investor styles and goals; they employ portfolio diversification to maximize returns for a given level of risk; they create cost efficiencies by allowing execution of multiple transactions through a single trade; and they generate continuity in the investment portfolio, particularly for assets with finite maturities or redemption dates. Funds are described by several key characteristics, including earnings type (current income, capital gains, or both), geographic focus, asset class, and sub-asset class, which can be applied to conventional, alternative, or private wealth schemes. Broad classes of investment funds include: open-end funds, or investment conduits that allow the creation of new shares on a continuous basis and which are quoted and redeemed at the end-of-day NAV; closed-end funds, which are investment conduits that issue a fixed number of shares and also trade at the daily NAV; hedge funds and other alternatives, which are speculative vehicles that can invest in a broad range of instruments and strategies, private companies or start-up ventures and which may only allow investors to liquidate every month or quarter; and ETFs, which are investment conduits that allow the creation of an unlimited amount of shares and that can be traded at will throughout the trading day. Funds feature varying degrees of liquidity: ETFs are the most liquid (with buying and selling possible on a continuous basis), followed by open-end funds, closed-end funds, and alternative funds.

FURTHER READING

Bogle, J., 2009, *Common Sense on Mutual Funds*, New York: John Wiley & Sons.

Cumming, D. and Johan, S., 2009, *Venture Capital and Private Equity Contracting*, Burlington, MA: Academic Press.

Darst, D., 2008, *The Art of Asset Allocation*, 2nd edn., New York: McGraw-Hill.

Gibson, R., 2013, *Asset Allocation*, 5th edn., New York: McGraw-Hill.

Lhabitant, F., 2007, *Handbook of Hedge Funds*, London: John Wiley & Sons.

Pozen, R. and Hamacher, T., 2015, *The Fund Industry*, 2nd edn., New York: John Wiley & Sons.

Rosenberg, L., Weintraub, N., and Hyman, A., 2008, *ETF Strategies and Tactics*, New York: McGraw-Hill.

7

DERIVATIVES AND INSURANCE

CHAPTER OVERVIEW

In this chapter we examine derivatives (a financial contract that derives its value from some underlying index) and insurance (a financial contract that seeks to indemnify against loss), which are tools that companies can use to manage different types of risks. We begin with a general review of risk management techniques and then turn to a review of why and how derivatives and insurance are used, the similarities and differences between the two, and the types of risks that each class is designed to create, reduce, or transfer. Following this, we consider speculation and arbitrage, two activities that are unique to derivatives. We conclude by analyzing the characteristics of derivatives and insurance; although the two share certain similarities, this section reveals in greater detail important differences between the two.

USES OF DERIVATIVES AND INSURANCE

RISK MANAGEMENT

As we know, prudent management of risk is an important corporate goal. If ABC Co. can keep its risk exposures properly balanced, then it stands a better chance of avoiding surprise financial losses, which reduces earnings volatility and ultimately helps boost enterprise value. The process of managing risk can be approached in a number of different ways, including loss control, loss financing, and risk reduction:

- Loss control: this class of risk management, sometimes known as risk mitigation, includes avoidance and resistance. Avoidance, as the name suggests, means prohibiting operation or expansion in an at-risk area, so that no possibility of loss might arise. Resistance, in contrast, means applying certain safety or control standards to minimize the negative effects of any risky event. In general, loss control techniques are applied to physical operating risks.
- Loss financing: this class of risk management, directly related to our discussion below, centers on risk retention, risk transfer and hedging. Risk retention is simply the degree to which a company is willing to accept a certain amount of risk in its operations. Risk transfer, in contrast, relates to shifting a defined amount of exposure to a third party, typically via a derivative or insurance contract. Hedging is an associated concept and refers to neutralizing a risk by creating an offsetting position, often by using a derivative. Loss-financing techniques can be applied to both physical operating risks and financial risks.
- Risk reduction: this class of risk management includes diversification and withdrawal. Diversification, as we have noted in the last chapter, involves creating a portfolio of uncorrelated or negatively correlated assets or businesses in order to help diffuse risks. Withdrawal is simply the decision to exit a particular business line that creates a given type of risk. Risk reduction is again applicable to both operating and financial risks.

The decision on which solution to follow is based on the costs of managing the risk, itself a function of risk frequency and severity, and implied benefits. We must consider an important point here: managing risks properly does not mean eliminating or shifting all risk. In fact, every risk management decision can be evaluated in a cost/benefit framework by focusing on the costs that a company incurs in reducing or eliminating the risk against the benefits it obtains from doing so; conversely, it may consider the

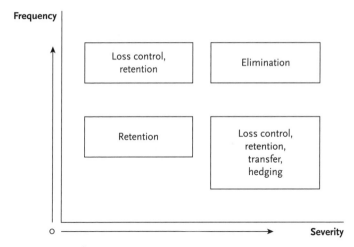

Figure 7.1 Risk management options

costs of retaining the risk versus the benefits that it derives from doing so.

In general, risks that are of low severity and low frequency are good candidates for retention as they are unlikely to damage a company financially. Those that are high severity and high frequency must be eliminated completely, as they can lead to financial ruin. Risks that occur frequently but have a low financial impact and those that occur only rarely but can have a large financial impact are more difficult to handle. In such cases a company must analyze the relative costs and benefits of applying loss control, retention, risk transfer, or hedging solutions. Figure 7.1 summarizes the available choices.

With this introduction in mind, let's turn our attention to the subclass of insurance and derivative-based loss financing. We begin with simple definitions of the two concepts (which we shall expand upon in subsequent sections):

- Derivative: a contract that derives, or obtains, its value from some other market or asset. In other words, it has no value on its own and must be tied to some other reference asset. For instance, a €/$ currency derivative is a contract that derives its value from the €/$ currency rate.

- Insurance: a contract that provides financial restitution when a loss-making event occurs. For instance, a fire insurance policy is a contract that provides a payment if a fire destroys valuable property.

On the surface, these two contracts may seem quite different. They do, in fact, have very different characteristics, as we'll discover later in the chapter. But they also share a significant commonality – namely, they can both be used to manage risks.

Though the actual nature and magnitude of risks can vary across companies, every firm is exposed to some type of risk. Some of the key risks that a company can encounter include:

- Operating risk: the risk of loss arising from a firm's inability to sell its goods or obtain raw material inputs; it can also include risk of loss stemming from plant and equipment damage or destruction, or technology/systems failure.
- Financial risk: the risk of loss coming from an adverse movement in financial markets/prices (such as interest or currency rates) or the failure of a client/counterparty to perform on its contractual obligations (such as accounts receivable or loans). The former is often referred to as market risk (and includes the important subclass of liquidity risk), while the latter is considered credit risk.
- Legal risk: the risk of loss arising from litigation (individual, regulatory, or "class action") or other legal/documentary conflicts or errors.
- Environmental risk: the risk of loss arising from the firm's willful, unknowing, or accidental damage to the environment (such as an oil spill).

Risk can also be distinguished more broadly as being either "speculative" or "pure." A speculative risk lends itself to three possible end results: profit, loss, or no profit/loss. A pure risk, in contrast, features only two end states: loss or no loss. In other words, there is no chance of generating a profit.

The basic decision states related to risk costs and benefits are summarized in Table 7.1.

Table 7.1 Risk decision framework

Decision	Cost	Benefit
Preserving risk	A possible loss from the source of risk	A possible profit from the source of the risk (if speculative) and no costs associated with a risk management solution
Reducing/ eliminating risk	Costs associated with a risk management solution (e.g. fee, insurance premium) and no possibility of profit from the source of risk (if speculative)	No/reduced potential for loss from the source of risk

A firm that is deciding how to manage its risks typically does so in a formalized way, as part of long-term financial planning. A proper risk management framework can be created by first defining a risk mandate, which reflects two important concepts:

- Risk philosophy: an explicit statement developed by the board of directors and executive management that reflects the nature of the risks that the firm is willing to bear.
- Risk tolerance: a quantification of the actual amount of risk that the firm is willing to bear.

The mandate can then be converted into a sequential, four-step process:

1 Risk identification: an analysis of the types of risks that the firm faces.
2 Risk quantification: a quantitative description of the size of the firm's risk exposures (or how large they may become) and the magnitude of the profit and/or loss that might be generated.
3 Risk management: a determination, based on cost/benefit analysis, of how the firm can best manage its exposures.
4 Risk monitoring: a process of tracking the company's risk exposures over time.

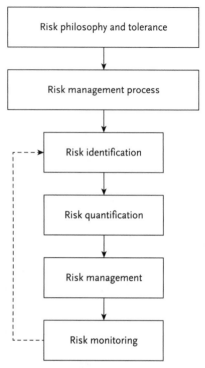

Figure 7.2 The risk management framework

The cycle then repeats, so that the process can be considered dynamic. The ultimate goal of the process is, of course, prudent management of risk that leads to value maximization.

Figure 7.2 summarizes the risk framework.

SPECULATION AND ARBITRAGE

Of course, not all risk-related activities are based on reducing or eliminating risk. Some firms are in business to actively take risk. Banks, securities firms, insurers, and investment funds, for example, regularly take financial risk, as this represents their core business and how they actually make money. They are motivated by speculation and arbitrage rather than pure risk reduction or minimization.

Speculation involves creating a risk position that has the potential for generating a profit or loss, depending on which way a particular market or reference asset moves.

Arbitrage is another form of risk-taking, though one that is generally considered less risky than pure speculation. The classic definition of arbitrage is the simultaneous purchase and sale of an asset that allows a "riskless" profit to be locked in.

RISK REFERENCES

Derivatives and insurance can be arranged on a broad range of risk references, making them suitable for companies from all industries. In general, derivatives are based on financial risks, while insurance contracts are based on insurable operating risks. That said, there are areas of "overlap" that are starting to emerge as the financial and insurance markets draw closer together.

Derivatives can be bought and sold on any of the following references:

- Equities: individual stocks, baskets of stocks, and broad indexes.
- Debt/credits: money market instruments/rates, government bonds/rates (e.g. risk-free bonds), and corporate bonds/rates (e.g. risky bonds).
- Currencies: industrialized and emerging market currency rates.
- Commodities: precious metals (e.g. gold, silver, platinum), industrial metals (e.g. copper, zinc, aluminum), energy products (e.g. oil/distillates, natural gas, electricity), agricultural products (e.g. corn, soybeans, coffee, sugar), commodity indexes, and other non-commodity references (e.g. inflation, gross domestic product, weather, catastrophe).

Insurance can be purchased on the following:

- Property and casualty (P&C): damage/destruction to property caused by non-catastrophic or catastrophic events, and losses related to liability.

- Business interruption: temporary loss of business revenues as a result of non-catastrophic or catastrophic events.
- Marine insurance: damage/destruction to hull, cargo, or freight, along with liability-related losses.
- Health and mortality: long-term disability and death.
- Automobile: damage/destruction, bodily injury, and liability caused by an auto accident.

From a corporate perspective, most focus is placed on the P&C, business interruption, and liability sectors; the health, life/mortality, and automobile sectors, while of vital importance, relate more specifically to individual insurance contracting.

INSTRUMENT CHARACTERISTICS: DERIVATIVES

While the derivatives sector is based on a large variety of unique contracts, we can condense the essential instruments to a more manageable number that includes over-the-counter (OTC) forwards, swaps and options, and exchange-traded (or listed) futures, options, and futures options. We shall not consider the subclasses of "exotic" derivatives (e.g. complex swaps and options, structured notes) as these are beyond our scope – they are, however, simply extensions of the basic building blocks. Figure 7.3 summarizes key types of derivative instruments.

Derivatives have certain features that can make them very appealing: some contracts are very actively traded and therefore cost-effective; transactions arranged through the listed (i.e. exchange-traded) market eliminate credit risk; transactions structured through the OTC market are highly customizable and flexible; and contracts serving as hedges don't require demonstration of "proof of loss" (as an insurance contract does). Some risks and disadvantages also exist, of course: credit risks for OTC transactions can be significant; the costs for exotic contracts can be high; and bilateral derivative contracts, like swaps and forwards, expose a firm to downside payments.

KEY CHARACTERISTICS

Derivatives can be defined by various key characteristics, including notional, reference asset, maturity, strike (for options) and

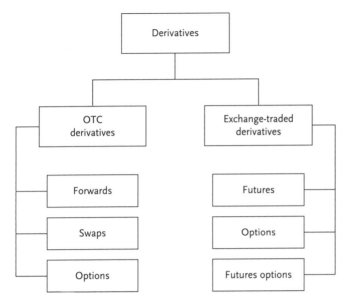

Figure 7.3 Derivative classes

payment/receipt flows (for swaps/forwards), settlement, and trading mechanism.

- Notional: the face value amount of the transaction being arranged. This ranges from several million dollars to more than $1 billion (or equivalent in other currencies), depending on the instrument, market, and motivation. For instance, ABC Co. may decide to arrange a swap with a notional value of £100 million to hedge its interest rate risk. It will not exchange the £100 million notional, but will just use the figure to compute the amount that it must pay, or expects to receive, each period.
- Reference asset: the specific financial asset to which the contract relates. We have noted above that a derivative can be arranged on a very broad range of reference assets from the debt, equity, currency, commodity, and credit markets. The reference asset must be defined specifically, rather than generally. Thus, if ABC Co. is arranging a £100 million notional swap on interest rates, the actual reference rates must be properly

defined, e.g. the company will pay 5 percent sterling fixed rates and receive sterling 6-month London Interbank Offered Rate (LIBOR).

- Maturity: the duration of the derivative contract. This can range from overnight to more than 10 years, though in practice most activity takes place in the 1- to 5-year range. ABC Co.'s £100 million swap, for instance, might have a 5-year maturity, indicating that it is contractually obliged to fulfill the terms of the deal for the full 5 years. The maturity of a derivative contract can sometimes be altered by mutual agreement of the contracting parties.

- Strike/payments/receipts: the relevant financial parameters that dictate the economic flows of a transaction. A strike price is used for options contracts, while pay/receive flows are used for forwards and swaps, as we shall discuss in the next section. For example, we have noted that ABC Co.'s swap involves a payment of 5 percent per year on £100 million versus receipt of LIBOR. If LIBOR at the end of year 1 sets at 4 percent, ABC Co. pays its counterparty £1 million (£100 million × (4 percent – 5 percent)); if LIBOR sets at 6 percent, ABC Co. receives £1 million (£100 million × (6 percent – 5 percent)).

- Settlement: the means by which the underlying economics of a transaction are settled at maturity. Settlement may be arranged in physical or financial terms. A physical settlement involves the actual delivery/acceptance of any asset or instrument that can be physically conveyed, such as oil, gold, or various types of financial instruments. A financial settlement involves a pure exchange of cash value. Thus, in ABC Co.'s sterling interest rate swap, any settlement of the fixed and floating interest rate flows is done in financial terms. Had ABC Co. sought to hedge an exposure to copper rather than interest rates, it could have selected a physical or financial settlement, depending on its need for, or access to, physical copper.

- Trading mechanism: the actual forum through which the derivative is arranged, revalued, and terminated. As we shall see below, this can be done through the OTC market (telephonically or electronically) or through the exchange-traded market; each trading mechanism has advantages and disadvantages. In arranging its swap, ABC Co. uses the OTC market, negotiating terms and conditions verbally with its bank, which then documents details through a written confirmation.

We begin our review of derivatives with a look at OTC contracts, or financial assets that are arranged on a customized basis between two parties.

OTC derivatives

OTC derivatives, as the name suggests, are arranged and traded between two parties on an off-exchange basis. Each contract represents a customized negotiation of terms and conditions, with the parties agreeing to specifics related to notional, term, reference market/asset, pay-off profile, and so forth. Since each contract is tailor-made, resaleability is very limited compared to markets where standardization is mandatory (i.e. the exchange-traded market that we consider below). Lack of liquidity adds to total costs, as expressed through the bid (buy) and offer (sell) spread. In fact, some OTC contracts can feature relatively wide spreads, which can impact the economics of a hedge or speculative trade. However, certain other contracts, such as standard, on-market interest rate, currency, and equity derivatives on major references, feature reasonably good liquidity.

Dealing occurs off-exchange (either telephonically or via electronic platforms) rather than through formalized exchanges; there is no "central forum" for OTC dealing, as activity is arranged and transacted by major financial institutions and their clients. Since OTC derivatives are arranged between two parties with no intermediate clearing house (or neutral clearing party), credit risk can arise.

Let us consider the essential instruments of the OTC derivatives market.

A forward contract is a single-period contract that allows one party, known as the seller, to sell a reference asset at a forward price for settlement at a future date, and a second party, the buyer, to purchase the reference asset at the forward price on the named date. A forward is considered a bilateral contract since either party may be obliged to make a payment at maturity. Market terminology indicates that the party that has sold the position is "short" and the one that has bought the position is "long"; this is true of all other derivative (and financial asset) positions, so we'll use the terms throughout this chapter. A notional amount is used as a reference to compute the amount payable/receivable at maturity; in fact, the two parties exchange no initial or intervening cash flows. Settlement of the contract at maturity may be set in physical or financial terms. If the market price at maturity is greater than the contracted forward price set at trade date, the buyer makes a profit and the seller a loss, and vice versa. These relationships hold true for all price-based forwards, including those involving equities, bonds, indexes, currencies, and commodities. The profit positions of generic long and short forwards are summarized below, and the flows are illustrated in Figure 7.4.

Table 7.2 describes how the value of long and short forwards change as the reference asset increases or decreases, while Figures 7.5 and 7.6 depict the same information in graph form.

We've noted that forwards can be used to neutralize, or hedge, other positions. To illustrate this in graph form, let's imagine that ABC Co. has a short position in some input that it uses in its production. For instance, the firm may use natural gas to power its assembly lines. As the price of natural gas rises, the firm suffers from an increase in its cost of goods sold, meaning its gross profit margins get squeezed. As the price of gas falls, its cost

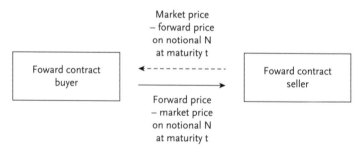

Figure 7.4 Forward contract flows

Table 7.2 Long/short forward relationships

Position	Reference asset ↑	Reference asset ↓
Long forward	Gains value	Loses value
Short forward	Loses value	Gains value

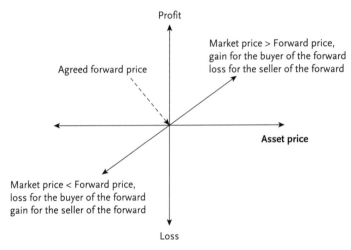

Figure 7.5 Long forward

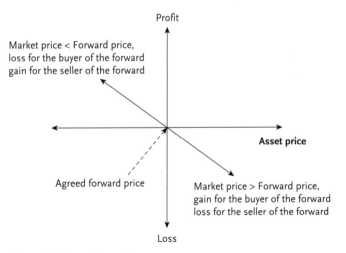

Figure 7.6 Short forward

of goods sold declines, allowing margins to expand. To hedge this input, ABC Co. can enter into a forward where it buys natural gas at the fixed forward price. If gas prices rise, it will suffer on the input position but gain on the forward, and if gas prices fall, it will suffer on the long forward position but gain on its input position. The net effect balances out to zero, meaning that ABC Co. is indifferent to the direction of gas prices: it has "locked in" the natural gas price and therefore crystallizes its profit result – lowering earnings volatility in the process. This relationship is shown in Figure 7.7.

SWAP

The swap, the second major product of the OTC derivatives market, is a package of forward contracts that mature at successive periods in the future, until the stated maturity date. Swaps, like forwards, are bilateral contracts and can be arranged on virtually any asset from any market sector. While interest rate swaps still account for the largest share of the market, active dealing occurs in equity, currency, commodity, and credit swaps. An emerging market has also started to appear in swaps based on inflation and other macro-economic indicators (e.g. gross domestic product), real estate, and weather references (e.g. temperature, precipitation).

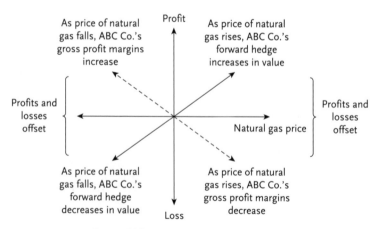

Figure 7.7 Long forward/short asset hedge position

Maturities in the swap marketplace typically range from approximately 1 to 10 years.

Let's examine the interest rate swap that we introduced earlier in the chapter to illustrate the mechanics of the structure. A conventional interest rate swap is a contract where one party agrees to pay a fixed interest rate and a second party agrees to pay a floating rate. The notional principal is used only to compute flows payable and receivable at each intervening evaluation period. On each date, which may be monthly, quarterly, semi-annually, or annually, the fixed and floating rates are compared and a net payment is arranged between the two parties. If the floating rate (generally a recognized index such as LIBOR) is greater than the fixed rate, the floating rate payer makes a net payment to the fixed rate payer in the amount of (floating rate – fixed rate) × notional principal, and vice versa. The process continues to the next evaluation/settlement period, and so forth, until maturity. Figure 7.8 illustrates these basic flows.

Let's consider how an interest rate swap can be used to hedge an interest rate exposure. Assume that ABC Co. has issued £100 million of 5-year floating rate bonds pegged to 6-month sterling LIBOR, which currently stands at 5 percent. Let's also assume that ABC Co.'s treasurer believes that interest rates will rise over the next 5 years. In order to guard against higher interest expense (which would squeeze profits) the company arranges an interest rate swap hedge with a bank where it pays fixed rates (let's assume 5 percent for simplicity) and receives 6-month sterling LIBOR over 5 years; this is illustrated in Figure 7.9. If LIBOR rises, ABC Co. will pay more for its LIBOR-based floating rate debt, but will receive a greater compensatory payment from the bank under the swap. So, if LIBOR rises to 6 percent after the first 6-month evaluation period, ABC Co. pays 6 percent on its floating rate debt, but receives a net 1 percent on the swap (e.g. 6-month sterling LIBOR – 5 percent fixed); this means that its net cost of debt is 5 percent (6 percent – 1 percent), which is precisely equal to the 5 percent fixed rate that it is paying on the swap. If the company's forecast is wrong and rates fall, it still faces the same 5 percent fixed cost of borrowing. For instance, if LIBOR declines to 4 percent, ABC Co. will pay a lower cost on its floating rate debt but will pay a higher cost on the swap; the two again net out

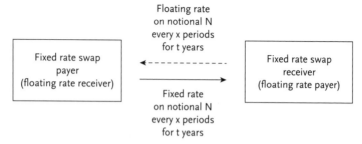

Figure 7.8 Interest rate swap flows

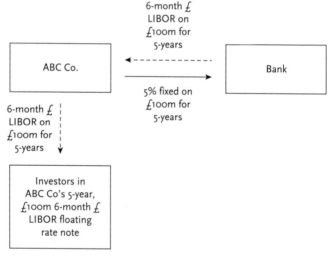

Figure 7.9 ABC Co.'s fixed/floating swap hedge

to 5 percent fixed payments. The process then continues for each of the remaining evaluation periods until maturity in 5 years. We see that, regardless of what happens to interest rates, ABC Co. has hedged itself at a 5 percent fixed rate. These simple scenarios are illustrated in Table 7.3.

OPTION

An option, the third major type of OTC derivative, is a contract that gives the purchaser the right, but not the obligation, to buy

Table 7.3 ABC Co.'s net cost of debt

LIBOR scenario	(a) Cost of floating rate debt (LIBOR)	(b) Gain/loss on swap (LIBOR – 5% fixed)	Net cost of debt (a) – (b)
3%	3%	–2%	5%
4%	4%	–1%	5%
5%	5%	0%	5%
6%	6%	+1%	5%
7%	7%	+2%	5%

(call option) or sell (put option) a reference asset at a particular price (known as the strike price). The option buyer can exercise its rights under the contact at any time until an agreed expiry date (American option), on the expiry date (European option), or on specified dates up to expiry (Bermudan option). In exchange for this right, the buyer pays the seller a premium payment. By accepting the premium the option seller has an obligation to sell (call) or buy (put) the underlying asset at the strike price if the option is exercised. These flows are illustrated in Figures 7.10 and 7.11.

If the buyer of a call option exercises (e.g. the price of the underlying reference asset is above the strike price), it delivers

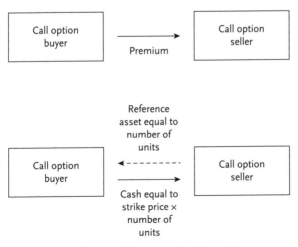

Figure 7.10 Call option flows: initial and exercise

the required amount of cash, which is defined by (strike price × number of units), and receives the underlying asset.

So, if ABC Co. purchases a call for $1,000 of premium that allows it to buy 1,000 barrels of crude oil at a strike price of $50/ barrel, it will be economically advantageous for the firm to exercise whenever the price of oil rises above $50. Let's assume the price of oil rises to $55. ABC Co. exercises the call option against the seller, and delivers $50,000 of cash (i.e. $50 strike price × 1,000 barrels) in exchange for 1,000 barrels of oil. Of course, the 1,000 barrels of oil are actually worth $55,000 in today's market (i.e. the market price is $55/barrel), so ABC Co. has a $5,000 profit on the position; the net profit is equal to $4,000 since the $1,000 premium payment must be deducted. The seller of the option is obliged to supply the 1,000 barrels of oil and accept the $50,000 of cash in exchange. Naturally, if the price of oil falls below $50/barrel, the option has no value to ABC Co. as the company can buy oil in the current market for less than the strike price of the option. If this happens, ABC Co. allows the option to expire and the seller has no further performance obligation. To help understand the economics of the call position, we can examine payoff profiles for ABC Co. as the call buyer and the bank as the call seller; these are illustrated in Figures 7.12

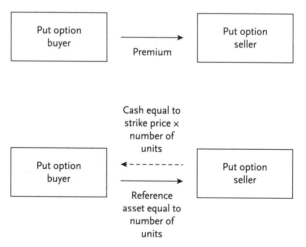

Figure 7.11 Put option flows: initial and exercise

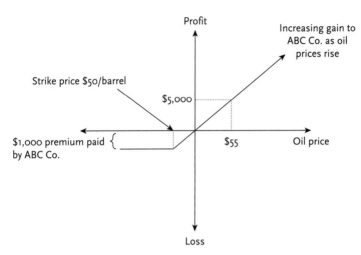

Figure 7.12 Long call option

and 7.13. It's worth highlighting the trade-offs: ABC Co. has a known downside loss (i.e. premium paid) and unlimited profit potential as the price of oil rises, while the bank has a limited gain (i.e. premium received) but potentially unlimited liability as the

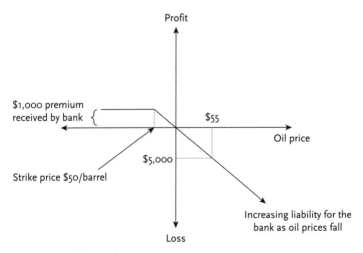

Figure 7.13 Short call option

price of oil rises. This payoff reveals the unilateral nature of the option contract.

A put option gives the buyer the right, but not the obligation, to sell a specified asset at a predetermined strike price. The buyer will exercise the put option when the market price is below the strike price, delivering the asset to the seller in exchange for the required amount of cash. So, if ABC Co. purchases a put option from a bank for $10,000 in premium that lets ABC Co. sell 1,000 oz. of gold at $900/oz. it will exercise when, and if, the price of gold falls below $900/oz. Let's assume that the price of gold falls to $875/oz. In this case ABC Co. can exercise the put option, delivering 1,000 oz. of gold to the bank in exchange for $900,000. The bank, as put option seller, is obliged to acquire the gold by delivering cash. If ABC Co. didn't have the put option and needed to sell the gold in the current market, it would only be able to do so for $875,000; this means that the option has created a $25,000 gain for the company. Again, if the price of gold remains above the strike of $900/oz., ABC Co. will be better off selling the gold in the current market, meaning that it will simply abandon the option. We can again summarize these payoff relationships via Figures 7.14 and 7.15.

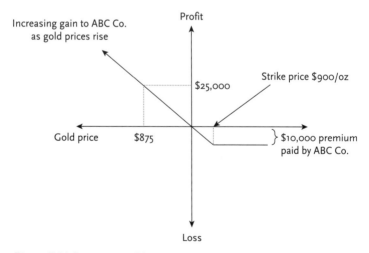

Figure 7.14 Long put position

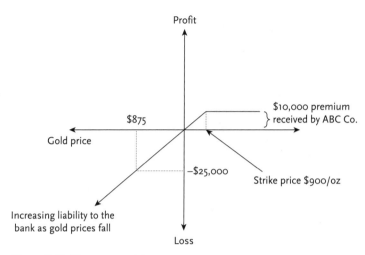

Figure 7.15 Short put position

Table 7.4 summarizes the discussion above by describing how the value of long and short calls and puts changes as the value of the reference asset increases or decreases.

Table 7.4 Long/short options relationships

Position	Reference asset value ↑	Reference asset value ↓
Long call	Gains Value	Loses value (but loss is limited to premium paid)
Short call	Loses value	Gains value (but gain is limited to premium earned)
Long put	Loses value (but loss is limited to premium paid)	Gains value
Short put	Gains value (but gain is limited to premium earned)	Loses value

FINANCE IN ACTION 7.1:   GROWTH OF THE OTC DERIVATIVES MARKET

The OTC market in derivatives has exploded in terms of size and participation, and is by now an essential component of global finance – a remarkable achievement considering that the market was in its formative stages as recently as the mid-1980s. The Bank for International Settlements tracks the growth in activities for each of three broad asset classes (currency/interest rates, credits, and equities/commodities), measuring the notional amount and gross market value of all dealings. While rates have been tabulated since 1987, equities and credits are relatively more recent additions to the marketplace, having come into increasingly widespread use during the new millennium. The growth trajectory for interest and currency rates has remained impressive, with notional activity topping $638 trillion in mid-2014 (versus some $400 trillion in 2008), as all manner of intermediaries and companies continue to use them for risk management or speculation. Credit derivatives, which became part of the financial mainstream around the middle of the decade, grew rapidly prior to the Credit Crisis of 2007–2009, reaching a peak of $59 trillion in 2007, but suffered some setback as a result of the dislocation; total activity declined to $19 trillion in mid-2014. Activity in equity and commodity derivatives has remained relatively stable in the region of $9 trillion over the same time period. Naturally, all of this activity is supplemented by dealing in the exchange-traded markets, which add to total outstandings.

Exchange-traded derivatives

Exchange-traded (or listed) derivatives – which include futures, options, and futures options – constitute the second major segment of the derivatives market. Exchange-traded derivatives can be used to achieve many of the same goals as OTC contracts, often at a cheaper cost, but with less structural flexibility. All trading occurs through regulated exchanges, such as the Chicago Mercantile Exchange, the Intercontinental Exchange, Eurex, Euronext, London International Financial Futures Exchange, and the Tokyo Commodity Exchange, among others (indeed, there are more than 400 registered exchanges around the world); some of these exchanges specialize in financial derivatives, others in commodities, and a few in both.

Each buyer and seller dealing with the exchange is required to post initial margin (i.e. collateral or security) with the clearing house to protect against possible credit losses. The initial margin is evaluated by the clearing house every day based on a client's open positions and market moves, and additional calls for margin may be made if a particular maintenance level is breached as a result of losses. Since the exchange serves as counterparty and participants must post margin, the counterparty credit risk that characterizes many OTC derivative contracts is eliminated; this is one of the central advantages of the listed marketplace.

All contracts listed on an exchange are standardized, meaning trade details cannot be customized as in the OTC market. All buyers and sellers deal in the same trading size/units, contract months/maturity, delivery date, deliverable asset, and settlement style. This homogeneity leads to a greater critical mass of liquidity, meaning the cost of arranging a hedge or speculative position can be lower than in the OTC market.

Let's review the key instruments of the listed market.

FUTURE

A future is a bilateral contract that allows one party, the seller, to sell a particular reference asset at a future price for settlement at a future date, and the second party, the buyer, to purchase the reference asset at the future price on the named date. Based on this description, the futures contract appears to be identical to the forward contract discussed above. In fact, the pay-off profiles of the two instruments are precisely the same, so the illustrations in Figures 7.4 and 7.5 are applicable to both futures and forwards. Indeed, the example of ABC Co. arranging a forward contract to hedge natural gas exposure can be replicated by substituting a natural gas futures contract in place of the forward; the ultimate economic outcome will be the same. However, as a result of the exchange mechanism, a futures position calls for a daily settlement of profit/loss rather than a single settlement at maturity: each futures position is revalued by the clearing house at the close of each trading day, and net debits/credits are made to the accounts of the two parties based on the day's losses/gains. Futures can be settled in physical or financial terms, and the precise settlement mechanism is specified as part of a contract's standardized features. Contract maturities vary, but typically span 1 week to 1 quarter. The most active futures references may be listed concurrently on a monthly or quarterly cycle out to several years (e.g. LIBOR/Eurodollar futures, S&P 500 futures, Brent crude futures).

OPTION AND FUTURES OPTION

The listed market features options that function much like the OTC options described above. In fact, there is no difference between the two contracts, apart from the general characteristics that distinguish listed products from OTC products. A unique subset of the listed options market centers on futures options, which are options that give the buyer the right to buy or sell an underlying futures contract and which require the seller to accept or deliver the futures contract upon exercise; this can be viewed as a type of compound derivative (i.e. a derivative on another derivative). The positions of the long and short futures options positions are summarized in Table 7.5.

The key differences between OTC and exchange-traded derivatives are summarized in Table 7.6.

INSTRUMENT CHARACTERISTICS: INSURANCE

The insurance sector, like the derivatives sector, features a large number of instruments (or contracts) that can be used to transfer

Table 7.5 Futures options positions

Position	If exercised . . .
Long futures call	Buyer acquires a futures contract at strike price
Long futures put	Buyer sells a futures contract at strike price
Short futures call	Seller obligated to sell a futures contract at strike price
Short futures put	Seller obligated to acquire a futures contract at strike price

Table 7.6 Primary differences between exchange-traded and OTC derivatives

	Exchange-traded	*OTC*
Terms	Standardized	Customized
Trading forum	Central exchange (physical or electronic)	OTC (telephonic or electronic)
Price transparency	Good	Poor/fair
Liquidity	Reasonable/strong	Limited/fair
Credit exposure	Negligible	Possibly significant unless collateralized
Margins	Required	None unless negotiated
Settlement	Generally closed-out	Generally held until maturity
Regulation	Regulated	Largely unregulated

risks from companies (which become "cedants" or "insureds") to insurance companies (insurers). In order to preserve our corporate focus we'll consider the essential contracts that are used to transfer corporate operating risks; we won't consider the very significant life, health, and auto insurance sectors that apply to individuals, though many of the same concepts we discuss below are equally applicable.

KEY CHARACTERISTICS

Before delving into the key characteristics that define any insurance contract, we must first consider several concepts related to insurance contracting. This is important because insurance contracts are intended to cover pure, rather than speculative, risks – a fundamental feature that distinguishes insurance from derivatives.

In order for a contract to be considered insurance, it must usually feature the following:

- The contract must cover an insurable risk with respect to a fortuitous event – an event that is unforeseen, unexpected, or accidental.
- A large number of similar risk exposures must exist so that insurers can measure the exposure with some degree of accuracy.

- The cedant must have an insurable interest and demonstrate proof of actual economic loss if a defined event occurs; this ensures that the cedant only receives compensation for losses and cannot create a profit.
- The risk of loss must be specifically transferred under a contract providing indemnity (i.e. financial restitution if a loss occurs) and it must involve the payment of an insurance premium.
- The right of subrogation must exist, meaning that the cedant must agree to transfer, to the insurer, any loss recovery rights.

Every insurance contract is defined by several key characteristics, including policy size (cap), premium, deductible, coinsurance, coverage and exclusions, and coverage period.

- Policy size (cap): the amount of insurance coverage being arranged, which can range from several million dollars to more than $1 billion (in equivalent currency terms), depending on the specific property being insured and the nature of the risk exposure. The smaller the size of the policy in relation to the amount of exposure, the greater the amount of risk that the cedant retains. For instance, ABC Co. may arrange P&C insurance based on a policy size of £300 million to protect against fire damage/destruction at one of its factories. Subject to the deductibles and coinsurance described below, ABC Co. will receive a maximum of £300 million in restitution if a fire occurs and damages or destroys its factory.
- Premium: the amount that the ceding company must pay the insurer for the policy. The premium is generally payable annually and is quoted in value terms (e.g. dollars or sterling). Once the premium is paid, the contract is activated and the company is protected by the insurer under the terms defined in the policy. For example, ABC Co. may pay a £100,000 premium for £300 million of fire insurance coverage.
- Deductible: the amount of initial losses that the cedant bears before the insurance coverage becomes effective. The deductible can range from a very small amount of the policy size up to more than 20 percent. The greater the deductible, the more risk the cedant retains (and the lower the premium, since the cedant bears more of the first losses); conversely, the smaller

the deductible, the less risk the cedant keeps (and the higher the premium). Under its £300 million fire insurance policy ABC Co. may be willing to bear a reasonable amount of the initial losses, setting a deductible of £5 million. This means that, if fire strikes and causes £25 million of damage to the company's plant and equipment, the net restitution to ABC Co. will amount to £20 million (£25 million of total losses minus the £5 million deductible).

- Coinsurance (copay): the amount of losses that the cedant and insurer agree to share. Coinsurance can range from 0 percent to more than 50 percent, though a range of 10–20 percent is quite typical. The larger the coinsurance, the greater the cedant's retention of risk and the lower the policy premium. Conversely, the lower the coinsurance, the greater the cedant's risk transfer and the higher the premium. ABC Co. may choose a 10 percent coinsurance on its fire policy. Assuming it also has a £5 million deductible, then £25 million of losses will result in net restitution to ABC Co. of £18 million (£25 million of losses minus £5 million deductible = £20 million × 90 percent = £18 million).
- Coverage and exclusions: the precise terms of risk coverage, including any events or circumstances under which the cedant is not covered. Coverage includes a detailed definition of the perils that can create losses for which the cedant will be indemnified. Exclusions, in contrast, relate to any specific or general circumstances under which a cedant's losses are not indemnified. The broader the coverage and the narrower the exclusions, the greater the risk transfer and the larger the premium. For instance, ABC Co.'s policy may cover against all physical damage or destruction caused by a fire in designated locations (e.g. the company's factories and warehouses). But it may exclude coverage for business interruption or the amount of business lost as a result of the company's inability to use its plant and equipment if fire creates damage/destruction.
- Coverage period: the period during which the insurance coverage is effective. In nearly all cases insurance policies are written for a 12-month period, after which the cedant and insurer can re-evaluate terms, conditions, and requirements and decide whether coverage renewal is necessary or desirable (and, if so, at what cost and under what terms).

The characteristics noted above are usually included as declarations in the insurance policy, which also contains important information on the actual property being insured.

KEY INSTRUMENTS/CONTRACTS

Since insurance is a risk transfer mechanism, the actual amount of risk transferred from cedant to insurer depends largely on how the characteristics noted above are defined. Policies may be created so that they transfer very little risk; these are more appropriately described as risk retention insurance contracts. Those that transfer some amount of risk are considered intermediate risk retention/transfer insurance contracts, while those resulting in a significant transfer are known as full risk transfer insurance contracts. Several other products, including loss financing contracts and captives, join these contracts.

Figure 7.16 illustrates instruments/contracts relative to the amount of risk retained or transferred.

Full insurance

A full insurance contract is an example of a maximum risk transfer contract where the cedant's goal is to shift as much insurable exposure as possible. Following from our discussion above, full insurance is created by crafting a policy with small (or even no) deductible, a large policy limit, limited (or no) coinsurance, and limited (or no) exclusions. Assume that ABC Co. wants full insurance coverage on its £300 million of fire exposure and is willing to pay a high premium if necessary. It can structure a policy with a £300 million limit, no deductible, no exclusions, and no coinsurance. If a fire strikes and causes £150 million of losses from destroyed property and £150 million of losses from business interruption, ABC Co. receives restitution equal to the full £300 million.

Standard insurance

A standard insurance contract is an example of an intermediate risk retention/transfer mechanism where the cedant retains some amount of exposure and transfers the balance. As we might

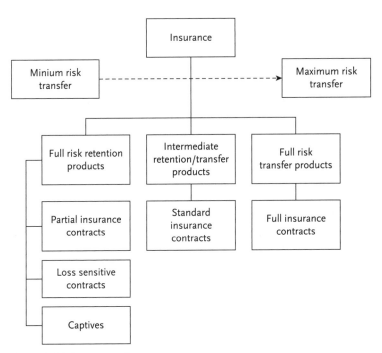

Figure 7.16 Insurance classes

expect, this coverage can be created by drafting a policy with a moderate deductible, a moderate policy limit, certain exclusions, and perhaps a modest coinsurance feature. Let's extend the example above by noting that ABC Co. is now willing to accept a larger amount of risk on its £300 million of fire exposure in exchange for paying a smaller premium. Accordingly, it sets a deductible of £10 million and lowers the policy limit to £275 million; it decides not to set any exclusions, but agrees on a 5 percent coinsurance level. If the same fire event noted above occurs, ABC Co.'s total restitution amounts to £251.75 million, or £48.25 million less than under the full insurance policy. The lower figure results from the fact that the company sets the maximum loss coverage at £275 million (meaning the additional £25m of losses that occur are excluded), it bears the first losses of £10 million through the deductible, and then receives 95 percent, rather than 100 percent, of the remaining losses as a result of the coinsurance.

Partial insurance

A partial insurance contract is an example of a risk retention contract, as it transfers the smallest amount of risk from cedant to insurer. This structure, which is best suited for companies that are not as risk averse as those purchasing standard or full insurance, features a very large deductible and perhaps a moderate policy limit, significant exclusions, and high coinsurance. It's relatively easy to see that under the partial insurance structure the ceding company bears the largest amount of first losses, faces limited coverage in the event of very large losses, may have no coverage if certain excluded events come into play, and must share in any losses that arise. In the most extreme version of our example, let's assume that ABC Co. is interested in accepting even more risk (i.e. transferring less risk) in exchange for paying a relatively small premium. Accordingly, it sets a £250 million policy limit, raises the deductible to £20 million, increases coinsurance to 10 percent, and excludes from the policy any losses created by business interruption. Once again, if the event described above occurs, ABC Co. will receive restitution of only £117 million, or £183 million less than the actual loss sustained.

These simple examples indicate that the optimal amount of insurance that a company like ABC Co. should purchase is a function of the cost of coverage (premium) and the expected benefits (coverage) should an event occur. The process of converting full insurance coverage to partial insurance coverage is summarized in Figure 7.17.

Loss sensitive contract

A loss sensitive contract is a partial insurance contract with premiums that depend on previous loss experience. Loss sensitive contracts are different from conventional insurance contracts as premiums are related to losses that occur during a specified period and claims are typically not determined until after some

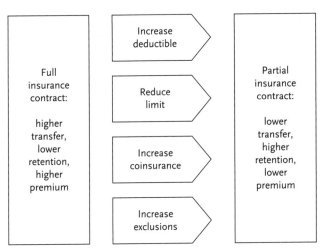

Figure 7.17 Converting full insurance to partial insurance

period of time has passed. For instance, ABC Co. may purchase an experience-rated fire insurance policy where the premium that it pays the insurer is a function of its past loss experience: the greater the losses and claims in previous periods, the greater the premium, and vice versa. Or, ABC Co. may choose a retrospectively rated policy, where it pays the insurer an initial premium and, depending on the occurrence/size of any fire-related losses, makes an additional premium payment (if a claim arises) or receives a refund (if no claims arise).

Captive

A captive is a company-owned (or controlled) insurance subsidiary that is used to facilitate a company's insurance program; it can be thought of as an in-house self-insurance company. The company (also known as a sponsor) provides capital to commence the operation, receiving interest and/or dividends in exchange. The captive then insures the company directly by accepting premiums to absorb particular types of risks. Though the nature and operation of captives vary, the focus is generally on high-frequency/low-severity risks – the highly predictable exposures

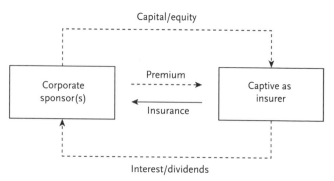

Figure 7.18 Structure of a captive

for which this form of self-insurance can be a cost-effective alternative.

Figure 7.18 illustrates the structure of the captive.

FINANCE IN ACTION 7.2:   EVEN INSURERS NEED INSURANCE

We've noted that individuals and companies often turn to the insurance marketplace to cover risks that they are uncomfortable keeping. But what about the insurance companies that provide coverage — how do they manage their own risks? In addition to the diversification and loss control mechanisms that we've described, they frequently buy insurance of their own – what is known as reinsurance. Reinsurance is simply insurance cover written by a reinsurance company for an insurer through one of the mechanisms described below. So, a primary insurer like State Farm, Aetna, or Prudential can buy reinsurance from a reinsurer like ACE, Swiss Re, Munich Re, or the Lloyds of London reinsurance market to achieve several goals: reduce risk in a particular peril or to a specific insurable event, increase portfolio diversification, or protect against high severity/low frequency catastrophic events (like hurricanes or earthquakes). Of course, in entering into a reinsurance agreement the insurer is exchanging an insurance risk for the credit risk of the reinsurer, because if a claim is made under the covered insurance policy, the reinsurer must be able to perform as required.

Insurance risk can be ceded to a reinsurer in different ways. First, we can distinguish between facultative and treaty reinsurance. Facultative reinsurance is customized, case-by-case reinsurance where the reinsurer examines, and either accepts or rejects, each specific risk. This approach is usually reserved for large and complex transactions where extra diligence is required, such as property and casualty coverage for a fleet of oil tankers or commercial property protection for a high-rise office tower against losses caused by an earthquake. Importantly, under this scheme the reinsurer is not obliged to accept the risk and the insurer is not obliged to cede the risk. Treaty reinsurance, in contrast, is an automatic process: the insurer and reinsurer agree on underwriting criteria for specific risks and, once agreed, the insurer automatically cedes and the reinsurer automatically accepts the risks, no questions asked, up to an agreed-upon limit. This, not surprisingly, is used for "run of the mill" risks for which the underwriting process is straightforward, such as ceding risk on a large portfolio of automobile policies. Second, we can distinguish proportional versus excess of loss (XOL) reinsurance. Under the proportional reinsurance scheme, quota share (fixed) and surplus share (variable) arrangements call for a proportional sharing of risks and returns between insurer and reinsurer. That is, both parties have an economic interest in every risk written based on a prearranged formula. In XOL, each party takes a preferred layer of risk. So, under a vertical XOL the insurer may keep the first $2 million of risk (through a deductible), Reinsurer A may take risk of loss between $2 million (attachment point) and $5 million (cap), and Reinsurer B may take the layer of $5 million (attachment point) to $10 million (cap). Alternatively, in horizontal XOL, the insurer and the two reinsurers may agree to those same layers, but may each take a percentage of a given layer, e.g. insurer takes $2 million, Reinsurer A takes 40% of $2 million to $5 million, and B takes the remaining 60 percent, and so forth. The proportional and XOL structures essentially allow the insurer and reinsurer(s) to customize the risk transfer as needed.

Knowing all of this, the next logical question is whether reinsurers can get insurance protection as well? In fact, they can: a reinsurer like

Swiss Re or ACE can use the same mechanisms described above to transfer risks to another reinsurer like Munich Re or Lloyds of London, in a process known as retrocession. Naturally, the ability to retrocede depends on the amount of available risk capital in the reinsurance market, and care must be taken not to pass the same risks around the same small group of reinsurers. Ultimately, however, reinsurance and retrocession allow insurable risks to spread widely through the financial markets, helping creating a more stable system.

CHAPTER SUMMARY

A derivative is a contract that derives its value from some market or asset, such as a stock, bond, currency, or commodity. Insurance is a contract that provides financial restitution against an event that creates a loss. Both instruments are widely used by companies to manage financial and operating risks: derivatives are used to hedge risks by providing a gain when an underlying risk exposure produces a loss; insurance is used to transfer risks to another party (i.e. an insurer) through the payment of a premium. While derivatives can also be used to speculate/arbitrage in the hope of creating profits, insurance can never be used to generate profits. Derivatives are characterized by notional, reference asset, maturity, settlement, trading mechanism, and, for options, strike price. Key classes of derivatives include standardized exchange-traded contracts (futures, options, futures options) that trade via exchanges and OTC contracts (forwards, swaps, options) that are customized between two parties. Insurance contracts are described by policy size (cap), premium, deductible, coinsurance, and coverage/exclusions. Key insurance categories include partial, standard, and full insurance contracts, as well as loss sensitive contracts and captives. Reinsurance is a vital component of the marketplace as well, allowing insurance companies to shift some of their own risk to reinsurers.

FURTHER READING

Banks, E., 2004, *Alternative Risk Transfer*, London: John Wiley & Sons.

Cox, J. and Rubinstein, M., 1985, *Options Markets*, Upper Saddle River, NJ: Prentice Hall.

Crouhy, M., Galai, D., and Mark, R., 2005, *The Essentials of Risk Management*, New York: McGraw-Hill.

Hull, J., 2014, *Options, Futures, and Other Derivatives*, 9th edn., Upper Saddle River, NJ: Prentice Hall.

Jorion, P., 2010, *The Financial Risk Manager Handbook*, 6th edn., New York: John Wiley & Sons.

MacDonald, R., 2012, *Derivatives Markets*, 3rd edn., Upper Saddle River, NJ: Prentice Hall.

Vaughan, E. and Vaughan, T., 2013, *Fundamentals of Risk and Insurance*, 11th edn., New York: John Wiley & Sons.

8

CORPORATE FINANCE

CHAPTER OVERVIEW

In this final chapter of Part 2 we alter our focus from products and instruments designed to directly fulfill funding, investment, or risk management goals, to specific financial transactions intended to boost enterprise value and meet other strategic, profit, or market share goals. We shall begin by discussing the uses of corporate finance and then examine the key characteristics of the most common transactions, including mergers, acquisitions, leveraged (management) buyouts, spin-offs, and recapitalizations and buybacks. We will then review the general process by which corporate finance deals are valued and conclude by examining the challenges that a company faces in arranging a transaction.

USES OF CORPORATE FINANCE

Corporate finance, which includes a broad range of financial engineering deals that can be used to alter the structure and scope of a company's operations, is a central part of long-term financial planning. The decision to acquire, or merge with, another company, sell a piece of the company, or restructure the capital base is achieved only after considerable planning and analysis. Corporate finance transactions, which are generally complex to arrange and execute, cannot typically be done as part of short-term, or tactical, operations. Rather, they are part of the long-term financial planning process and must often be sanctioned by the board of directors and, in some cases, even shareholders. Though a company may sometimes respond quickly to a market opportunity that presents itself at short notice, the strategic analysis related to any such action is part of long-term strategic planning.

We'll examine corporate finance transactions in more detail later in the chapter to gain an understanding of both uses and challenges. We begin, however, with some basic definitions:

- Merger: a transaction where one company combines with another company on an equal basis to create a "new" company.
- Acquisition: a transaction where one company buys another company.
- Leveraged (management) buyout: a transaction where a publicly listed company takes itself private by borrowing to purchase outstanding shares.
- Spin-off: a transaction where a company sells one or more of its units or divisions to the public (in an initial public offering – IPO) or to a third party (in a private equity transaction).
- Recapitalization: a transaction where a company restructures its capital base, sometimes dramatically.

Each one of these may be driven by slightly different motivations. All, however, are intended to enhance stakeholder value. Let's consider some of the key reasons why a company like ABC Co. might consider arranging a "generic" corporate finance transaction.

- Expanding product/market share: ABC Co., an established company with a full product line, may be reaching a point in its product and market cycle where it can no longer grow simply by adding more workers or plant and equipment. To continue its expansion, it may need to look to new geographic areas in the same industry or absorb other parts of the production chain. By acquiring or merging with another company, ABC Co. has the potential of increasing its revenue base more rapidly and efficiently. In some cases the combination of two companies can produce growth through "synergies" – the creation of new cross-market products or services that can only be done by joining two different firms; and in some cases the deal can produce some areas of overlap, which can lead to rationalizations and cost reductions.

- Creating earnings stability: we have already noted that the worth of a company can decline when earnings are volatile or unpredictable. Investors don't like surprises, and if the earnings stream cannot be relied on to a significant degree, the company's stock will trade at a lower price. ABC Co. may be able to dampen its earnings volatility by acquiring, or merging with, a company that has a different pattern of earnings. This goal can only be achieved, however, if ABC Co. and its partner company have different earnings cycles; if they have the same cycle, the earnings volatility effect will be compounded, as illustrated in Figure 8.1.

- Reducing costs: while ABC Co. may be managing its costs as efficiently as possible, it may find opportunities to create even greater cost savings by combining with another company. We recall from Chapter 2 that a company can increase its enterprise value by reducing cost of goods sold, SG&A expenses, and other operating expenses. Economies of scale, which arise when large producers negotiate large (and cheaper) input purchases and eliminate duplicative resources (e.g. personnel, real estate, technology), are a key driver of cost savings. Cost savings can also be achieved by divesting inefficient operations or eliminating duplicative areas. Tax benefits may also factor into the process. For instance, a profitable company that buys an unprofitable company with accumulated tax loss carry forward can reduce its tax liability, thereby increasing its after-tax earnings.

- Acquiring intellectual property: ABC Co. may want to expand its product line into areas that require a higher degree of technical specialization and knowledge. While it may be able to do so through "organic" development, i.e. adding technical capabilities by hiring individuals with the proper mix of skills, it can also use a corporate finance transaction, such as an acquisition or merger, to obtain the same level of intellectual expertise. Speed is the main benefit of obtaining intellectual

Different earnings cycles

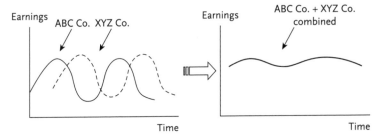

Identical earnings cycles

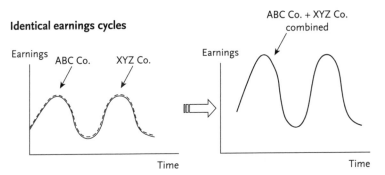

Figure 8.1 Earnings cycles and earnings stability

property via a merger or acquisition: rather than waiting for years for the proper base of intellectual property to develop through hiring, training, and development, ABC Co. may be able to gain the advantage it seeks within months.

• Altering the capital structure: ABC Co. may wish to change its capital structure, either by increasing equity if it believes it has too much debt, or increasing debt if it believes that it is not taking full advantage of the tax shield generated by bonds and loans. In more extreme scenarios it may increase its debt dramatically to purchase outstanding shares and take the company private; this is the initial step in a leveraged buyout (LBO), which must then be accompanied by radical internal cost restructuring. It can use also use other corporate finance techniques, such as arranging a buyback of its stock (which increases leverage), acquiring a company with low levels of debt (which decreases leverage), or divesting a portion of the company (which injects cash and allows debt to be reduced).

As we've said, each of these factors tells us why companies use corporate finance techniques. Of course, the ultimate measure of whether or not a transaction is useful becomes evident in enterprise value: if a company can increase its worth by acquiring intellectual property, altering capital, gaining market share, and so forth, then the financial decision-making process is likely to support a deal. That said, corporate finance transactions can be difficult and complex to arrange and execute; we'll discuss some of the potential pitfalls later in the chapter.

TRANSACTION CHARACTERISTICS

MERGERS AND ACQUISITIONS

Mergers and acquisitions (M&As) are relatively common corporate finance transactions. Over the past century these deals appear to have gone through various stages: the earliest deals (1900 to 1950s) were "friendly" rather than "hostile," based initially on horizontal expansion (i.e. of competitors), and then vertical expansion (i.e. in the supply/production chain). These were followed by conglomeration (1960s and 1970s), and then a turn towards hostile transactions (1980s and 1990s). More recent activity (1990s into the new millennium) has returned to friendly transactions, often on a cross-border basis.

Let's begin with a review of acquisitions. An acquisition, as the name suggests, occurs when one company buys another company on an outright basis. An acquisition can be arranged within or outside the industry, depending on the specific goal the acquiring firm is attempting to achieve. For instance, if ABC Co. wants to gain market share within its own product line of specialty goods, it may decide to acquire rival competitor XYZ Co., which makes the same goods; this is known as horizontal integration. The "new" ABC Co. will thus have a larger market share in specialty goods than it did before the acquisition. Alternatively, ABC Co. may be interested in expanding its production chain by acquiring its main raw material supplier, Acme Supply. This is a form of vertical integration. Though ABC Co.'s market share won't immediately increase as a result of the Acme purchase, it will give the company an opportunity to control more parts of its input and production processes, perhaps allowing it to drive down costs in the process. If it wants to continue expanding vertically, it may then acquire a product transportation and distribution company, Transport Co. Again, by combining Transport Co.'s operations with its own, ABC Co. may be able to achieve greater operating efficiencies. Efficiencies can lead to lower operating costs, larger earnings, and greater enterprise value. Of course, ABC Co.'s management must be very certain that it can actually achieve the efficiencies and cost savings proposed through the merger before it commits resources.

While many acquisitions are based on horizontal or vertical integration, some are based on conglomeration. This occurs when a company purchases a firm operating in an entirely unrelated industry and this is intended to diversify the firm's revenue base. For instance, ABC Co. may want to expand its revenue base from specialty goods to consulting services in order to protect its earnings, should demand for specialty goods decline during the next business cycle. After much analysis of Consult Co.'s business and earnings, it may conclude that Consult Co. can provide the proper earnings protection during particular market cycles and proceed to buy the firm. It's worth noting that some con-glomerations are successful and others are not. The market may not be convinced of a company's ability to properly manage and integrate an unrelated firm into its overall operations and may "penalize" the acquiring company's stock by assigning it a lower value. Major types of acquisitions are shown in Figure 8.2.

An acquisition can be arranged in various ways. For instance, the acquiring company (e.g. ABC Co.) can buy the shares of the target company (e.g. Acme Supply Co.) for cash. Or, it can use its own shares, or a mix of shares and debt, to acquire the target. Though less common, the acquirer can purchase the majority of the target company's assets (rather than the whole company).

As we've noted, an acquisition can be arranged on friendly or hostile terms. A friendly acquisition, which is the most common type of deal, occurs when the executives and directors of the acquiring company and the target company negotiate, and then

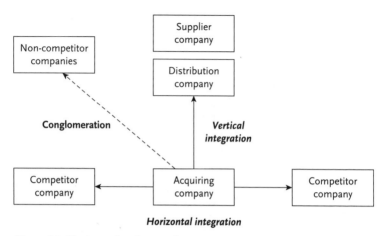

Figure 8.2 Horizontal and vertical acquisitions

agree to, a transaction. In such cases the target company's board of directors recommends acceptance of the deal to its investors. A hostile acquisition occurs when the target company wants to remain independent, doesn't like the terms of the deal, or would prefer to merge with, or be acquired by, another firm. While these transactions are rather less common, they do occur. The law in many countries provides for certain legal anti-takeover defenses that are designed to provide a modicum of protection again unwelcome approaches. However, these defenses (which may include "poison pills," or legal clauses that trigger post-acquisition asset sales or other value-destroying measures) are not always sufficient to deter a full battle. The target company may ultimately succumb or force a proxy fight (i.e. a vote by shareholders on whether to proceed). Alternatively, it may search for a friendly partner to take over a minority stake (a so-called "white squire") or a majority stake ("white knight") in the company.

A merger occurs when two companies, often of roughly equal size and strength, combine their operations to create a new company. The motivations follow along the lines described above (i.e. vertical or horizontal expansion, or conglomeration to boost enterprise value). For instance, ABC Co. and one of its main rivals, JKL Inc., may decide to join forces in order to create a dominant market position and generate cost savings. If we assume that the two companies are about the same size, the transaction may be considered a "merger of equals," yielding an entirely new firm comprising the consolidated operations of the two.

LEVERAGED BUYOUTS

An LBO, sometimes known as a management buyout (MBO), is another common form of corporate finance transaction. An LBO is arranged when a public company, with shares listed on a stock exchange, is "taken private" – that is, all of the shares held by the public are purchased by a small group of the company's managers and/or a sponsoring private equity group and the stock is de-listed from the exchange. Once the company is private it no longer needs to answer to a broad base of shareholders regarding performance and strategy issues, thereby gaining valuable operating freedom. The team taking the company private need only satisfy a small number of stakeholders, primarily those that are involved in financing the deal.

The strategy and rationale behind the LBO is to repurchase outstanding shares from investors by using a great deal of borrowed money (hence the term "leveraged" in LBO) and then begin a multi-year (e.g. 3–5 year) program of reshaping the operating structure of the firm. Reshaping is typically based on reducing the cost of goods sold and operating/selling, general and administrative (SG&A) expenses, introducing new efficiencies, and perhaps realigning or eliminating product lines that no longer produce the desired margins. In some cases entire portions of the company may be sold to generate cash for eventual repayment of debt. In fact, firms that require significant financial restructuring are good LBO candidates: companies with little outstanding debt, a relatively high cost base, and a mature and recognized product base generally fit in this category.

Since the firm's interest expense becomes so much greater under an LBO, reducing costs is essential. The end goal of the successful LBO is crystallized after the restructuring program is completed: the newly restructured company, which may still have a reasonably large amount of debt but a leaner cost structure and a more focused operation, is either recapitalized through an initial public offering or is sold to a third party (e.g. another company).

In either case, cash raised is used to pay down the remaining debt, and the new company that ultimately emerges is financially strong. The LBO group sponsoring the deal generates its own profit from the sale proceeds. Figure 8.3 illustrates the LBO and post-LBO flows.

SPIN-OFFS

A spin-off is a public or private sale of assets that provides a company with a valuable cash injection or allows it to increase efficiencies and focus its operations. A spin-off can be managed as a carve-out or disposal, and is intended ultimately to boost enterprise value.

(a) LBO phase

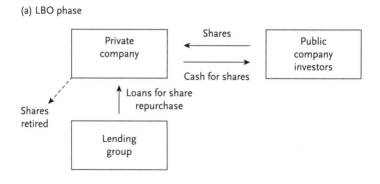

(b) Post-LBO phase (recapitalization via IPO)

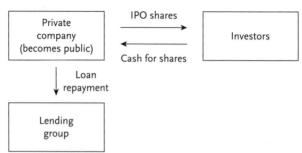

Figure 8.3 Leveraged buyout (LBO) structure

A carve-out involves the sale of some part of a company's existing operations, such as a profitable and well-regarded subsidiary that can be readily split from the balance of the firm. By selling one of its units, the company hopes to earn a premium over book value (i.e. the value at which the asset or unit is carried on the company's balance sheet) that will increase its own worth. Naturally, such a sale is only contemplated when management believes that the transaction will add value and will not impair its ability to operate efficiently and profitably. Indeed, there is little point in selling assets if the value of the company will be permanently damaged. Let's assume that ABC Co. has a highly profitable subsidiary, ABC Sub Inc., and that management believes it can create value for ABC Co. shareholders by carving out the subsidiary. It may thus work with a bank, a private equity fund or even a competitor to structure a private sale of ABC Sub Inc., or it may decide to float ABC Sub Inc. publicly through an IPO. In either case, ABC Co. will receive the financial benefit of the sale, while ABC Sub Inc. will continue its operations as part of another firm or as an independent entity.

Divestiture is another form of spin-off. While the divestiture shares certain similarities with the carve-out – namely, the sale of a portion of a company – the value driver is somewhat different. In the case of a carve-out, a company believes that it can create value by selling a valuable asset to the public or a third party, while in a divestiture it seeks primarily to exit a business line that is no longer essential to its operations or which is not performing up to financial expectations. The sale may or may not generate an immediate gain for the company. In fact, the divestiture in some cases may be done at a loss to book value, creating a one-time charge against the income statement. However, if the decision proves ultimately to be correct, the value of the firm should rise over time as an underperforming operation ceases to hamper the firm's progress or tie up its capital.

RECAPITALIZATIONS

A recapitalization is a corporate finance transaction that is used to restructure the form and size of a company's capital base. This generally involves using debt and equity to create a capital base that is more appropriate for a firm's circumstances at a particular stage in its corporate life, or in light of changing market circumstances (including competitive pressures and potential takeover threats).

A recapitalization is often associated with deleveraging of the corporate balance sheet. A firm may, over time, become overly dependent on debt, causing its financial position to weaken – perhaps to the point where financial pressures from a large interest burden set in and the credit rating is threatened. In such instances a company may implement a recapitalization program to overhaul its funding structure. For example, if ABC Co. finds itself with too much debt and not enough equity, it may arrange for simultaneous issues of common and preferred stock, using the proceeds to repay a variety of medium- and long-term loans and bonds. While this may initially lead to a higher cost of capital, it will give ABC Co. greater financial strength and flexibility, both of which can boost corporate value.

In some cases a firm may have too little leverage. This means, of course, that it may not be taking full advantage of the tax shield that is generated through the use of debt. If we assume that ABC Co. is now underleveraged rather than overleveraged, it can again arrange a recapitalization program where it issues new debt (or borrows from its bankers) and uses the proceeds to buy back some amount of stock.

But recapitalization needn't only focus on a rebalancing of debt and equity. In some instances these transactions involve restructuring of the voting rights accorded to investors. Again, depending on the specific nature of a company's control structure and its ultimate goals, directors may authorize distribution of voting power by diluting the voting rights of a small block of control investors and expanding those of a larger base of minority shareholders. This places greater legal control in the hands of small investors. Alternatively, directors may propose a dual-class recapitalization that creates two classes of shares: those where minority shareholders are given less (or no) voting power and those where control shareholders are given virtually complete voting power.

VALUING CORPORATE FINANCE DEALS

A company must only arrange a corporate finance deal when it makes financial sense to do so. In other words, a deal must create value for stakeholders. The valuation process centers on examining what a company looks like before a deal (ex-ante) and forecasting what it might like look after a deal (ex-post). This is typically done by developing a detailed analysis of operating and financial risks, current and future cash flows, current and anticipated cost of capital, and current and expected earnings per share. However, since the process relates to estimates of future events, it can never by completely accurate. In fact, a good valuation process incorporates multiple scenarios (i.e. base case, worst case, and best case), so that the "value range" of the transaction can be properly considered in the financial planning process.

Let's consider, as an example, the basic steps involved in valuing an acquisition: ABC Co., expanding horizontally, wants to buy Acme. In the first step, ABC Co. examines the present value of Acme's future (after-tax) income. The actual process takes us back to our discussion in Chapter 4: the present value (PV) of future earnings is estimated over some reasonable horizon period (e.g. 5 years) and then the terminal value of the flows for the period extending beyond the horizon is computed. This yields the minimum value that ABC Co. will have to pay for Acme.

The second step is to add in an estimate of the PV of future gains expected from any synergies. This is a critical component as it reflects the perceived benefit that management believes can be obtained by combining ABC Co. and Acme. But it is a complicated process that should really be approached with a fair degree of conservatism. The essence of this step is to consider the incremental benefits that will be achieved via the acquisition – those above and beyond the pure "summation" of the two component parts. This can include increased revenues (e.g. from leveraging multiple sales forces), increased cost efficiencies (e.g. from eliminating duplicative efforts), increased depreciation (e.g. from greater asset revaluations), and so forth.

Naturally, Acme's investors are unlikely to sell their shares to ABC Co. without receiving some premium. Naturally, ABC Co.'s directors need to protect their own shareholders by minimizing the size of this premium. We can summarize the theoretical value of the deal, before the payment of any premium, as:

$$\text{theoretical value of acquisition} = \text{PV of future earnings of target} + \text{PV of future earnings from synergies} \qquad [8.1]$$

So, if ABC Co. estimates that the PV of Acme's future earnings amounts to £500 million and conservatively believes that a further £100 million of synergies can be obtained from the purchase, then Acme's shareholders will receive £600 million, plus any premium negotiated between the boards of the two companies.

The process above works well for an "all cash" deal. But what happens if ABC Co. wants to buy Acme using ABC shares? Such stock acquisitions are actually quite common. In fact, the same general principles apply, but an extra step is needed to determine the number of shares that ABC Co. will have to offer to Acme's shareholders. This is estimated by computing a ratio based on the price offered for the target (Acme) and the price of the acquiring company (ABC Co.). Assume that Acme currently has 100 million shares outstanding, meaning that the per share purchase price is £6. Assume further that ABC Co.'s current share price is £12. This means that the exchange ratio is 0.50. That is, ABC Co. will give up 0.50 shares of its shares for 1 share of Acme. Let's now assume that ABC Co.'s share price is £20 rather than £12. This yields an exchange ratio of 0.30 – meaning that ABC Co. has to give up fewer shares to acquire Acme. Not suprisingly, when the acquiring company has a strong and rising stock price, it will pay "less" in shares than if it has a low and falling stock price. In fact, stock-based acquisitions are very popular when the stock market is strong and the prices of potential acquirers are on the rise.

Valuing corporate finance deals is quite tractable when the parties involved are publicly traded, as the quoted stock prices give an indication of market value. But what happens when one or both companies are private? The process in such cases must turn to the use of a proxy method, such as the constant dividend growth model we discussed in Chapter 4. While this assumes that the private companies pay dividends and requires assumptions about dividend growth and the cost of capital, it can provide some estimate of value. We can therefore adapt the constant dividend growth model (assuming that all earnings generated are paid out as dividends):

$$\text{proxy value of shares} = \frac{\text{dividends } (1+ \text{growth rate})}{\text{cost of common} - \text{growth rate}} \quad [8.2]$$

Assume, therefore, that ABC Co. and Acme are private, rather than public, companies (with all shares held by management and employees) and that ABC Co.'s finance team has prepared estimates of the data reflected in Table 8.1.

The fair value of ABC Co. would equal £43.33, while the fair value of Acme would amount to £14.88. This would suggest a swap of 0.34 "shares" of ABC Co. for a single "share" of Acme based on a pure exchange ratio. However, since the earnings per share (EPS) estimate doesn't include any synergy effects, some additional gain has to be factored in. If we assume that synergies will add 20 percent to the value of the acquisition, Acme's share value is adjusted by 20 percent to yield a fair value of £17.85. The new exchange ratio is thus 0.41.

Proper accounting treatment is vital in corporate finance deals, especially for mergers and acquisitions. Though specific details differ across systems, the essential points center on accounting via the pooling of interest method and the purchase acquisition method. The pooling method is used when two companies involved in a deal exchange stock on a tax-free basis. The resulting "consolidation" is simply an addition of the balance sheets of the two firms. Thus, if ABC Co. and Acme merge by swapping stock, the resulting ABC Co.–Acme balance sheet is a simple summation of the individual parts. If the transaction is an

Table 8.1 Company estimates

	ABC Co.	Acme
EPS	£2.50	£1.30
Cost of capital	10%	12%
Dividend growth	4%	3%

outright acquisition, such as ABC Co.'s purchase of Acme, then the purchase acquisition method must generally be used. If the purchase price is precisely equal to the target's company net worth (i.e. assets minus liabilities), then the consolidated balance sheet is again an addition of the two components. However, if the purchase price exceeds the target's net worth the balance sheet must reflect an upward valuation of assets to reflect the differential. This value is reflected in the goodwill account; goodwill premium is typically amortized (or reduced) over a period of time.

CORPORATE FINANCE CHALLENGES

We've considered the logic behind corporate finance deals, the nature of key transactions, and how they can be valued to ensure that a company is not over- or under-valuing a deal. If the deal makes tactical and strategic sense and is successfully arranged and managed, then shareholders should over time reap the benefits of a higher share price. But corporate finance is a challenging discipline. Companies face a number of hurdles in their pursuit of good deals and must be aware of the potential pitfalls. Some of the most common challenges include:

- Overpaying for an acquisition: the history of mergers suggests that companies acquiring other firms can overpay for their targets. We've noted that valuing deals is not an exact science, because much depends on estimates of unknown future earnings. However, when an acquirer takes an aggressive stance and pays a large premium for a target by assuming overly optimistic future earnings flows and/or synergy effects, it may undermine the financial rationale for the transaction and ultimately destroy, rather than create, enterprise value.
- Creating too broad a focus: managing corporate operations is a difficult task, and one which can be made more difficult by adding other operations that are only loosely connected with core operations or which are completely unrelated. Many conglomeration-based transactions – created through mergers or acquisitions of very different companies – have proven over the years to be ill-advised; in the extreme, failed attempts at

conglomeration have actually reduced, rather than enhanced, enterprise value.

- Failing to capitalize on synergies: we know that the value of certain types of deals lies in the creation of synergies. If the management team of a company that has just merged with, or acquired, another company cannot crystallize these synergies, any premium paid on the deal will be lost. When a firm can't convert "theoretical" synergies into true economic value, the financial decision driving a deal will have been made in error.

- Failing to properly integrate operations: integrating the operations of two (or more) different companies can be a very difficult task – even when they are in the same industry. Firms tend to have unique corporate cultures, human resource requirements, technology platforms, business strategies/approaches, and so forth. Lack of proper attention to these individual characteristics, and how they need to be handled in order to create a proper strategic operation and add corporate value, can again jeopardize a transaction.

- Lacking discipline to reduce expenses or sell assets: the financial justification for certain kinds of deals, including acquisitions and LBOs, is often based on cost reductions and/or asset disposals. If a firm is unable to implement a disciplined regimen of post-deal cost controls or is unable to complete a program of asset sales, it may again undermine the rationale for executing the deal.

- Treating investors unfairly: investors supply capital and capital drives corporate operations. If board directors and executives arrange a deal that is not in the best interests of investors (e.g. significantly overpaying for another company, merging on bad terms, attempting to reallocate voting rights), they risk breaching their fiduciary duties, alienating shareholders, and/ or jeopardizing access to future capital. Dissatisfied investors may try to oust directors or sell their shares and put downward pressure on the company's stock.

If these challenges are well understood in advance, then a company's managers can help ensure that proper steps are taken to avoid problems. Naturally, even such diligence is not an absolute guarantee for success, as we can see in the Finance in action 8.1.

FINANCE IN ACTION 8.1:   CHALLENGES OF CORPORATE FINANCE DEALS

The financial markets have been witness to many mergers and acquisitions over the years, including some that can be classified as "mega-deals" – multi-billion-dollar mergers, acquisitions, or buyouts that capture the spotlight. Some of these transactions have been very successful, others unfortunately less so – either because the price paid to acquire another company has been too high, cost savings haven't been realized, synergies have failed to materialize, or corporate cultures have clashed.

Indeed, some of the biggest corporate finance deals have turned sour some years after completion, as reflected in low or falling post-merger stock prices (which, as we know, is a direct measure of shareholder value). We need only think of some of the biggest ones to realize just how difficult it is to conclude a good corporate finance transaction. Consider, for instance, the $25 billion 1988 LBO/merger between tobacco company RJ Reynolds and foods company Nabisco: after competitive bidding for the companies between rival banking groups pushed the cost of the deal up, the winning bidders saddled the newly combined company with an enormous amount of debt, placing tremendous financial strain on its operations for many years. To gain relief, RJR Nabisco's international tobacco operations were sold to Japan Tobacco in 1999, and the US tobacco and the Nabisco food businesses were placed in separate companies. One year later, Philip Morris (later renamed Altria) acquired Nabisco and merged it with its own Kraft Foods, leaving RJ Reynolds back where it started, as a US-based tobacco company; Altria itself eventually spun off Philip Morris in a separate deal. In another example, Daimler and Chrysler, the much-touted $39 billion 1998 combination of the two auto giants, failed to produce the returns so widely expected. Daimler abandoned the venture in 2007, actually paying $650 million to transfer an 80 percent stake in Chrysler to private equity group Cerberus (which then had its own stake taken over by the US Government in a 2009 bailout; Fiat of Italy eventually stepped in to take a controlling stake in Chrysler). Similarly, the merger of AOL and Time Warner – which was billed as a transformational new millennium deal uniting new media with conventional media – became something of a financial disaster for Time Warner investors. The world's largest M&A deal of the time was both strategically flawed and wildly expensive ($166 billion), executed at a very high premium at the top of the "dot-com" bubble. After less than a decade the deal was unwound, at a significant cost to shareholders. Worldcom, the high-flying telecom darling of the 1990s, bought MCI Communications in 1997 for $42 billion. Unfortunately, the debt burden was so great that Worldcom managers began committing financial fraud to "enhance" the company's earnings – culminating in a spectacular bankruptcy in 2002. And, in the banking sector, a series of mergers and acquisitions within the Citigroup universe eventually had to be reversed or abandoned; the Travelers insurance unit was sold off, the Smith Barney retail broker was ultimately transferred to Morgan Stanley, the Salomon Brothers investment bank was integrated and downsized, and the Nikko Japanese venture was sold – all at the expense of Citigroup shareholders. We can also point to the £71 billion acquisition by Royal Bank of Scotland and its partners of the Dutch banking giant ABN Amro as another example of a failed deal. The transaction was completed at a very high premium just prior to the Credit Crisis of 2007, and required partners Fortis and Santander to take up portions of the target bank. The deal was so large and expensive that it ultimately contributed to RBS's undoing – the collapsing financial markets caused the British government to step in to bail out the bank. This is a small sampling of deals that just haven't worked as anticipated, either because of excessive premiums, flawed strategies, or failed integrations.

Of course, many deals have proven successful. We need only think of giant M&A transactions like Exxon and Mobil (energy), JP Morgan and Chase (banking), Pfizer and Warner Lambert (pharmaceuticals), British Petroleum and Amoco (energy), Smithkline Beecham and Glaxo Wellcome (pharmaceuticals), and American/US Airways and Delta/Northwest (airlines), along with literally thousands of small and middle-market transactions, to realize that the right deal can be beneficial to all parties. But creating a successful transaction takes rigorous financial analysis, thorough understanding of strategy, support of key stakeholders, proper timing, and discipline in pre-deal and post-deal execution and integration.

CHAPTER SUMMARY

Corporate finance transactions are designed to optimize a company's operations through expansion, rationalization, or restructuring. The most common classes of deals include mergers (where one company combines with another company on a relatively equal basis to create a "new" company), acquisitions (where one company buys another company), leveraged buyouts (where a publicly listed company takes itself private by borrowing to purchase outstanding shares), spin-offs (where a company sells one or more of its units or divisions to the public in an IPO or private equity transaction), and recapitalizations (where a company restructures its capital base). Deals can be arranged to expand market share, create earnings stability, reduce costs/generate operating efficiencies, acquire intellectual property, and/or alter the capital structure. Valuation generally centers on examining the impact of a deal on future earnings; since this involves unknown events, it requires analysis of a range of scenarios. Corporate finance deals are fraught with challenges that must be considered during the planning phase. These can include overpaying for another company, creating too broad a business focus, failing to properly integrate newly acquired operations into existing operations, failing to reduce expenses or sell assets as needed, and treating investors unfairly.

FURTHER READING

Bruner, R., 2004, *Applied Mergers and Acquisitions*, New York: John Wiley & Sons.

—— 2009, *Deals from Hell: M&A Lessons that Rise Above the Ashes*, New York: John Wiley & Sons.

DePhampilis, D., 2013, *Mergers, Acquisitions and Other Restructuring Activities*, 7th edn., Waltham, MA: Academic Press.

Gaughan, P., 2014, *Mergers, Acquisitions, and Corporate Restructurings*, 5th edn., New York: John Wiley & Sons.

Rosenbaum, J. and Pearl, J., 2013, *Investment Banking: Valuation, Leveraged Buyouts and Mergers and Acquisitions*, 2nd edn., New York: John Wiley & Sons.

PART

PARTICIPANTS
AND MARKETPLACES

FINANCIAL PARTICIPANTS

CHAPTER OVERVIEW

Chapter 9 begins the first of two chapters focused on macro-finance issues, where we consider how concepts from Parts 1 and 2 influence, and can be influenced by, a range of individual, institutional, and sovereign parties. We begin by analyzing how key groups of participants – including intermediaries, end-users, and regulators – rely on financial dealings to conduct their daily activities, the role that each one plays in supporting the entire cycle of finance, and the motivations that drive activity. We then assemble a complete picture of how the groups interact, and conclude by considering forces of disintermediation that can affect financial intermediaries.

THE ROLE OF PARTICIPANTS

Macro-finance, which involves the study of finance at the systemic level, is concerned with both participants and marketplaces. We'll consider participants in this chapter and reinforce the discussion with an overview of marketplaces and financial market variables in the next chapter. Both, as we'll discover, are integral to a complete understanding of finance.

The concepts, tools, instruments, and transactions that we've discussed in the past chapters form the backbone of micro-based finance. They are the essential ingredients that allow companies to make decisions about how to optimize their operations and put in motion strategies that lead to the best possible funding, risk management, liquidity, and enterprise value solutions.

Such micro-level financial concepts and instruments exist because of, and in service of, a range of participants. If these participants didn't exist, or were uninterested in the overarching corporate goals that we've discussed, there would be little point in studying finance. And if they didn't exist, there would be no need to develop the tools, instruments, and transactions that we've considered.

Fortunately, these participants exist and are able to fulfill the crucial roles required to create a workable financial process. Understanding their specific roles is important in gaining a perspective on the macro-financial framework. Specifically, we are interested in understanding how key financial participants rely on financial dealings to conduct their activities, the specific functions that they play in supporting the financial "life cycle," and the motivations that drive them to participate. This framework allows us to tie together many of the individual topics that we've already discussed.

KEY PARTICIPANTS AND THEIR OBJECTIVES

To build the macro-finance picture we need to divide our discussion into three broad categories: intermediaries, end-users, and regulators. We can then atomize these classifications to gain greater insight into specific roles and responsibilities.

INTERMEDIARIES

Our review begins with intermediaries, or institutions that intermediate (stand between) those providing and those using capital, those acquiring and those purchasing assets, and those transferring and those accepting risks. Though the intermediation function might sound rather simple (i.e. matching up two different parties), it is actually quite complex; the function in its most developed form features product development, risk-taking, sales/marketing, and advisory services. To understand the full scope of intermediation we can consider the different functions that intermediaries perform and the types of intermediaries that are active in the financial markets.

Let's first consider the functions that intermediaries, as a group, perform. Though the depth and sophistication of these services vary considerably across national systems, intermediaries operating in the world's most advanced financial sectors are able to offer most or all of the services described below.

- Capital-raising and lending: while all services provided by financial intermediaries may be considered important, none is perhaps quite as vital in creating enterprise value as the raising of capital and financing. We know that companies regularly raise debt and equity capital and obtain loans and other forms of credit in order to finance balance sheet operations. Intermediaries are uniquely positioned to provide this essential service: they have access to investors, depositors, and other banks that are willing to supply capital, they have rosters of clients that need to raise capital, and they have the market knowledge required to properly arrange and execute all manner of financings. If intermediaries did not exist to perform this function, individual companies would be left trying to raise their own funds in an inefficient, and almost certainly more expensive, manner.
- Trading and liquidity provision: many intermediaries are active in trading securities and other assets, either as agent or principal (through the electronic trading mechanisms that we have reviewed previously). When an intermediary acts as an agent (or broker), it simply matches buyers and sellers of securities, taking a small spread as a commission (but taking no risk itself). When it acts as a principal (or dealer), it assumes risk by taking one side of the transaction (e.g. purchasing a security) and then either retains that risk, hedges the position, or separately arranges an offsetting deal (e.g. selling the security that it purchased); in this capacity the intermediary effectively provides liquidity to the market at large. If intermediaries did not perform this function, the secondary markets for

trading of securities and other assets would be far less liquid (if not completely illiquid), meaning that investors would be unable to quickly sell or rebalance their portfolios without suffering significant losses.

- Corporate finance advice: intermediaries often play a leading role in detecting, and then arranging, mergers, acquisitions, leveraged buyouts (LBOs), and other corporate finance deals. They are again uniquely positioned to serve as advisors in such matters as they have strong market and industry knowledge regarding potential corporate financing opportunities, and they have the expertise to evaluate the fair value of potential transactions. Again, if intermediaries did not provide this advice, companies seeking expansion or merger opportunities or some other form of restructuring would be unable to do so efficiently.

- Risk management advice: we have described the importance of risk and the use of derivatives and insurance in managing risk. Not surprisingly, since many intermediaries are in the business of taking and managing risk, they are well placed to provide risk management services to their clients. By analyzing a client's financial risk picture, an intermediary can help craft a risk management/hedging program that meets stated risk/return and risk transfer goals. In addition, the financial engineering capabilities of major intermediaries permit them to offer clients unique, and sometimes complex, solutions. If intermediaries did not perform this role, clients would be forced to analyze, and then manage, their financial and operating risks directly; for many this would be costly and inefficient.

- Asset management: we have previously discussed the process of creating investment portfolios to give investors an opportunity to allocate their capital in a professionally managed setting. Some intermediaries focus on creating asset management strategies for clients on a customized basis. Others provide similar services to investors at large, allowing a broad base of clients to benefit from the intermediary's research and portfolio risk management expertise. If intermediaries did not provide such asset management functions, client investors would again be responsible for identifying potential investment opportunities and creating their own investment portfolios, which would be a difficult, time-consuming, and potentially expensive task for all but the most sophisticated.

- Custody: the financial business is founded on trust and reputation, and the safekeeping of financial assets is one element of this process. Many intermediaries provide clients with custody services that include asset safekeeping, valuation, and reporting, and principal, interest, and dividend collection. Again, if intermediaries did not supply this service, clients would be forced to create their own processes, which would be costly.

One of the recurring themes in our brief descriptions above relates to costs: though intermediaries charge fees, premiums, or spreads for the services they provide, attempts by clients to replicate the same services (if even possible) would almost certainly come at a much higher price. Accordingly, by providing economically rational alternatives, intermediaries indirectly help corporate clients to achieve their enterprise value maximization goals.

With that background in hand, let's now consider the different types of intermediaries that constitute an advanced financial system.

- Commercial banks: these are regulated banking institutions that in most nations accept deposits from retail and institutional customers and use those funds primarily to grant commercial and industrial loans and residential mortgages. This is, of course, a "traditional" banking model that focuses heavily on the creation of credit. Commercial banks generally feature a full spectrum of clients: individuals seeking mortgage loans, credit cards, or personal loans; middle-market companies interested in working capital loans and lease financing; and large companies interested in revolving credit facilities, leases, and medium- to long-term acquisition loans. Though commercial banks may also be involved with securities and asset management, such business lines generally constitute a smaller portion of their activities.
- Investment banks/securities firms: these are involved primarily in the capital markets business, including issuing and trading securities and providing corporate finance and risk management advice. These institutions focus heavily on primary

issuance of debt and equity securities, along with secondary trading and market-making, and maintain extensive client relationships in both the retail and institutional sectors so that they can distribute securities. Within the advisory sector, the most sophisticated investment banks offer corporate finance advice, including mergers and acquisitions (M&A) and LBO structuring; they may also act as principals in private equity investments in support of such transactions. Some are also active in providing hedging services and derivative-based risk management advice.

- Universal banks: though relatively few in number, these can be considered a hybrid of the commercial and investment bank models. These institutions, which are usually constituted as large international financial conglomerates, provide clients with the broadest range of financing and advisory products and services. Most are active in the issuance and trading of securities, development and execution of risk management, investment management, and corporate finance programs, and extension of short- and long-term credit. Major universal banks often offer traditional retail banking services as well as more exclusive, higher margin, private banking services.

- Thrifts/building societies: thrift institutions, also known as savings and loans and building societies, are active primarily in the residential mortgage market. Thrifts accept retail deposits, mainly from individuals, and use the funds to grant residential home mortgages. Though they may provide additional forms of credit to individuals and may even grant commercial mortgages to middle-market enterprises or property developers, most keep quite a strict focus on the residential market. Thrifts can thus be regarded as specialized forms of commercial banks, though they may be governed by different rules and regulations to reflect their unique retail focus.

- Insurance companies: these provide individual and institutional customers with risk transfer advice and policies/products, including the full range of insurance contracts described in Chapter 7. The largest insurers operate on a global basis, insuring risks across national boundaries through one or more subsidiaries. National or local insurers, in contrast, concentrate their business within a particular country or even within a single state or province. Some insurers specialize in writing life and health coverage, others on property and casualty coverage, and still others on the entire range of insurable risks. Insurers may also offer customers annuities and other savings/investment products.

• Reinsurance companies: these act as insurers of insurers, providing risk transfer coverage to insurers that are writing primary coverage to their individual and corporate clients. In fact, reinsurers can be regarded as wholesale institutions, as they have no dealings with individual customers on a primary basis; their business focus is strictly on the professional insurance market, where they provide different classes of reinsurance. Since reinsurers deal at the institutional level, they tend to operate with a fairly broad geographic focus, reinsuring risks across borders and exposure classes.

There are, of course, various other types of intermediaries, including dedicated bancassurance companies (combinations of banks and insurers), asset managers, private equity funds, non-bank financial institutions (e.g. captive finance and leasing companies associated with an industry or parent company engaged in the provision of loans or leases), government and quasi-government finance entities, and so forth. These institutions tend to be more specialized in their activities, though many are quite large when measured by assets, revenues, or profits. It is worth noting that all of these financial intermediaries are heavily supported by a broad base of technology, which allows functions such as debit/credit payments, merchant payments, cash transfers, investments, and trading to be executed in the electronic sphere (see Finance in action 9.1).

So, what motivates financial intermediaries to provide the products and services noted above? We can point to two general objectives: maximization of profits and management of risks. Maximization of profits is simply a reiteration of our familiar theme: financial intermediaries are most often constituted as corporations and thus seek to generate as much income as possible for their shareholders, within the confines of their business models and risk-taking abilities. Thus, commercial and investment banks, universal banks, insurers, and other non-bank financial intermediaries are in business to generate fees, premiums, spreads, and commissions, and their shareholders will benefit as long as they can offer useful products and services.

Management of risk is a second key objective. By linking diverse pools of clients that have different views and requirements, and developing new financial products, intermediaries can manage their own risks more effectively. For instance, if one firm seeks to raise capital through the committed underwriting of bonds, an investment bank can supply the required capital, earning a fee in the process. However, at this stage the investment bank still holds the company's bonds, meaning that it is fully exposed to market and credit risks. By using its investor distribution network or certain derivative contracts it can lower its risk profile dramatically – while still locking in some amount of profitability. Since intermediaries are in business to take risk, they must actively search for ways of reducing, hedging or restructuring such risks.

FINANCE IN ACTION 9.1:   A CASHLESS SOCIETY

Money implicitly or explicitly underpins every financial transaction that occurs every day. And while the conventional notion of physical money as a fungible medium of exchange and store of value supported by government fiat is certainly still relevant, it is also clear that, in an age of advanced technologies and widespread cross-border dealings, electronic forms of money have become more important than ever. Indeed, how many of us still carry around cash to buy anything substantial? Though differences obviously exist between countries and across income levels – Japan, for instance, is heavily cash oriented, while Sweden and Canada are very cashless, and lower-income earners are more cash dependent than higher earners – real cash is increasingly reserved for small retail point-of-sale transactions, like buying coffee, a newspaper, or a subway ticket – and even those simple purchases are increasingly handled by a variety of electronica. Many of us have come to rely on cashless mechanisms like ATM cards, bank debit cards, digital wallets, and SMS payments via smartphones to buy things. Indeed, we often don't even have to touch cash: employers can directly deposit salaries into bank accounts, after which electronic bill payments, direct debits, automated investments, and credit/debit card purchases add to and subtract from the bank account balances. And the "e-money" concept is even more pervasive at the corporate level where, apart from some petty cash transactions, virtually all dealings occur electronically.

Though the taxonomy of this cashless society is evolving, for our purposes we can introduce the concept of the electronic funds transfer (EFT), an all-encompassing category that involves any monetary exchange between accounts occurring in the electronic sphere. Thus, an EFT includes credit card and debit card transactions, direct deposits, direct debits, electronic bill payments, wire transfers, and digital currency payments (directly and through digital wallets, like ApplePay and GoogleWallet, which are essentially "thin layer" storage for digital credentials). While most of us have used credit cards and direct debits for a long time, digital currencies and digital wallets are becoming increasingly ubiquitous as well – their flexibility means that they can be used to purchase goods and services in a store or online and even to send money via email to other merchants or friends and family.

Digital currency (or digital cash) can be structured and used in various forms. In its most basic retail construct, a consumer uses cash or a credit card to buy "credits" online, which can then be used to make purchases on various sites. In some instances the cash purchases a unique number known as a digital certificate, which is transmitted from buyer to seller at the time of the purchase. The digital certificate is then effectively presented to the bank or credit card provider to complete an electronic funds transfer. Within the digital cash world we can distinguish between so-called hard currencies (which are most like cash as they permit no reverse capability, e.g. no refund or reversal) and soft currencies (which have reverse capabilities). We can also speak of centralized and decentralized digital currency systems. A centralized system, like PayPal, has a central hub that is managed and maintained by a single party and which supports digital payments at its hub. So, if a consumer wants to make a payment to a seller through PayPal, relevant bank or credit card information or preloaded cash card value is input into a digital layer, after which the hub confirms and then debits and credits the corresponding accounts. Decentralized systems feature no central hub and are instead widely distributed amongst those who use the currency. For instance, Bitcoin, a digital currency developed in the new millennium, is a peer-to-peer mechanism where transactions are verified by network nodes rather than a central administrator. In this case, a purchaser wanting to use Bitcoin must first "own" some amount of Bitcoin (either from participating in the "mining" process that creates Bitcoin or from having accepted Bitcoin from another party in settlement of a transaction) and must then find a seller or merchant willing to accept the currency. Thereafter the buyer digitally signs a transaction with a private key, which is verified by the network node using a public key – after which the Bitcoin value is effectively transferred.

These simple examples are, of course, just small representations of a much larger, and growing, world involving the digital exchange of value. We may be sure that, as technology and encryption continue to progress, the use of physical cash will continue to give way to all manner of cashless mechanisms.

END-USERS

If intermediaries represent the supply of financial services, then end-users represent the demand for those services. To consider the demand side of the equation, we describe major classes of end-users and the kinds of financial transactions that they are most likely to be involved in.

- Industrial and service companies: these are the single largest non-financial users of financial services. Large capitalization and middle-market companies from virtually all sectors (e.g. technology, automotive, energy, pharmaceuticals, consumer goods, and so on) rely on access to financial services to manage their business affairs. These companies regularly borrow funds from commercial/universal banks and issue debt/equity securities via investment banks in order to fund their expansion plans; the significant amount of capital financing that companies require is a key source of primary and secondary activity for intermediaries, and also allows the investment demand of investors (noted immediately following) to be met. These companies are also often users of M&A and risk advisory/hedging services; this allows them to efficiently incorporate acquisition, spin-off, or other corporate restructurings into their strategic plans, and to hedge or transfer financial and operating risks via derivatives and insurance. Obviously, if these corporate end-users did not borrow funds or issue securities, the global financial markets would be considerably smaller; similarly, if they didn't avail themselves of M&A services, expansion or restructuring opportunities would be limited.

- Institutional/professional investors: institutional investors, comprising open-end and closed-end funds, hedge funds, and pension funds, as well as the investment or trust operations of insurance companies and banks, are significant users of primary and secondary investment and risk management services. Institutional investors are the single largest group of capital providers in the financial system, routinely absorbing the greatest amount of debt and equity capital securities issued on a primary basis, and actively buying and selling securities on a secondary basis. In recent years they have also become important players in the secondary loan market, buying portions of loans originated by banks for their clients. The intent of all of these asset purchases is to generate returns for their own clients, including other institutional investors, individual investors, and pensioners. Of course, if institutional investors didn't provide capital to the financial system, corporate end-users (as well as financial institutions) would be unable to fund their balance sheets appropriately. In addition to acquiring capital instruments, institutional investors often use risk management solutions and products developed by intermediaries in order to hedge or synthetically create particular risk exposures.

- Sovereigns and government agencies: governments are important borrowers in the global debt markets and they are periodically active in the corporate finance market through privatization of state-owned assets. Governments and their central banks regularly issue securities to meet various goals.

For instance, they may issue short-term securities (e.g. treasury bills) to meet liquidity needs and help manage aspects of monetary policy (which we'll consider in Chapter 10). They may also issue medium- and long-term securities: since nations may have significant spending and investment programs that cannot be adequately funded with tax-based revenues, they may have to issue medium- or long-term securities. In practice, most governments use intermediaries to raise capital; though many could issue directly to investors, the use of intermediaries (so-called primary dealers) is an efficient and effective way of distributing securities. Government agencies are also periodic sellers of state-owned assets that they wish to place into the private sector. Intermediaries may conduct private or public sales of these assets in order to help a governmental agency maximize value.

- Individuals: we have deliberately excluded discussion of individuals in the financial process in order to maintain our corporate focus. It is clear, however, that individuals are an important element of the marketplace, acting as small-scale investors and borrowers. Though each transaction arranged by a single customer may appear small, the collective portfolio of transactions across all individuals quickly becomes very significant – meaning that individuals are an influential market force. Individuals invest in debt and equity securities and investment fund shares via their savings and retirement accounts. If individuals didn't participate, capital issuers and borrowers would face periodic capital supply shortages and/or would place excessive demands on the institutional investor base. Individuals are also active in the risk management area, primarily through health, home, auto, and/or life insurance policies that transfer unwanted risks to the insurance sector. They are also frequent, and significant, borrowers through consumer/credit card debt, auto loans, student loans, and home mortgages.

What motivates end-users to participate in the financial marketplace? First, end-users need capital in order to fund public (government) or private (corporate) operations or, at an individual level, to make significant purchases (e.g. homes, automobiles, education). Access to this supply of capital is essential and can only be gained by tapping into the financial marketplace. In fact, if end-users were unable to access the capital and loan markets, their ability to grow would be severely curtailed. Second, end-users that have an excess of capital to invest require access to conduits that provide the opportunity of creating real returns. Simply put, it would be impossible for this base of end-users to generate profits on their resources if they were unable to access capital instruments. Third, end-users want to be able to efficiently manage their risks. This, as we have noted, can be accomplished by using a professional risk transfer mechanism, where the benefits of diversification can lead to lower premiums and fees.

While much of what we have discussed in the book so far relates to Western concepts of finance – including risk, return, and profits – intermediaries and end-users operating in the economically significant Islamic world must adhere to special tenets of Islamic law (see Finance in action 9.2). This approach adds to the concepts, tools, and solutions that are available to participants.

FINANCE IN ACTION 9.2: THE WORLD OF ISLAMIC FINANCE

For those living in Western societies the concepts of interest, risk, and speculation are well established and almost second nature. The Islamic world, in contrast, embraces a very different kind of practice, commonly known as Islamic finance or alternative finance arrangements. While Islamic finance obviously has a long history of development and use in the relevant local markets, it became part of modern global finance starting in the mid-1970s, and has expanded steadily since that time.

Islamic finance can be regarded as a form of structured finance that is designed to adhere to religious interpretations and legal rulings that govern permissible financing and investment. Under Islamic finance, contracts are permissible unless they are characterized by one or both of *riba* (interest) or *gharar* (uncertainty), which renders them null and void. Put differently, *haraam* relates to any action or objective that is forbidden under Islamic law (e.g. interest or risk), while *halal* represents any action or objective that is permissible. This means that a standard loan or derivative contract, such as might be used by individuals and companies outside the Middle East, Malaysia, or other Islamic centers, would not be legally binding, or even permissible, under Shari'a, or Islamic religious, law.

To overcome these hurdles, structures have been developed that permit trading of goods or assets today for a sum of money in the future (*bai' muajjal*, a *de facto* credit sale) or the trading of money today for goods or assets in the future (*bai salam*, or a prepaid forward), where the sale of an asset under one contract is matched by the purchase of the asset under a second contract for a greater value. *Sukuk* (or rent certificates) are popular "bonds" that grant the investor a share of an asset, along with the associated cash flows, instead of interest payments. Other common Islamic structures include the *ijarah* (secured lease), *murabaha* (trust sale), *wadiah* (deposit safekeeping), and *takaful* (Islamic insurance). Regardless of structure, it is important to stress that interest is never explicitly paid, though it can be incorporated as a "profit" in a credit sale or as a "rent" in a lease or certificate and may even be benchmarked to a recognized market rate. Naturally, each product is vetted and approved by Islamic scholars to ensure adherence to Shari'a law. In addition, the Islamic Financial Services Board, which was created early in the millennium, provides guidance related to consistency of products, services, and rules.

Islamic finance is becoming well established in the global financial system, with active markets developing around the world to serve an estimated 40 million customers. According to various research studies, approximately 60 percent of Islamic financial contracts and assets are located in key Middle East financial centers such as Qatar, Saudi Arabia, United Arab Emirates, Turkey, and Kuwait, with the balance spread among regional Muslim financial centers (e.g. Malaysia, Morocco, Indonesia) and international financial centers (e.g. London, New York). Total assets held by Islamic banks reached approximately $2 trillion in 2014, representing an annual growth rate of more than 20 percent since 1994; additional assets are expected to accumulate through banking "windows" and other non-Islamic bank conduits. Total outstandings in the *sukuk* "bond" market exceeded $300 billion in mid-2014, and the first Shari'a-compliant master agreement for "derivatives" has been introduced (such Islamic derivative contracts are designed for hedging, so that uncertainties can be removed from financial dealings). Though the sector can still be regarded as nascent in terms of the overall financial markets, growth has been impressive and expansion appears set to continue.

REGULATORS

Those dealing in the financial marketplace cannot generally do so without some level of guidance and oversight from government regulators. Most modern financial systems have some type of regulatory "watchdog" to provide end-users with an appropriate level of protection so that they don't become victims of unintentional losses or fraud.

The most effective and efficient way of providing end-user protection is to set minimum standards for those supplying financial services. These may relate to the minimum required financial strength for institutions supplying services, the minimum level of disclosure that must accompany deals or offerings, minimum protections that must be granted to clients, and/or the maximum amount that can be charged for specific services; in some cases such protection may even restrict or prohibit the sale of certain financial products to particular segments of the market.

The national regulatory system can be arranged in different ways, depending on the depth and breadth of the local financial services base. In the most advanced systems, however, we can point to at least three classes of regulatory oversight:

- Bank regulator: this regulator is responsible for ensuring that all financial institutions in the local system (either domestic institutions or domestic branches of foreign institutions) operate prudently by maintaining a minimum level of capital and reserves, minimum level of liquidity, minimum standards of asset quality, and maximum amount of leverage. The bank regulator may also require banking institutions to contribute to an insurance fund that provides depositors with protection against losses. Some countries feature regulators for individual segments of the banking sector. Thus, one body may be responsible for regulating commercial banks, another for regulating thrifts/building societies, and still another for reviewing non-bank financial institutions.

- Insurance regulator: this regulator may operate at a state/ provincial level, a national level, or both, and is typically responsible for reviewing the capabilities of insurers writing specific classes of insurance and ensuring that they maintain a minimum level of statutory reserves/capital. It also makes certain that insurers conduct their dealings with policyholders in a fair and equitable manner when settling loss claims.

- Securities/exchange regulator: this regulator is typically responsible for overseeing the financial soundness and operations of local financial markets, including those created by securities exchanges and/or derivative exchanges. Specifically, it ensures that market-making, trading, execution, and settlement occur in a transparent and orderly fashion so that investors (especially individuals) are adequately protected. Securities regulators are often also responsible for establishing minimum levels of disclosure for stock and bond issues that are to be floated in the public markets, and may also be responsible for the activities of investment banks/securities firms, helping to ensure that they remain properly capitalized and keep leverage at prudent levels.

Though countries differ in how they apply the financial regulation model (see Finance in action 9.3), it should be clear that regulators are essential players that help ensure that intermediaries and marketplaces for intermediation adhere to minimum standards of financial and professional conduct so that end-users are not prejudiced or financially damaged.

FINANCE IN ACTION 9.3:   DIFFERENT REGULATORY MODELS

While every country with a meaningful financial system has some form of regulation, the range of models used to enforce that regulation varies: some countries have opted for the single, consolidated "super-regulator" model, where all activities are housed under one

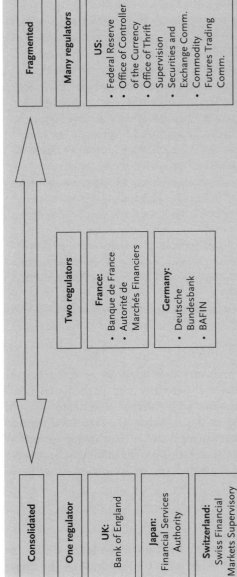

Figure 9.1 Sample financial regulatory models

authority. Others have chosen to follow the fragmented "multiple regulator" model, relying on a large number of specialized regulators to police markets and institutions. And still others have opted for the "middle road" model, granting regulatory powers to perhaps two or three authorities. Proponents of the "super-regulator" model believe that a single authority enhances communications, coordination, and efficiencies. Supporters of the "multiple regulator" model argue in favor of the need for greater specialization, particularly when the national financial sector is very complex. Each approach has advantages and disadvantages, and there is no particular evidence to suggest that any one model is superior; in fact, individual countries have different degrees of financial sophistication and development, implying that there is no "one size fits all" solution. It is worth noting that these models are not static, but changeable over time. Indeed, governments, in the aftermath of some national or global financial dislocation, often take the opportunity to change or fine-tune their regulatory coverage models to address actual or perceived shortcomings. Some representative examples of different regulatory models are illustrated in Figure 9.1.

THE COMPLETE PICTURE

We now have the components that allow us to construct the complete picture of financial activities and participants (we'll supplement this discussion with further comments on the financial markets at large in the next chapter). Figure 9.2 features a simplified and conceptualized view of the major groups of participants and the role that each plays in the financial process. Note that end-users are separated into two classes to simplify the discussion.

Let's briefly summarize the key roles and activities noted in the diagram:

- Block 1 indicates that institutional and individual investors act as suppliers of capital. This capital flows through the group of intermediaries (who may supplement it with their own capital) and on to the group of end-users that demands capital,

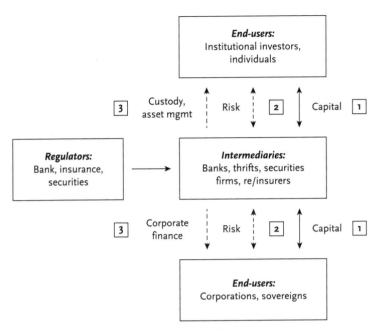

Figure 9.2 The complete picture of financial participants

including companies and sovereigns/agencies. This represents the essential debt and equity capital funding process. Associated with the capital flow function is an implicit trading function. Many investors continue to direct their trading through intermediaries, which execute on exchanges or in the over-the-counter (OTC) market on behalf of investors. Block 1 reflects the fact that individuals may also be users of capital, borrowing from financial institutions via mortgages, credit cards, and other loans.

- Block 2, which centers on risk transfer, is less transparent. Corporate and sovereign end-users often wish to transfer financial and operating risks via derivatives and insurance. The same is true of individuals (though in most cases this is limited to insurance transfers). Accordingly, intermediaries can expect to receive risk exposures from these end-users and must then manage the resulting positions by hedging, diversifying, or buying insurance/reinsurance. However, some end-users are willing to accept risk. For instance, hedge funds and certain pension and investment funds take risks (primarily financial ones) in order to boost their returns, and must therefore be considered risk-takers. In fact, intermediaries often transfer certain types of financial risks to these end-users in order to reduce their own exposures. There are times, of course, when even sophisticated risk-taking institutions reverse their positions and shed, rather than accept, risk; when this happens intermediaries must be prepared to react.

- Block 3, which focuses on specialized services, is group dependent. We have noted that companies and sovereigns are active end-users of corporate finance advisory services, and would expect to receive the benefit of any such advice from intermediaries. Individual and institutional investors may use custody services (e.g. securities safekeeping) as well as specific asset management programs and strategies.

The activities supplied by intermediaries are, of course, overseen by the appropriate regulator(s). Naturally, this illustration is simplified, as institutions may be involved in other financial activities or may act in a manner opposite to the ones indicated above. Alternatively, they may perform multiple roles (e.g. a bank may supply capital directly to end-use companies, and may also do so indirectly by financing a private equity fund, which then invests in the capital of an end-use company). Nevertheless, the general structure holds true and allows us to understand the dependencies and relationships.

FORCES OF DISINTERMEDIATION

Intermediaries obviously play a vital role in the financial system: they stand between demanders and suppliers of capital, and between companies seeking partners and those willing to be acquired; they create investment and risk management solutions through their financial engineering expertise; and they provide the custody services that allow assets to be safely held.

But all of these services come at a price – intermediaries are in business to make a profit. End-users must therefore address, as part of their financial planning activities, the relative cost/benefit trade-off attached to the services provided by intermediaries. If the benefits obtained from efficiently raising capital or completing a corporate finance transaction outweigh the fees/expenses that must be paid, then the decision rule framework will suggest proceeding. If, however, the costs appear too large, then end-users may seek alternative solutions. This gives rise to disintermediation, or the process of removing intermediaries from their traditional roles in raising capital, granting advice, and providing other financial services.

Disintermediation arises when end-users are presented with alternatives or substitutes. For instance, if ABC Co. can issue commercial paper or bonds directly to investors, rather than via an investment bank, it saves on the underwriting fees. Or, if it can trade assets in its portfolio through an electronic trading platform with direct market access rather than via a securities firm, it saves on commissions and asset management fees (institutional and individual investors can, of course, do the same thing). If the firm can identify and arrange its own acquisition or merger partners, it can avoid paying advisory fees. Or, if it can detect a predictable pattern of small losses within its employee health or disability benefit portfolio, it can self-insure via a captive and save on insurance premium costs. Figure 9.3 presents a decomposition of the illustration presented earlier to demonstrate how financial institutions can be removed from aspects of the process.

The concept of disintermediation sounds very appealing from the perspective of the end-user. So why not eliminate the "middle man" from all financial transactions? The short answer is: inefficiency. It is very difficult, in practice, for most companies to replicate the types of skills, services, relationships, and networks that financial intermediaries have spent decades cultivating.

Forces of disintermediation are still somewhat limited, certainly in the fullest sense of the word. While "partial" disintermediation has occurred (e.g. replacing bank lending with the issuance of bonds, which cuts banks out of their traditional credit-granting role, but still leaves them involved in the issuance and trading of bonds), full disintermediation is still rather uncommon. In general, only the largest companies have the ability to remove financial intermediaries from the process and even then tend to do so very selectively. In practice some large firms issue short- and

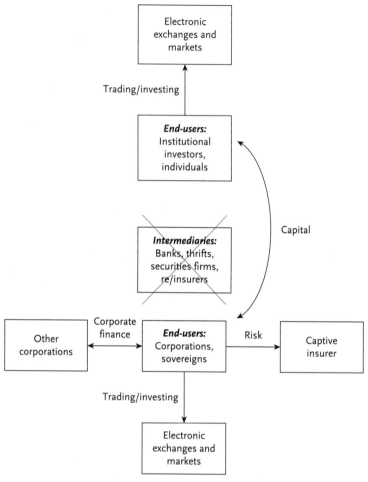

Figure 9.3 Disintermediation of select financial functions

medium-term liabilities directly to end-users; this, however, is confined to firms with strong name recognition and healthy financial standing. Note that small companies (and individuals) have no practical, cost-efficient way of directly accessing credit other than through intermediaries. Some large firms feature in-house corporate finance teams that actively seek out acquisition opportunities, and some medium and large firms manage portions of their operating risks via captives. There are greater signs of disintermediation in aspects of trading and asset management, where large and small investors now use electronic platforms and direct market access to handle elements of trading and portfolio management.

CHAPTER SUMMARY

Intermediaries, end-users, and regulators are the main participants in the financial marketplace. Intermediaries are institutions that raise capital, provide trading and liquidity services, develop corporate finance and risk management advice, manage assets, and supply custody services to their clients. The main types of intermediaries include commercial banks, investment banks/ securities firms, universal banks, thrifts/building societies, insurance/reinsurance companies, and bancassurance conglomerates. End-users include all firms that demand the financial products and services created by intermediaries. These include industrial and service companies, institutional/professional investors, sovereigns and government agencies, and individuals. Those dealing in the financial marketplace cannot generally do so without some level of guidance and oversight from government-related regulators. Most modern financial systems have one or more regulators to keep an eye on the activities of firms/marketplaces supporting banking, insurance, and/or securities activities. While the services that intermediaries provide to end-users are valuable, the specter of disintermediation – or removal of intermediaries from the traditional role as "middle man" – exists. Disintermediation can theoretically help reduce costs for end-users, which leads to an increase in enterprise value. That said, the process of disintermediation is still limited to medium-sized and large firms that arrange some of their own financial transactions, and investors/ investment managers that execute trades directly into the market.

FURTHER READING

Davies, H. and Green, D., 2008, *Global Financial Regulation*, London: Polity.

Hubbard, G. and O'Brien, A., 2011, *Money, Banking and the Financial System*, Upper Saddle River, NJ: Prentice Hall.

Kidwell, D., Peterson, R. L., Blackwell, D. W., and Whidbee, D. A., 2011, *Financial Institutions, Markets, and Money*, 11th edn., New York: John Wiley & Sons.

Saunders, A. and Cornett, M., 2011, *Financial Institutions and Markets*, 5th edn., New York: McGraw-Hill.

THE GLOBAL FINANCIAL MARKETS

CHAPTER OVERVIEW

Chapter 10 continues our discussion of macro-finance issues. In this chapter we consider the macro-structure of the global financial markets and their role in promoting capital flows and economic growth. We then discuss the impact of key financial variables – including interest rates, inflation, and economic growth – on the markets and analyze the effect of monetary policy on financial variables. Next, we consider elements of the financial markets that give rise to their fluidity and dynamism, including deregulation, capital mobility, volatility, and technology, and discuss how financial crises can enter the picture. We conclude by considering the practical impact of dynamic forces on the marketplace.

MACRO-STRUCTURE OF THE FINANCIAL MARKETS

In Parts 1 and 2 of the book we have considered aspects of finance from a micro perspective; in the last chapter we have extended the discussion by examining the macro roles of end-users, intermediaries, and regulators. We now build on that macro picture by considering different segments of the financial markets and how they are impacted by financial variables.

To begin, we may note that the global financial markets comprise broad capital pools and asset classes that are linked through a series of intricate relationships:

- Money markets: these markets, as we've noted in Chapter 5, consist of short-term liabilities issued by banks (e.g. certificates of deposit, bankers' acceptances), companies (e.g. commercial paper), and sovereigns (e.g. treasury bills). In the private sector these instruments are used for liquidity management purposes, while in the sovereign sector they may be used for both liquidity management and monetary policy management, which we describe below. Virtually all industrialized and emerging nations feature some type of money market sector.
- Debt markets: these markets, which include medium- and long-term bonds and loans, constitute the single largest element of the global capital markets. As we know, bonds and loans are used for capital investment, acquisitions, and expansion and may be renewed on a regular basis – making the capital appear semi-permanent. Of course, these markets also include loans granted to individuals for mortgages, automobiles, education, and so forth. The largest debt markets are found in industrialized nations.
- Stock markets: these markets include common and preferred stock issued by corporations to fund productive operations/ permanent investments, and ensure that balance sheet leverage remains reasonable. All market-based economies feature companies that are capitalized via equity instruments, making the overall market deep and broad. As we might expect, the stock markets of industrialized nations tend to feature the greatest breadth and depth of both securities and participants.
- Foreign exchange market: this market, in which currencies are exchanged for other currencies, represents the single most actively traded element of the financial markets, with intermediaries and end-users dealing in very large amounts of spot (i.e. current market) and forward transactions every business day (see Finance in action 10.1). Market activity is centered on both major and emerging exchange rates.
- Commodity markets: these global markets are broad and deep, and feature a significant amount of spot and forward dealing;

hedgers (e.g. commodity producers and commodity users) and speculators (e.g. any institution seeking a profit) are both active in this marketplace. Key traded commodities include precious metals (e.g. gold, silver, platinum, palladium), industrial metals (e.g. iron, copper, aluminum, zinc), energy (e.g. oil/products, natural gas, electricity), agricultural products (e.g. corn, wheat, soybeans), and softs (e.g. cocoa, coffee, sugar).

• Derivative markets: these markets, as noted in Chapter 7, include financial contracts that are linked to specific asset classes, including interest rates, equities, foreign exchange, credits, and commodities. Hedgers and speculators use the markets to achieve specific goals, injecting liquidity in the process. In fact, derivatives can serve as substitutes for, or complements to, other financial instruments.

FINANCE IN ACTION 10.1: THE 24-HOUR GLOBAL FOREIGN EXCHANGE MARKET

The global foreign exchange (FX) market, which combines spot and derivative trading in both major and emerging currencies, is the most actively traded segment of the financial markets. The Bank for International Settlements has estimated that daily spot, forward, and swap trading volumes exceeded $5 trillion at the end of 2013, up from $3.3 trillion a day in 2007. Since the abandonment of fixed exchange rates and the turn towards floating exchange rates in the early 1970s, the market has evolved into a multi-center marketplace, where all dealing is done via voice or electronically – apart from currency futures and options contracts offered by certain derivative exchanges, we may regard the market as being truly over-the-counter.

London has long been the center of global FX trading and continued its dominance with a 41 percent market share in 2013, followed by New York (19 percent), and Singapore and Tokyo (5 percent each); the balance is split among various other financial centers. A typical trading day begins in Sydney and Auckland, after which dealing is taken up by institutions in Tokyo, Hong Kong, and Singapore. Trading books may then be passed through Mumbai or directly into the Middle East centers of Dubai and Bahrain, where many international banks have a presence. Activity then shifts to the European centers of Zurich, Frankfurt, and London (with some additional trading also occurring in Moscow, Paris, Milan, and Amsterdam). European trading overlaps for a few hours with the North American opening, after which New York, Toronto, and Chicago take over. From there books may be passed to the West Coast centers of Los Angeles and San Francisco, marking the end of the 24-hour business day.

The FX market attracts a range of participants, including individual and institutional speculators in search of short- or long-term profits, along with companies seeking to hedge or otherwise manage their international exposures and government agencies attempting to optimize their foreign exchange reserves and funding. More than 50 percent of foreign exchange dealing is done between banks in the so-called interbank market. The remainder is split between activities involving hedge funds and other institutional investors, central banks, corporations, and individual customers. Most dealing still involves quoting against the US dollar (e.g. more than 88 percent of all transactions have a dollar "leg"). However, there is also an active market for "cross rates," such as euro versus sterling, euro versus yen, Swiss franc versus euro, and so forth. The most actively traded currency pairs are dollar/euro (24 percent of all trading volume), dollar/yen (18 percent), and sterling/dollar (9 percent).

While much of the activity in the global foreign exchange market is speculative in nature, an important component relates to corporate end-use transactions. In fact, corporate foreign exchange management is central to the financial decision-making that we have discussed in Part 1, and any company with an offshore presence must consider the impact of foreign currencies on core operations. When a company deals in offshore markets on a per-transaction basis (e.g. importing from one country and/or exporting to another country), it must contend with so-called transaction exposure, where currency arising from individual cash flows can be managed individually. When a company has an entire operation in a foreign country, it must deal more broadly with a local currency balance sheet; this means that it must manage translation exposure, or conversion of the local balance sheet back to the home currency for accounting and disclosure purposes.

Let's consider a simple example of a situation where ABC Co., as a UK-based company managing its operations in sterling, sources components from the USA, payable in dollars, which it transforms and distributes in Continental Europe, generating euro receipts. Under this scenario the company must consider the potential effects of deprecation or appreciation in the US dollar versus sterling, and the euro versus sterling. Assume, for simplicity, that ABC Co. can purchase inputs in the USA for $85 million and sell them in Europe for €100 million. Let's examine two scenarios: the current market scenario, which features a $/£ exchange rate of 1.56 and a £/€ exchange rate of 0.90, and a second scenario where the dollar strengthens to 1.36 (meaning that the company pays more in sterling to source the inputs) and the euro weakens to 0.80 (meaning that it receives less in sterling from its sales). The results are summarized in Table 10.1, which reflects how ABC Co.'s profit compresses dramatically from this unhedged transaction exposure. We can, of course, imagine the opposite scenarios as well, where sterling strengthens against the dollar and weakens against the euro, which would result in a larger profit.

Table 10.1 ABC Co. foreign currency exposures

		Inputs ($85m)	Sales (€100m)	
Scenario 1	$/£ = 1.56 £/€ = 0.90	£55m	£90m	Profit £35m
Scenario 2	$/£ = 1.35 £/€ = 0.80	£63m	£80m	Profit £17m

If we now assume that the products supplied from the USA are coming via Acme Supply (a subsidiary of ABC Co.) and are sold via ABC Europe Distributors (another subsidiary), then ABC Co.'s treasurer must move the analysis and decision-making from transaction risk to translation risk. This is a more involved process, which essentially requires the treasurer to make decisions on how best to manage its multi-currency operations so that, when dollar and euro balance sheets are translated back into sterling, the resulting effects do not have a negative impact on the parent company's own balance sheet. In order to do this, analysis is likely to focus on a number of issues, including whether to:

- Raise short-term funds for Acme in dollars directly in the US market or raise them via ABC Co. in sterling and swap them into dollars for on-lending to Acme.
- Pay Acme for goods supplied for resale in sterling swapped to dollars on a forward basis (locking in a known rate) or do so in the spot market as needed.
- Convert the euros from sales proceeds from Acme Europe into sterling on a forward basis (locking in a known rate) or do so in the spot market as they occur.
- Make available long-term loans in sterling that are swapped on a long-term basis into dollars and euros, respectively.
- Hedge the local equity accounts of each subsidiary to eliminate or minimize the effects of accounting translations.

This is just a sampling of the foreign exchange issues that a typical multinational company must address as part of the financial process. Much of the decision-making invariably returns to the decision by the company on how much financial risk it wishes to take in its operations.

Each of the market sectors noted above is linked to the other sectors directly or indirectly. In fact, the relationships between different sectors are complex and sometimes unstable: changes in one market can impact capital flowing into, or out of, another market. Let's consider some simplified examples of what might happen to the financial markets under "normal" market scenarios as key macro variables – including interest rates, inflation rates, and economic growth rates – change.

Consider, for instance, that, when a country's short-term interest rates rise, the general cost of public and private borrowing rises in tandem. Rising interest rates tend to attract a greater amount of investment capital – investors in other asset classes, including equities, sell their existing investments and redeploy capital in the higher earning asset. This puts downward pressure on stock prices (and the prices of other financial assets), making money market and debt capital market investments look that much more attractive – at least for a time.

Several "ripple effects" may then appear. First, higher interest costs can lead to greater corporate profit pressures, which can put additional pressure on stock prices. Reinvestment in productive ventures may also slow, as the internal hurdle rate that a company must achieve increases. Second, higher domestic interest rates will attract foreign investors, for the same reasons cited above. Accordingly, foreign investors will convert (sell) their home currencies and buy the domestic currency, causing the latter to appreciate in value. We may also note that a strong currency has important implications for a country's trade balance, causing goods exported abroad to appear expensive in foreign markets; this can lead to a decline in demand, which can also negatively impact export-oriented corporate earnings. There is, of course, a limit to this process. As more domestic and offshore investors acquire fixed income assets, they force prices up and yields down. This will eventually cause investors to stop allocating additional capital to fixed income assets and may generate a temporary equilibrium.

The opposite scenario can also appear: when interest rates fall, fixed income investments appear less attractive, causing capital to flow into other asset classes, including stocks and diversified investment funds (as well as "hard assets," such as real estate). Corporate interest expense declines, allowing companies to boost their earnings and reinvestment activities, which helps increase stock prices. Under this scenario, the domestic currency may appear less attractive to foreign eyes, and will lose value as offshore investors liquidate their fixed income holdings and repatriate capital (the amount repatriated depends, of course, on their perception of domestic stock market opportunities). Separately, a weaker domestic currency makes export goods appear more competitive on the global stage, meaning that global demand for corporate goods and services can rise and earnings can grow. This can also lead to higher stock prices. There is, of course, an equilibrium under this scenario as well: at some point stock prices may trade at unsustainably high future earnings multiples, causing investors to pull back and search for other opportunities. This slows, and may even halt, the rise in stock prices, perhaps to the point where fixed income investments begin to appear attractive once again. Sometimes the halt is sudden rather than gradual, as in the bursting of a bubble. This type of phenomenon is not, unfortunately, unusual – asset bubble collapses happen every few years, as the effects of "cheap credit" and subsequent asset price inflation take their toll.

The generalized impact of interest rates on financial markets is summarized in Table 10.2.

Let us also consider an example based on inflationary forces. Inflation measures the price of goods and services at the wholesale level (via indexes such as the producer price index) and at the consumer level (through the consumer price index or retail price index). Rising inflation can result from excess demand for goods/services during a strong phase of economic expansion. Higher commodity prices can be a benefit to commodity producers (e.g. oil and natural gas companies, resources/mineral companies), which may see their stock prices trade at strong earnings multiples, but can be detrimental to commodity users (e.g. every company that relies on commodity inputs to produce finished goods), which may suffer from weaker earnings and/or be forced

Table 10.2 Interest rates and financial market impact

Scenario	Key financial market impact
Rates ↑	• Capital is attracted to fixed income assets, causing stock (and other asset) prices to fall • Borrowing costs rise, causing corporate profits to decline and reinvestment to slow • Domestic currency strengthens, causing export goods to become less competitive
Rates ↓	• Capital is diverted from fixed income assets to stocks and other alternatives, causing their prices to rise • Borrowing costs decline, causing corporate profits to rise and reinvestment to increase • Domestic currency weakens, causing export goods to become more competitive

to hedge their input exposures. During a period of growing price inflation, the national central bank may be forced to deal with the problem by raising interest rates; in fact, this is an important tool of monetary policy, as we shall discuss below. Higher interest rates create two "anti-inflation" effects: they make corporate borrowing more expensive, which causes investment in production to slow, and they make debt-financed purchases of goods more expensive, again leading to a slowdown. Rising rates are thus used to "cool" an overheated economy and lower prices, hopefully in a gradual and methodical fashion. Naturally, the opposite scenario occurs when inflation is under control.

The generalized effects of inflation on financial markets are summarized in Table 10.3.

Let's analyze a third scenario where economic growth, as measured by gross domestic product – GDP, or the total output of goods and services produced within a nation's borders – weakens. When

Table 10.3 Inflation and financial market impact

Scenario	Key financial market impact
Inflation ↑	• Prices of core commodities increase, causing corporate earnings and stock prices of non-resource companies to decline
	• Short-term interest rates begin to rise as the central bank combats the price pressures, causing capital to be diverted to fixed income assets
	• Borrowing costs rise, causing corporate profits to decline and reinvestment to slow
	• Domestic currency strengthens, causing export goods to become less competitive
Inflation ↓	• Prices of core commodities decrease, causing corporate earnings and stock prices of non-resource companies to rise
	• Short-term interest rate hikes will cease, causing capital to flow from fixed income assets to stocks and other financial assets
	• Borrowing costs decline, causing corporate profits to rise and reinvestment to increase
	• Domestic currency weakens, causing export goods to become more competitive

a national economy is contracting, corporate profits decline and stock prices fall. In order to help restart economic activity, monetary authorities may lower interest rates, hoping to spur borrowing for both corporate investment and consumer purchases. Lower rates, as we know, also lead to an increase in the prices of fixed income securities and weaken the domestic currency relative to other currencies, making export goods appear more attractive on the world markets; the latter can ultimately help boost earnings, and stock prices, of companies active in the export sector. Inflation is unlikely to be much of a problem when the economy is weak: companies and customers will curtail demand for goods, easing price pressures. In addition, the prices of many commodities may decline. With less price pressure, the central bank can lower interest rates without fearing a rise in inflation. The cycle of lowering rates will continue until there is some evidence that consumer spending and capital investment are building once again. When the economy begins its upturn – as evidenced by growing sales, consumer debt, and corporate inventories – the central bank will become more vigilant about inflation. Again, the opposite scenario plays out when the economy is expanding.

Table 10.4 summarizes the financial market impact of GDP scenarios. We must, of course, be careful about generalizing these relationships, because exceptions appear during specific market-driven cycles.

MONETARY POLICY AND FINANCIAL VARIABLES

Monetary policy can be defined as the set of financial actions taken by a country, generally through its central bank, that allows it to manage inflation and economic growth (and, indirectly, employment levels). Most countries try to promote steady economic growth while keeping inflation under control. The latter point is very important, as an economy that is growing rapidly but which also features high inflation is in an unsustainable position: as noted above, the purchasing power of consumers and companies will eventually decline, leading to an economic slowdown (and an associated rise in unemployment as workers are dismissed). Conversely, an economy that is expanding at a steady pace while inflation is held in check represents a far more balanced system.

Table 10.4 GDP and financial market impact

Scenario	Key financial market impact
GDP ↑	• Corporate profits rise, causing stock prices to rise • Short-term rates are increased (gradually), causing fixed income asset prices to fall • Domestic currency strengthens, causing export goods to become less competitive • Inflation pressures build, causing commodity prices to rise
GDP ↓	• Corporate profits fall, causing stock prices to decline • Short-term interest rates are lowered, causing fixed income asset prices to rise • Domestic currency weakens, causing export goods to become competitive • Inflation pressures abate, causing commodity prices to fall

Implementing monetary policy is a delicate task. Those responsible, generally a group of officials within a country's central bank, must analyze and interpret a great deal of economic information, some of which may offer conflicting signals on the health of the economy. A small sampling of the key data that officials may use to gauge the state of economic affairs is summarized in Table 10.5. Proper interpretation of this data is vital, as any misreading may cause officials to take the wrong actions regarding interest rate adjustments.

In order to actually match policy to stated goals, central banks rely on several different tools, including changes in the discount rate, open market operations, and changes in bank reserve requirements. Let us consider each one.

• Changes in the discount rate: the most visible, and frequently used, tool of monetary policy involves changing official short-term interest rates (i.e. the official discount rate). For instance, the central bank may raise interest rates to slow an economy that is showing signs of inflation. We know from Part 1 that, when the central bank raises its short-term rates, all other risky short-term rates (e.g. LIBOR) rise as well.

Table 10.5 Sample of key economic measures

Measure	*Indication*
Gross domestic product	• Amount of goods and services produced within a country, overall size and pace of economic growth
Economic/business sentiment	• The overall level of confidence in the economy demonstrated by businesses
Employment/unemployment	• The level of the employment pool and the amount of workers who are unemployed
Producer price index	• Level of wholesale prices/inflation in the wholesale sector
Consumer price index	• Level of wholesale prices/inflation in the consumer sector
Industrial production	• Level of production in the wholesale sector and the degree to which productive processes are utilized
Durable goods orders	• The amount of durable goods, plant, and equipment processed
Capacity utilization	• The degree to which an economy is using its productive capacity, and the amount of any excess or deficit
Merchandise inventory	• The level of inventory on hand
Merchandise trade	• The balance of trade (exports minus imports)
Housing starts	• The amount of new home construction started
New home sales	• The amount of new homes sold
Construction spending	• The amount spent on commercial and residential construction
Retail sales	• The amount of sales conducted at the consumer level
Consumer confidence	• The degree to which consumers are confident of their financial and employment situation, and thus willing to spend

As we've already noted, higher rates cause firms and individuals to borrow less. Less borrowing, in turn, means less investment/expansion in productive endeavors, a slowdown in production, and less debt-financed purchases by consumers and companies. A smaller amount of purchases translates into less price pressure, which leads to a gradual slowing of the economy and a decline in inflation. The opposite scenario holds true.

- Open market operations: a subtle, but effective, tool that central banks frequently employ centers on open market operations, or management of liquidity in the financial system. For instance, when the financial system at large is awash with liquidity (e.g. an excess of cash) banks continue making loans, spurring economic activity and placing upward pressure on prices. To keep inflation in check, the central bank's dealing desk may issue government securities to financial institutions. Since banks and dealers must pay cash for the securities, the central bank draws liquidity out of the system, giving banks less cash with which to make loans; this flows through the system and leads to some curtailment of lending and, ultimately, economic activity. The opposite is also true: when a central bank wants to boost the economy in a period of low inflation, it can buy securities from the financial community, injecting cash into the system and lowering rates. While most of the time open market operations tend to be short term in duration and modest in scope, more extreme versions are used in times of great crisis (see Finance in action 10.2).

- Changes in bank reserve requirements: central banks can also implement monetary policy through a third tool, though they tend to do so infrequently. Specifically, they can influence the level of interest rates, inflation, and economic growth by altering the reserve requirements applied to banks operating in the national system. In most financial systems banks must set aside in non-interest-bearing assets a particular percentage of their balance sheets. For instance, if the current reserve requirement is 10 percent, a bank is able to create €90 of new loans with €100 of new deposits; the remaining €10 of reserve requirements must be held in the form of non-interest-bearing assets. If the central bank is concerned about an overheated economy, it will try to slow the amount of new credit being created by banks. Rather than (or in addition to) increasing short-term rates, it may raise the reserve requirement (e.g.

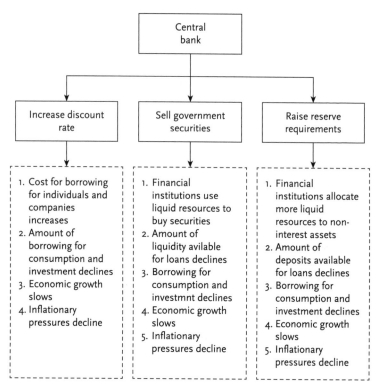

Figure 10.1a Tools to slow economic growth/inflation

from 10 percent to 15 percent); this means that a bank that previously granted €90 in new loans for every €100 of new deposits taken in can now only make €85 in new loans. The credit phase is thus less expansionary and should lead to a slowdown in the purchasing and investing activities of borrowers. The opposite can also occur, of course: if the central bank wants to stimulate economic growth it can reduce the reserve requirement.

These elements of monetary policy are summarized in Figures 10.1a and 10.1b.

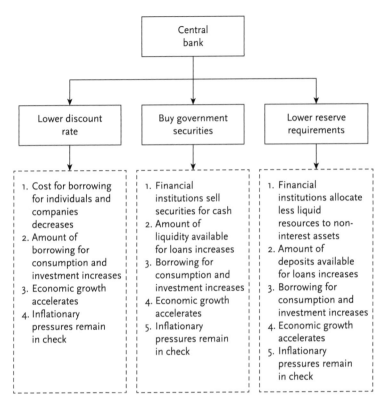

Figure 10.1b Tools to expand economic growth

FINANCE IN ACTION 10.2:   THE AGE OF QUANTITATIVE EASING

When a financial concept is discussed regularly on the evening news, you may be sure that its role in the functioning of daily life has become truly important. So it has been with quantitative easing, the name given to actions taken by a central bank to expand the money supply, lower interest rates, and stimulate the national economy. More specifically, we know from our discussion in this chapter that central banks regulate the level of money supply (and thus interest rates) through open market operations, buying and selling government securities to absorb cash from or inject cash into the financial system. Quantitative easing is a "turbo-charged" version of this process (though it tends only to happen in one direction):

- A central bank buys from financial institutions acceptable securities in large quantities on a regular formulaic basis (the "quantitative") in order to pump cash into the system and lower short-term interest rates (the "easing").
- Banks, flush with cash, will lend to businesses and consumers at the new lower short-term rates.
- The new borrowing causes businesses to expand further and consumers to buy more, thus stimulating the economy and creating new jobs, in a virtuous cycle.
- The process continues until the economy has stabilized; the central bank then gradually halts it securities purchases and begins pursuing its traditional monetary policies.

QE, as the process is commonly known, is implemented when all other central bank stimulus measures have failed to kick-start a weak economy and when short-term rates can no longer be cut further (i.e. they are already close to zero). Not surprisingly, this tends to happen during or immediately after a financial crisis when rates are already low, credit creation is negligible, and economic activity is either slowing or contracting.

During the QE process, a central bank doesn't actually print new banknotes to buy securities from banks, it simply creates electronic cash to effect purchases. This still has the effect of inflating the central bank balance sheet, eroding the value of the national currency and setting the stage for possible inflation. And, while the intentions may be good, there is no guarantee that financial institutions will actually use the newly minted funds in their lending operations. Indeed, sometimes banks just use the central bank cash to buy new securities, earning a positive spread with very little risk – hardly the best way to try and "jump start" an anemic economy. Moreover, the purchase of these new securities (e.g. bonds and stocks) can create speculative asset pressures which might create more problems down the road.

While QE may not be a foolproof way of boosting an economy, it has been used to a significant extent in the past few years. For instance, during and after the Credit Crisis of 2007–2009, most major central banks around the world implemented such programs to try and stave off recessions (or worse) and to try and inject some modicum of stability into otherwise fragile financial systems. Consider that the US Federal Reserve saw its bank balance sheet increase from $1 trillion in 2007 to $4.5 trillion at the end of 2014 when it concluded its 3-part QE program. In effect, the Fed pumped $3.5 trillion in cash into the US financial system through the purchase of securities from banks. Banks, in turn, used some portion of the money to on-lend to individual and corporate customers, and some portion to reinvest in other assets. During this 6-year period, US short-term rates were near zero, the money supply expanded, economic growth began to recover (albeit at a very slow pace) and stock and bond values rocketed. The Bank of England, for its part, purchased £200 billion in securities from banks in 2009 in an attempt to shore up its economy; evidence suggests 1.5–2% growth in the economy in the aftermath of the program. Similar QE programs have been put in place over the years in Switzerland, the Eurozone, and Japan.

The final verdict on the efficacy of QE is still open and may ultimately depend on how individual countries manage in the aftermath of massive easing. While some nations have successfully used these monetary programs to lift their fragile economies and create some level of financial stability in the short term, the medium-term effects of potential speculative pressures, inflation, and currency devaluation remain unclear.

In addition to monetary policy, nations can use fiscal policies to guide their economies. Fiscal policy, in which a government attempts to influence inflation and economic growth (and, by extension, employment levels) through changes in taxes and government spending, is generally agreed to be a medium- to long-term process. Indeed, the effects of changes in tax policy (such as the creation of new taxes or an increase or decrease in tax rates) or government stimulus measures (such as new spending on infrastructure or defense) may not be apparent in economic indicators for months or even years. Thus, while fiscal policy is an important part of the "toolkit" and features prominently during particular market cycles, it cannot typically be relied on to produce short-term results.

FINANCIAL CRISES

Global financial systems are not perfect and are, in fact, subject to all manner of pressures. Sometimes these pressures can build to unsustainable levels, culminating in financial crises. These crises may be of varying severity and breadth, but the end result in most cases is some amount of financial damage to investors, companies, intermediaries, and even governments. Of course, these crises are nothing new: economic history shows us that financial disasters have occurred since the dawn of trading and commerce, typically as a result of economic fragility, asset bubble collapse, risk mismanagement, debt mismanagement, currency attacks, bank runs, and institutional flaws.

Financial crises can be categorized in many ways, but for our discussion we can summarize them in three subclasses: banking/credit crises, currency crises, and debt crises.

- Banking/credit crisis: this crisis represents a severe state of dislocation in which a national banking system ceases to function normally, making impossible the proper allocation of credit – which we know is the fuel of any economic engine. This kind of crisis can be created through a consistent mispricing of risk during the growth phase of an economic cycle (e.g. the boom period), which tends to become more extreme as euphoria spreads. Once economic fortunes turn (e.g. through some catalyst, such as the bursting of an asset bubble built atop cheap financing), the mispricing evident in the extension of risk becomes clear – losses sustained by banks at the heart of the financial system are no longer covered by the returns generated in previous years. Banks may then start rationing credit: borrowers that previously enjoyed favorable borrowing terms may be forced to repay their loans, creating liquidity problems and jeopardizing their own operations. In more extreme situations, the complete lack of credit in the downward cycle leads to growing corporate defaults, further losses within bank loan portfolios, and so forth, in a self-fulfilling cycle. Borrowers who have used funds to pursue speculative ventures, such as real estate development or equity investments, may become forced sellers of assets in order to repay their loans, which leads to asset price devaluation. Recessionary conditions may sweep into the economy, creating a period of economic uncertainty, corporate defaults, heightened unemployment, and so forth.

- Currency crisis: this crisis is a form of financial disaster that relates more narrowly to a significant devaluation in a country's national currency as a result of inconsistencies between its exchange rate regime and its macro-economic policies. The dislocation centers on a change in currency parity, dissolution of a peg, or migration from fixed to pure floating rates, leading to a very large devaluation. Although a currency crisis can be considered to be a narrower form of a financial dislocation than a banking/credit crisis, we should not underestimate its potential for damage – it can be a devastating event which can have significant spillover into the real economy.

- Debt crisis: this form of crisis occurs when a country can't support its debt obligations. When a country can no longer pay its principal and interest, it moves into a very precarious position: its national balance sheet comes under pressure, its currency may suffer a similar fate, and a restructuring or default may shut down access to the international capital markets (sometimes for years). In addition, national equity and debt markets may collapse, along with the value of other tangible assets such as real estate. Local companies relying on external financing for their own operations may see their borrowing abilities restricted entirely and their costs of borrowing rise to the level suggested by the distressed sovereign; in more extreme situations they may also be forced into restructuring or default. Debt crises appear on a reasonably frequent basis; while some are relatively minor, others are quite major and can involve the restructuring of tens of billions of dollars of outstanding debt.

FINANCE IN ACTION 10.3: THE CREDIT CRISIS OF 2007–2009

The Credit Crisis, which began in 2007 and carved a very destructive path through the global economy for more than 2 years, was the most devastating since the Great Crash/Depression of the 1930s, literally reshaping the face of banking, commerce, and the national economies. The origin of the Credit Crisis is generally attributed to a decline in the overheated US housing market, which triggered widespread defaults on subprime mortgages (home loans granted to borrowers of less than desirable credit history or financial capacities). The reality is a bit more complicated, and involves a confluence of players and events, including loose monetary policies, rising (and then falling) real estate prices, complex risk structures, punitive mark-to-market accounting principles, lax regulatory oversight, poor corporate governance, and inadequate risk management practices.

Let's take a step back to review the salient points of this case. From a macro-economic perspective, the US Federal Reserve's low interest-rate policy, put in place in 2001 to reverse the weak economy, permitted excess liquidity to build within the system. From 2001 until the eve of the crisis in mid-2007 this excess liquidity was channeled into the purchase of goods and services and, more importantly, hard assets such as residential and commercial real estate. In addition to this bank-based leverage, additional debt was injected into the system by hedge funds, non-bank financial institutions, and a variety of off balance sheet vehicles, which together acted as a *de facto* "shadow" banking system. Not surprisingly, property prices escalated steadily throughout many parts of the country during this period, with average housing prices in some areas nearly doubling in nominal terms (e.g. Florida, Las Vegas, California, and Arizona). While this provided some homeowners with true gains as they sold or "traded up," it also fueled the mistaken belief that real estate prices would continue on the same upward trajectory.

Flaws at the institutional level compounded the macro-economic pressures. Many large banks based their business models on the "originate and distribute" scheme, whereby assets that they "originated" (including subprime and prime home mortgages) were repackaged in securitized form (as described in Chapter 5), with different tranches "distributed" to a range of investors. As the housing boom seemed unstoppable, banks were all too happy to lower their underwriting standards and accept subprime mortgages in their pools under the assumption that they would not keep these pools on their balance sheets and that, even though default experience would invariably be higher than normal, the average would still be sufficient to repay the securitized tranches when grouped together with thousands of other loans. Both of these assumptions proved ultimately to be wrong.

The US housing market reached its peak in mid-2006 and began a fairly rapid descent from that point on. The first significant losses attributable to US housing appeared at HSBC Finance in February 2007. Credit spreads on structured credit products based on mortgages then started to widen steadily, spilling over into broader "vanilla" credit indexes, including those based on strong corporate borrowers. Significant losses mounted in all manner of structured credit products and investment vehicles managed by global banks, and most became completely illiquid – meaning that they could not be sold, and could not be properly valued. Intervention by Bear Stearns in two of its mortgage hedge funds followed in June 2007. The global extent of the problem became clearer by August 2007, when institutions in the UK and Germany declared large losses from credit-related activities (i.e. Northern Rock, Sachsen Landesbank, and IKB). Forced sales of assets by some funds and banks put more price pressure on illiquid credit assets, lowering prices and compounding losses for virtually all institutions – in a self-fulfilling cycle.

Of course, the excess liquidity was not confined to the housing and real estate markets – capital was also put to work in other asset classes. For instance, private equity funds accumulated a great deal of extra capital from investors, which they channeled into debt-finance leveraged buyouts and other public-to-private transactions. The excessive leverage flowing through the financial system in support of LBOs and public-to-private deals reached an all-time high in the first half of 2007. Many major banks financing such LBO deals had multi-billion-dollar commitments on their books which they hoped to syndicate to end investors. As the market weakened in the summer of

2007, arranging banks were left with tens of billions of dollars of unsold leveraged loans on their balance sheets, many of which would ultimately be written down, creating additional losses.

Throughout late 2007 major global banks such as UBS, Citibank, Merrill Lynch, Deutsche Bank, RBS, Bank of America, JP Morgan Chase, Barclays, and others reported significant losses coming from their structured credit and LBO portfolios, as well as any off balance sheet vehicles they may have been sponsoring. Many banks admitted failures of their risk management processes on many fronts (including business dominating risk control, flawed models and stress tests, and so forth).

In response to the unfolding disaster, central banks engaged in a series of liquidity injections and rate cuts; these commenced in a rather uncoordinated fashion in September 2007, and truly synchronized efforts did not appear until the first quarter of 2008. Central banks made available funds through special borrowing facilities and repurchase agreement facilities that allowed banks to pledge certain structured assets in exchange for cash. This, however, did little to ease tightness in the interbank markets, which remained frozen – from late 2007 and into 2008 banks simply refused to lend to one another as they moved into a "defensive mode." This had the critical effect of halting credit to individuals and companies, leading the system into a classic credit crisis.

The situation remained dire into the first quarter of 2008, with credit spreads continuing to widen and liquidity in credit-related assets remaining scarce. In March 2008 US investment bank Bear Stearns became the subject of liquidity and capital rumors, and was forced into a "shotgun bailout" by JP Morgan. Financial losses in the banking sector continued to mount throughout 2008, and the IMF's estimate of $1 trillion in losses (which it published in April 2008) soon became a reality; even ignoring the recessionary spillover effect into the global real economy and the additional burdens imposed on taxpayers for a variety of bailouts, the dislocation represented a financial catastrophe to rival that of the Great Crash/Depression of 1929.

The second half of 2008 became a critical period for financial institutions as systemic risk mounted. The US government was forced to bail out the US housing agencies Fannie Mae and Freddie Mac but that was insufficient to quell market fears. As the market spiraled downward, the US investment bank Lehman Brothers was forced into bankruptcy, which then triggered various other rescues and hastily arranged corporate marriages: UBS was rescued by the Swiss government, RBS was *de facto* nationalized by the UK government, Merrill Lynch sold itself to Bank of America, Wachovia was taken over by Wells Fargo, HBOS was taken over by Lloyds TSB, Alliance & Leicester was taken over by Banco de Santander, Fortis was rescued by the Dutch and Belgian governments (with portions of the bank being acquired by BNP Paribas), AIG was *de facto* nationalized by the US government, and so forth. In addition, the governments of the UK, Netherlands, Belgium, France, Germany, Ireland, Austria, and Italy, among others, provided *de facto* "safety nets" for their banking systems by guaranteeing deposits, providing capital, and/or guaranteeing second loss positions on bad bank assets. Iceland, unfortunately, was not as lucky, and saw all of its major banks collapse. In late 2008 the US Treasury introduced the Troubled Asset Relief Program (TARP), a $700 billion package designed to purchase "toxic assets" (but which was eventually used to provide preferred capital to most large banks). This was accompanied by additional measures in late 2008 and early 2009, including a residential mortgage relief program to avert a further rise in foreclosures and the Term Asset Backed Securities Lending Facility (TALF), a government program providing investors with financing to purchase a range of qualifying securitized assets. Figure 10.2 illustrates the widening US investment grade credit spreads apparent during different phases of the crisis (similar trends existed for European and Asian credits).

The panic phase of the crisis subsided in 2009 as the commitment of governments to support their financial systems became clear and undoubted. In the immediate aftermath it became clear that most major global economies had entered a recessionary phase as a result of the financial crisis; continued instability in the financial sector (with major banks still holding billions of dollars' worth of "toxic" assets), frozen credit conditions, growing corporate defaults, steady foreclosures, lack of a "bottom" in real estate prices, and increasing job losses combined to create an economic contraction of

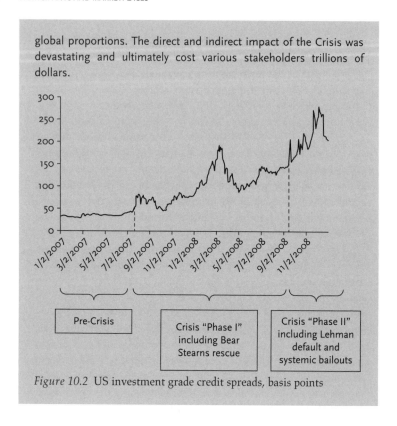

global proportions. The direct and indirect impact of the Crisis was devastating and ultimately cost various stakeholders trillions of dollars.

Pre-Crisis

Crisis "Phase I" including Bear Stearns rescue

Crisis "Phase II" including Lehman default and systemic bailouts

Figure 10.2 US investment grade credit spreads, basis points

THE DYNAMIC MARKETPLACE

The financial markets of the twenty-first century are built on the concepts and activities that we have considered throughout the book. In fact, many of the financial tools, instruments, and transactions have existed for decades, sometimes even centuries, and have become part of the fabric of the financial process. But events of the past two decades, in particular, have altered fundamentally certain aspects of the marketplace. Specifically, the financial system has become more dynamic, flexible, and innovative, primarily as a result of forces of deregulation, capital mobility, volatility, and technology:

- Deregulation: as we've observed in Chapter 9, financial regulations exist to help control the behavior of intermediaries and protect end-users. While regulations may have good intentions, they can also create inefficiencies, particularly in free market economies that operate on the basis of market forces. In fact, while some regulations have been useful in providing proper protection (e.g. mandatory deposit insurance offered by banks), others have actually led to the development of competitive barriers (e.g. forbidding commercial banks from offering investment banking services, prohibiting offshore insurance companies from offering insurance in the local marketplace or across state lines, placing interest rate ceilings on deposit accounts, and so on). Such barriers can have the effect of stifling competition and creating inefficiencies – which can hurt end-users through higher costs and reduced selection. There has, however, been a greater turn towards deregulation in many markets over the past few decades, making the operating environment more competitive and innovative as a result.

- Capital mobility: we have seen at various points that capital is the essential ingredient in corporate expansion and economic progress. When capital can be raised at reasonable rates, companies (and others) are likely to borrow or issue stock/bonds in order to fund their investment and expansion plans; this, in turn, helps boost production, consumption, and economic growth. When capital is mobile, it is able to freely search for the best possible return opportunities. The advent of electronic trading has helped make capital even more mobile, as the process of buying and selling all manner of securities has become cheap and efficient.

- Volatility: financial market volatility drives investment, funding, and risk management decisions. If the financial markets were perfectly stable, there would be no risk and little need to make complicated financial decisions. The very forces of deregulation and capital mobility mentioned above have led to steady increases in the volatility of asset prices and market indicators over the past few decades, meaning that the marketplace at large has become much more dynamic. The seminal event contributing to the rise of financial volatility was the dismantling of the fixed exchange rate regime that had pegged the value of major currencies for decades. Once the major global economies moved to a floating exchange rate regime, financial asset volatility began to rise. Various subsequent events have compounded the volatility effect, i.e. elimination of interest rate ceilings, removal of commodity price controls, dismantling of fixed stock commissions, and deregulation of energy prices, to name but a few. Naturally, this volatility can act as an amplifier during periods of financial stress, helping to fuel or prolong a crisis.

- Technology: advanced computing, communications, and networking technologies have been instrumental in changing the shape of the financial landscape, and there is certainly no indication that the pace of change will slow. The creation of new technology allows intermediaries, end-users, and regulators to conduct their business and duties more efficiently and accurately, generating cost savings in the process.

The dynamism created by these forces has changed the face of finance over the past few decades, and there is little to suggest that things will slow in the coming years. The effects of market impact are widespread and include:

- Greater competition: deregulation and the race for new business in various international financial markets have intensified the level of competition amongst traditional intermediaries (banks, insurers) as well as "new" intermediaries (e.g. non-bank financial institutions, private equity, and hedge funds). A key result of this competition is a gradual erosion of margins and profits among intermediaries and greater economic advantages for end-users, who become the beneficiaries of cut-rate pricing.
- More innovation: the financial markets have long provided participants with innovative ways of solving financial problems. Intermediaries are likely to develop increasingly innovative solutions as technology advances permit more precise pricing of risks, the capital bases and risk-taking abilities of intermediaries continue to expand, and competitive pressures threaten profits. In fact, there is already substantial evidence that this is

occurring: many new derivative instruments and corporate financing techniques have been created in recent years, and electronic trading platforms have become ubiquitous.

- Greater transparency: we have stressed the importance of financial statements in the analysis and decision-making process, and we've noted some of the efforts that have occurred in recent years to inject a greater level of transparency into the corporate accounts (moving off balance sheet items back on the balance sheet, disclosing more information about risks, and so on). As the major accounting approaches of the world begin to harmonize and as investors and analysts continue to demand more information as part of the governance and accountability process, financial statement transparency should continue to improve.

- Increased efficiencies: enterprise value can be enhanced through improved efficiencies. We know that companies that are able to reduce expenses and manage their working capital and risks more efficiently can boost value. Technology is, of course, central to enhanced efficiencies. We can consider just a few of many examples: workplaces are increasingly automated, meaning that firms spend less time and expense on manually intensive work processes; computer-based real-time inventory management is also increasingly common, allowing firms to keep a minimal amount of raw materials on hand, leading to smaller inventories and lower inventory financing costs; e-commerce distribution/ sales solutions, an important channel of revenue generation for small and large firms, are now used to shrink or eliminate aspects of the physical distribution system, and so forth.

- Deeper global penetration: the concept of the global corporation has been mooted for many decades and appears now to be a reality. Firms with a national focus have long sought to expand their geographic presence by creating/acquiring operations in other countries or partnering with foreign entities. Deregulation and mobile capital, coupled with increasingly simple and efficient forms of technological communication across borders, mean that companies choosing to establish a global footprint can do so with greater ease.

- More frequent/deeper crises: the complex system of relationships that exists within the financial sector, the speed of communications, and the flexible and mobile attributes of capital suggest that the financial crises that have appeared in the past years will continue to occur, perhaps with greater frequency and severity. The transmission of a crisis from one market to another – so-called "contagion" – is much more likely to occur in an era where information and decision-making appear in real time. Despite the best efforts of regulators to try and contain these crises, past evidence suggests that in some cases they, too, may be overwhelmed by the speed and ferocity of some of these dislocations. Forces of change and market impact are summarized in Figure 10.3.

Our list here is not, of course, all-inclusive. Other benefits will invariably accrue to companies that use the financial techniques, products, and instruments that we have discussed in the management of their daily operations. And others as yet unknown will appear over time as the landscape continues to evolve. However, many of the core financial operating principles that we have discussed in this book will continue to remain a relevant, and important, cornerstone of prudent management.

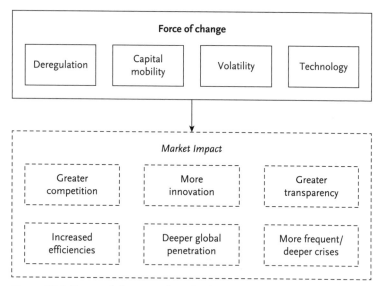

Figure 10.3 Forces of change and market impact

CHAPTER SUMMARY

The key sectors of the global financial system include the money, bond and loan, stock, foreign exchange, commodity, and derivative markets. The relationships between different segments of the financial markets are complex and dynamic: changes in one market can impact capital flowing into, or out of, another market. While such relationships may hold true under most market conditions, they may also vary during times of market stress, causing previously held notions of "normal behavior" to be brought into question. Rising and falling interest rates, inflation rates, and economic growth rates can affect the performance of different asset classes. In order to help manage aspects of the financial markets and national economy, countries can employ fiscal and monetary policy techniques. Fiscal policy, which relates primarily to changes in taxes and spending, is a medium- to long-term approach. Monetary policy, generally conducted by the national central bank, is a shorter-term mechanism for managing inflation and interest rates and, by extension, economic growth and employment levels. Key tools of monetary policy include adjustments to bank reserve requirements, open market operations, and discount rate changes. Financial crises must also be recognized as a key element of the twenty-first-century financial system, and may appear in the form of credit, currency, and/or debt dislocations. The marketplace of the new millennium is dynamic, and subject to a variety of forces that alter its structure; these include deregulation, capital mobility, volatility, and technology. The dynamism of the marketplace can lead to greater competition, innovation, transparency, efficiencies, and global penetration, but perhaps also more frequent and severe periods of dislocation.

FURTHER READING

Banks, E., 2009, *Risk and Financial Catastrophe*, London: Palgrave Macmillan.

Carnes, W. S. and Slifer, S., 1991, *The Atlas of Economic Indicators*, New York: HarperCollins.

Cassidy, J., 2009, *How Markets Fail: The Logic of Economic Calamities*, New York: Farrar, Strauss and Giroux.

Minsky, H., 2008, *Stabilizing Unstable Markets*, New York: McGraw-Hill.

O'Brien, T., 2005, *International Financial Economics*, 2nd edn., Oxford: Oxford University Press.

Taleb, N., 2007, *The Black Swan: The Impact of the Highly Improbable*, New York: Random House.

APPENDIX

INTERNET RESOURCES

The Internet contains a vast amount of valuable information on different aspects of the financial world, and this appendix contains a very small sampling of sites that may prove valuable to those interested in further information, research, and data. Note that, in addition to the sites we have listed in Table A1, individual companies and financial institutions feature sites of their own; these often contain a great deal of financial and strategic information and thus serve as useful references.

Table A1 Selected Internet listings

Name	Site	Type
African Development Bank	afdb.org	Supranational finance, data
American Bankers Association	aba.com	Education and data – banking
AnnualReports.com	annualreports.com	Financial reporting
Asian Development Bank	adb.org	Supranational finance, data

(Continued)

Table A1 (Continued)

Name	Site	Type
Association of Corporate Treasurers	treasurers.org	Education – corporate treasury
Bank for International Settlements	bis.org	Regulation, central banking, data
Bank of England	bankofengland.co.uk	Regulation, central banking, data
Bloomberg	bloomberg.com	Financial news
Central Bank Hub	bis.org/cbanks.htm	Central bank portal
CEO Express	ceoexpress.com	Financial news portal
CFA Institute	cfainstitute.org	Education – financial analysis
Economist	economist.com	Financial news
Euro Banking Association	abe-eba.eu	Education – banking
Euromoney	euromoney.com	Financial news
European Association of Corporate Treasurers	eact.eu	Education – corporate treasury
European Bank for Reconstruction and Development	ebrd.org	Supranational finance, data
European Central Bank	ecb.europa.eu	Regulation, central banking, data
European Corporate Governance Institute	ecgi.org	Corporate governance
Federal Reserve Bank	federalreserve.gov	Regulation, central banking, data
Financial Accounting Standards Board	fasb.org	Accounting standards
Financial Conduct Authority	fca.org.uk	Regulation
Financial Post	financialpost.com	Financial news
Financial Times	ft.com	Financial news
Fitch	fitchratings.com	Financial ratings and analysis
Forbes	forbes.com	Financial news
Fortune Money	fortune.com	Financial news
Global Association of Risk Professionals	garp.com	Education – risk management
Global Treasury News	gtnews.com	Financial news
Google Finance	Google.com/finance	Financial news, data
Hoover's	hoovers.com	Financial data – public/private companies

Name	Site	Type
Inter-American Development Bank	iadb.org	Supranational finance, data
International Corporate Governance Network	icgn.org	Corporate governance
International Finance Corporation	ifc.org	Supranational finance, data
International Financial Reporting Standards	ifrs.org	Accounting standards
International Financing Review	ifre.com	Financial news, data
International Monetary Fund	imf.org	Supranational finance, data
International Swaps and Derivatives Association	isda.org	Education and data – derivatives
Investopedia	investopedia.com	Financial dictionary
Investor's Business Daily	investors.com	Financial news
Market Watch	marketwatch.com	Financial news, data
Moody's	moodys.com	Financial ratings and analysis
Money	money.cnn.com	Financial news
Morningstar	morningstar.com	Financial news, data
National Association of Corporate Treasurers	nact.org	Education – treasury
Organisation for Economic Co-operation and Development	Oecd.org	Economic and financial data
Professional Risk Managers' International Association	prmia.org	Education – risk management
Reinsurance.org	reinsurance.org	Education – reinsurance
Reuters	reuters.com	Financial news
Risk and Insurance Management Society	rims.org	Education – corporate risk management
Risk.net	risk.net	Financial news
Risk World	riskworld.com	Education – insurance
Securities and Exchange Commission	sec.gov	Regulation
Securities Industry and Financial Markets Association	sifma.org	Education – financial Markets

(Continued)

Table A1 (Continued)

Name	Site	Type
Standard & Poors	standardandpoors.com	Financial ratings and analysis
The Street	thestreet.com	Financial news
Wall Street Journal	wsj.com	Financial news
World Bank	worldbank.org	Supranational finance, data
Yahoo Finance	finance.yahoo.com	Financial news, data

GLOSSARY

Accounts payable: A form of credit accepted by a company from its suppliers which arises when it chooses to pay in the future for goods or services received today.

Accounts receivable: A form of credit extended by a company to its customers which arises from delayed customer payments for goods or services sold today.

Acquisition: A corporate finance transaction where a company purchases another company in order to expand its market presence/share or develop some other competitive advantage. Also known as Takeover.

Add-on: A secondary offering of a company's shares that is offered to the market at large rather than to existing shareholders.

Agent: In the financial markets, a party that matches buyers and sellers of securities, taking a small spread as a commission but taking no risk itself. Also known as Broker.

Alpha: In an investment portfolio the absolute returns that exceed pure index returns.

Amortizing repayment: Any debt mechanism where the borrower repays a portion of the principal on every interest payment date, so that there is no large principal payment due at maturity.

Annuity: A contract that pays equal cash installments over an extended period of time.

Arbitrage: The simultaneous purchase and sale of an asset that allows a "riskless" profit to be locked in.

Asset: An item of value legally owned by a company.

Auditor: An external or internal specialist who is responsible for regularly and independently reviewing the accuracy and veracity of a company's financial statements.

Balance sheet: A financial statement that reflects a point-in-time status of a company's assets, liabilities, and equity.

Balloon repayment: Any debt mechanism where the borrower makes small principal repayments for the first few years of the borrowing, followed by a large final repayment at maturity.

Bank: A financial institution that is primarily involved in accepting deposits and granting loans.

Bank regulator: A national authority that is responsible for ensuring that banks in the local system operate prudently by maintaining a minimum level of capital, reserves, and liquidity, minimum standards of asset quality, and maximum amount of leverage.

Banking/credit crisis: A form of financial crisis representing a severe state of dislocation in which a national banking system ceases to function normally, making impossible the proper allocation of credit.

Basis point (bp): 1/100th of 1 percent, and a common way of measuring interest rates.

Behavioral finance: The study of the actions of investors and companies when they must deal with the realities of a real-world environment, which often leads to abandoning of "rational" actions and optimal decision-making.

Beta: A measure of the riskiness of an individual security in comparison with the overall market.

Bid: The price at which an investor is willing to purchase a security.

Board of directors: In a corporate structure, external and, sometimes, internal professionals charged with independently representing investor interests.

Bond: Debt issued by a company in the form of a tradable security.

Bond optionality: The inclusion of issuer or investor options in bonds to enhance yield or lower funding costs, as in callable bonds and puttable bonds.

Book value: The value at which an asset is carried on the company's balance sheet.

Broker: See Agent.

Building society: See Thrift.

Bullet repayment: Any debt mechanism where the borrower makes no principal repayment until the final maturity of the financing.

Call option: The right to buy a reference asset at a particular strike price in exchange for payment of a premium.

Callable bond: A bond that grants the issuer the right to call (buy back) the bond from investors, generally at par value.

Capital: See Equity.

Capital appreciation: Rise in the value of a security or other asset.

Capital asset pricing model (CAPM): A financial framework that relates non-diversifiable risk to the expected return of a security, project, or investment, stating that the actual risk of a stock is equal to a constant (the base risk-free interest rate) plus a market return that is adjusted by beta.

Capital investment: The process of managing long-term investment projects, research and development, and capital expenditures.

Capital lease: A long-term, non-cancelable, lease where the lessee is responsible for maintenance and repairs on the asset being leased.

Captive: A company-owned (or controlled) insurance subsidiary that acts as a self-insurer by keeping insurance premiums within the subsidiary and using them to cover any potential losses arising from insurable events.

Carve-out: The sale of some part of a company's existing operations, such as a profitable and well-regarded subsidiary, which can be readily split from the balance of the firm.

Cash: Ready money, or the most liquid part of a company's asset accounts.

Cash flow: The amount of cash flowing into, and out of, a company's operations, typically defined to include operating cash flow, investing cash flow, and financing cash flow; or, an amount of cash used in a time value of money calculation.

Cash flow-based model: An equity valuation model that uses cash flow estimates to project a value for a company's stock.

Cash flow statement: See Statement of cash flows.

Cedant: A party that is transferring risk exposure to an insurer under an insurance contract.

Certificate of deposit (CD): An unsecured, discount- or coupon-bearing negotiable debt security issued by a bank, with a maturity ranging from short to long term.

Closed-end fund: An investment fund that accepts capital from investors and uses the proceeds to buy securities, but where the amount of capital accepted is limited to a specified size.

Coefficient of variation: A common measure of risk, computed as the standard deviation divided by the expected return.

Coinsurance: The amount of losses that an insured and an insurer agree to share.

Collateralized debt obligation (CDO): A form of securitized bond, where the bond is backed by a pool of debt instruments, such as payables, loans, or bonds and which pays interest to investors in relation to the specific tranche purchased.

Commercial bank: A regulated banking institution that accepts deposits from retail and institutional customers and uses those funds primarily to grant commercial and industrial loans, personal loans, and residential mortgages.

Commercial paper (CP): Senior, unsecured, discount-based short-term negotiable debt issued almost exclusively by high grade companies.

Commodity market: The global market for spot (i.e. current) market and forward dealing in precious metals, industrial metals, energy, agricultural products, and soft commodities.

Common stock: A form of ownership capital issued by a company to investors, generally characterized by rent rights and legal rights. Also known as Ordinary shares.

Comparables analysis: A method for valuing the cost of equity for a company that has not yet gone public, typically by comparing the company's pro-forma financial statements with those of public firms that are engaged in similar activities.

Contagion: The transmission of a financial dislocation or crisis across different financial markets and/or national borders.

Convertible bond: A hybrid bond that pays a minimum coupon, generally on a fixed rate basis, and allows the investor the option of converting the bond into common shares if a conversion level is reached; if converted, the bond is extinguished and bondholders become equity investors.

Corporate finance: The broad range of financial transactions that can be used to alter the structure and scope of a company's operations, such as mergers, acquisitions, buybacks, and spin-offs.

Corporation: An enduring business structure where shares are sold to multiple investors and where liability for losses is limited to share capital committed.

Correlation: A statistical measure that is computed from the covariances and standard deviations of variables a and b.

Cost of capital: The amount a company must pay for its semi-permanent and permanent financing, i.e. debt and equity.

Cost of goods sold: The amount a company must pay to produce or convey the goods/services it sells, generally defined to include raw materials and other inputs as well as labor/production costs.

Coupon: The periodic interest rate paid by a borrower to the lender or investor on a loan or bond.

Coverage: In insurance, a detailed definition of the perils that can create losses for which the cedant will be indemnified.

Credit rating: An independent financial analysis and scoring of the financial strength of a company.

Credit rating agency: An independent company that performs financial analyses of companies and/or countries and assigns corresponding credit ratings.

Credit spread: See Debt risk premium.

Cross rate: A foreign exchange quotation between two currencies that does not include the US dollar.

Cumulative preferred stock: Preferred stock that accumulates dividends that are due to preferred investors in cases where the company is unable to make a current dividend payment; no other dividends can be paid to other equity investors until dividend arrears have been settled.

Currency crisis: A form of financial crisis centered on a significant devaluation in a country's currency as a result of inconsistencies between its exchange rate regime and its macro-economic policies.

Current assets: The total of a company's cash, securities, accounts receivable, prepayments, and inventories, which together represent the most liquid portion of the balance sheet.

Current liabilities: The total of a company's accounts payable and short-term debt, which together represent the most immediate portion of the company's obligations.

Current ratio: A financial ratio that measures the liquidity of a company's balance sheet by dividing current assets by current liabilities.

Custody: Fiduciary services provided by certain financial intermediaries on behalf of clients that can include asset safekeeping, valuation and reporting, and collection of principal, interest, and dividends.

Dark pool: Any exchange or off-exchange mechanism that permits anonymous, unadvertised trading in stocks, thus ensuring confidentiality and reducing the chance of market price impact.

Dealer: See Principal.

Debt: An obligation to repay a lender or investor any amount borrowed, plus interest, in the future and which may take the form of a loan, payable, or tradable security.

Debt crisis: A form of financial crisis in which a country cannot support repayment of its debt obligations, leading to instances of debt restructuring or default.

Debt markets: The national and global markets for medium- and long-term liabilities, including bonds and loans issued by companies, agencies, and sovereign nations.

Debt risk premium: The basis point spread above the base risk-free rate prevailing in the market that a company must pay to obtain debt. Also known as Credit spread.

Debt service: The amount a company must regularly pay in interest/principal to fulfill its contractual debt obligations.

Debt to assets: A financial ratio measuring the amount of financial leverage being supported by a company's asset base, computed as total debt divided by total assets.

Debt to equity: A financial ratio measuring the amount of financial leverage being supported by a company's equity base, computed as total debt divided by total equity.

Deductible: The amount of initial losses a cedant must bear before insurance coverage becomes effective.

Default: The act of not paying on debts contractually owed to third parties.

Deferred payments: Payments a company is required to make which have not yet been made, classified on the balance sheet as a liability.

Depository receipts: Equity securities that are issued by a depository on behalf of the issuing company; the company lodges shares with the depository, which then issues tradable receipts to investors.

Depreciation: The reduction in the value of a physical asset that occurs over time as a result of normal use (or "wear and tear").

Derivative: A financial contract that derives its value from some underlying asset or market, and which can be used to hedge or speculate.

Derivative market: The national and global market for trading in financial contracts linked to interest rates, equities, foreign exchange, credits, and commodities.

Digital currency: An electronic store of value that can be used to make purchases or transfers, and which may be supported through a centralized hub or a decentralized network.

Dilution: The diminishing of legal and rent rights through the addition of new stock investors.

Disintermediation: The process of removing intermediaries from their traditional roles in raising capital, granting advice, and providing other financial services, allowing companies to perform these roles by themselves.

Diversifiable risk: A risk that is unique to a project/investment, and which can therefore be changed by adding other projects/investments.

Diversification: The process of adding uncorrelated investments, projects, or risks in order to reduce the overall riskiness of a portfolio.

Divestiture: A form of spin-off where a company disposes of assets related to a business it is seeking to permanently exit.

Dividend: A periodic, voluntary income distribution made by a company to its common stock and preferred stock investors.

Dividend-based model: An equity valuation model that uses future dividend estimates to project a value for a company's stock.

Dividend payout ratio: A measure of how much of a company's earnings are paid in dividends, typically computed by dividing dividends per share by earnings per share.

Dividend yield: The return provided by the dividends on an equity security, computed by dividing the current dividend by the current stock price.

Earnings before interest and taxes (EBIT): An important corporate profitability measure computed as gross profit minus selling, general, and administrative expenses, essentially reflecting core operating performance before any interest or taxes are paid.

Efficient market hypothesis (EMH): A theory stating that information is not regularly or accurately absorbed by financial markets, suggesting that the market prices of assets may not be accurate and that portfolio managers can routinely outperform the market at large.

Efficient portfolio: A portfolio of assets that provides the maximum level of return for a given amount of risk.

Electronic funds transfer (EFT): The broad class of financial transactions that involves monetary exchange between accounts in the electronic sphere.

Environmental risk: The risk of loss arising from the firm's willful, unknowing, or accidental damage to the environment.

Equity: An ownership interest in a public company, entitling the investor to certain legal and rent rights. Also known as capital, shares, and stock.

Eurobond: A bond issued by a company, agency, or sovereign in the offshore (non-domestic) markets.

Euro-commercial paper (ECP): Senior, unsecured, discount-based short-term negotiable debt issued almost exclusively by high grade companies and issued in the offshore (non-domestic) market.

Euro medium term note (EMTN): An offshore (non-domestic) bond issued from a pre-filed "shelf" registration, allowing for quick and easy launch.

Excess of loss (XOL) reinsurance: A form of reinsurance where the insurer and reinsurer take preferred "layers" of risk though deductibles (attachments) and caps, either on an outright basis (vertical) or a shared basis (horizontal).

Exchange: A centralized physical or electronic forum that brings together buyers and sellers of securities and other assets, helping promote price discovery and orderly settlement.

Exchange-traded derivative: A standardized derivative contract that is traded through an established exchange, and which does not permit any customization in the terms and conditions related to notional, term, reference market/asset, or payoff profile.

Exchange-traded fund (ETF): An investment fund that allows new shares to be created and redeemed at will and permits continuous intra-day trading (just as in stocks and bonds).

Exclusions: In insurance, any specific or general circumstances or conditions under which a cedant's losses are not indemnified.

Expected value: The expected future return of an investment or project multiplied by the probability that the return will be achieved.

Facultative reinsurance: A form of customized, case-by-case reinsurance where the reinsurer examines and either accepts or rejects each specific risk proposed by the ceding insurer.

Finance: The study of concepts, applications, and systems that affect the value (or wealth) of individuals, companies, and countries over the short and long term.

Financial decision-making: The use of financial tools and concepts, along with financial analysis and financial planning, to make decisions that affect a company's future activities.

Financial distress: A state where a company is in jeopardy of bankruptcy, generally as a result of persistent financial mismanagement, including operating losses, illiquidity, and/or excessive financial leverage.

Financial leverage: The degree to which debt is used to fund the balance sheet.

Financial planning: A process based on the actions that a firm needs to take over the short term and long term to meet its financial goals.

Financial process: A multi-stage cycle centered on financial reporting/analysis, financial planning, and financial decision-making.

Financial reporting/analysis: A process based on the structure and trend of a company's financial position, most often conveyed through three key financial statements (or accounts), the balance sheet, income statement, and cash flow statement.

Financial risk: The risk of loss coming from an adverse movement in financial markets/prices (i.e. market risk) or the failure of a client/counterparty to perform on its contractual obligations (i.e. credit risk).

Financing cash flow: The degree to which a company uses external funding to cover its operating and investing activities, computed as new debt and stock issuance (cash inflows), debt repayment (outflow), dividend payments (outflow), and treasury stock repurchases (outflow).

Fiscal policy: Tax and government spending policies enacted by a national government over the medium term to influence the level of inflation and economic growth.

Fixed assets: See Property, plant and equipment.

Fixed rate: An interest rate that remains unchanged for the life of the contract.

Flat yield curve: A state of the yield curve where short-term rates are the same as long-term rates.

Floating rate: An interest rate that sets or resets to a level specified by an index, such as the London Interbank Offered Rate (LIBOR).

Flotation: The act of issuing shares or bonds to the market.

Foreign exchange: A currency bought or sold for a second currency.

Foreign exchange market: The global market for the exchange of one currency for another, on either a spot (current) or forward basis.

Forward: A single-period over-the-counter contract that allows one party, known as the seller, to sell a reference asset at a forward price for settlement at a future date, and a second party, the buyer, to purchase the reference asset at the forward price on the named date.

Full risk transfer insurance contract: An insurance policy that transfers a great deal of risk from cedant to insurer.

Funding management: The process of arranging financing through the loan or capital markets.

Future: A single-period exchange-traded contract that allows one party, the seller, to sell a particular reference asset at a future price for settlement at a future date and the second party, the buyer, to purchase the reference asset at the future price on the named date.

Future value: The value of one or more cash flows paid or received today compounded to the future using the appropriate rate or cost of capital.

Futures option: An exchange-traded option that gives the buyer the right to buy or sell an underlying futures contract, and which requires the seller to accept or deliver the futures contract upon exercise.

Generally accepted accounting principles (GAAP): Common standards and procedures used by companies in compiling their financial statements.

Goodwill: The excess amount over book value paid by a company when it acquires another company.

Gross domestic product (GDP): The total output of goods and services produced within a nation's borders.

Gross margin: A financial ratio indicating how much of each dollar, pound, or euro of revenue (from sales of goods/services) remains after removing the costs of producing the goods/services, which is calculated as gross profit divided by revenues.

Gross profit: The difference between the revenues earned by a company and the cost it incurs in producing those revenues.

Gross revenues: The total amount of goods/services sold by the company to its customers. Also known as Turnover.

Hedge: A risk management technique which allows a company to neutralize a financial risk by using an off-setting position, such as a derivative.

Hedge fund: A flexible investment vehicle intended primarily for sophisticated investors which often buys risky assets, uses borrowed funds to magnify leverage, takes concentrated positions, short sells assets and buys/sells illiquid securities and derivatives.

High grade debt: The debt issued by companies rated between AAA and BBB–. Also known as Investment grade debt.

High yield debt: The debt issued by companies rated BB+ and below.

Horizontal expansion: An acquisition strategy where a company grows by acquiring direct competitors.

Income statement: A financial statement reflecting a company's revenues, expenses, and profits. Also known as Profit and loss account.

Indexing: A common fund management technique based on creating an investment portfolio that replicates a specific benchmark index.

Inflation: A measure of the price of goods and services at the wholesale level and the consumer level.

Initial public offering (IPO): The first launch of a company's shares in the stock market, which converts it from a private company to a public one.

Insolvency: A state where a company's assets are worth less than its liabilities (e.g. negative equity), indicating that it can no longer operate as a going concern.

Insurance: A contract that provides financial restitution when a loss-making event occurs.

Insurance company: A regulated institution that provides individual and institutional customers with risk transfer advice and policies/products, including the full range of insurance contracts.

Insurance regulator: A national, state or provincial authority that is responsible for reviewing the capabilities of insurers writing specific classes of insurance, ensuring that they maintain a minimum level of statutory reserves/capital and making certain that their dealings with policyholders in settling loss claims are fair and equitable.

Intangibles: Assets that cannot be physically seen or touched, but which add value to the firm, such as trademarks, patents, intellectual property, and goodwill.

Interbank market: The marketplace for foreign exchange dealing and short-term deposit placement between international banks.

Interest coverage: A financial ratio measuring the degree to which a company's core operating profitability covers its interest expense, typically computed as earnings before interest and taxes divided by interest expense.

Interest expense: The amount a company pays its creditors for the use of borrowed funds, such as those from short- and long-term loans and bonds and accounts payable.

Interest income: The amount that a company earns in interest from its investments in short- or long-term securities.

Interest rate: The general cost of borrowing money or the amount that can be earned by lending money or depositing funds.

Intermediate risk retention/transfer insurance policy: An insurance policy that transfers a fractional amount of risk from cedant to insurer.

Intermediation: The process of facilitating and arranging the provision and use of capital, the acquisition and purchase of assets, and the transfer and acceptance of risks, tasks which are commonly performed by financial institutions.

Internal rate of return (IRR): The cost of capital that forces a net present value computation to zero.

International Financial Reporting Standards: A set of international accounting standards indicating how companies should treat and present transactions in their financial statements.

Inventory: Accounts comprising the items needed to manufacture physical goods that are ultimately sold to customers, often classified according to their stage in the production process (e.g. raw material, work-in-progress, and finished goods). Also known as Stock in British English.

Inverted yield curve: A state of the yield curve where short-term rates are higher than long-term rates.

Investing cash flow: The amount of cash a company uses in pursuing productive ventures or investments, computed as the purchase of other companies or property, plant, and equipment (outflows of cash), the purchase of securities/other financial assets (outflow), the sale of existing assets, subsidiaries, or joint venture stakes (inflow), and the sale of securities (inflow).

Investment: The commitment of capital in a venture, project, asset, or security in order to create more value.

Investment bank: A regulated financial institution that is primarily involved in the capital markets business, including issuing and trading securities and providing corporate finance and risk management advice. Also known as Securities firm.

Investment funds: Financial products that combine into managed portfolios a range of assets, such as debt and equity securities.

Investment grade debt: See High grade debt.

Investment mandate: The specific investment parameters to which a fund manager must adhere in investing capital on behalf of clients.

Islamic finance: A form of structured finance that is designed to adhere to religious interpretations and legal rulings governing permissible financing and investment.

Joint venture: A commercial business that is operated by two or more corporate partners, each of whom retains and runs its own operations separate and apart from the venture.

Laissez-faire: A free market economic system characterized by a minimum of government regulation and widespread participation by the private sector.

Lease: A financing transaction between the lessor, which owns an underlying asset, and the lessee, which wishes to use/rent the asset in exchange for lease payments; at the end of the lease contract the lessee returns the leased asset, though it may be given the option to purchase the asset at a pre-defined residual value.

Legal rights: In a corporate setting, specific rights granted to every equity investor, including voting on issues important to the continuing success of the company (e.g. selection of board directors) and receiving periodic audited financial statements.

Legal risk: The risk of loss arising from litigation (individual, regulatory, or "class action") or other legal/documentary conflicts or errors.

Leverage: Any balance sheet or off balance sheet structure or mechanism that magnifies profits and losses, and which may come from financial or operating sources.

Leveraged buyout (LBO): A corporate finance transaction where a publicly listed company takes itself private by borrowing to purchase outstanding shares. Also known as Management buyout.

Liability: An amount legally owed by a company to a third party, or the amount of loss exposure to which a capital provider is exposed.

Limited liability: A legal tenet of corporate structure indicating that the owners of a corporation's shares are not liable for more than the amount they have invested.

Liquid assets: Assets, such as cash and short-term marketable securities, which can be used with immediate effect by a company to cover expected or unexpected obligations.

Liquidity: A sufficiency of cash or cash equivalents (i.e. liquid assets) to pay bills and cover any surprises or emergencies.

Loan: A debt financing granted by a bank to a corporate or individual borrower, which is defined by a specific maturity and periodic interest and principal payments.

London Interbank Offered Rate (LIBOR): The rate paid on short-term interbank deposits by the world's largest banks, and the most common short-term interest rate reference in the financial markets, used to price floating rate loans, floating rate notes and bonds, interest rate swaps, deposits, foreign exchange transactions and certain kinds of mortgages.

Long-term debt: Credit extended to a company via long-term loans and securities with maturities ranging from 10 to 30+ years.

Loss control: A technique of risk management based on avoidance (i.e. refusing to participate in risky activities) and resistance (i.e. imposing safety measures to reduce risk). Also known as Risk mitigation.

Loss financing: A technique of risk management centered on risk retention (i.e. the amount of risk a company is willing to take), risk transfer (i.e. the amount of risk a company wishes to shift to others), and hedging (i.e. the use of instruments/strategies designed to offset certain risks).

Loss sensitive contract: A partial insurance contract with premiums that depend on previous loss experience.

Macro-finance: The study of finance at the systemic level with a focus on participants, marketplaces, financial market variables, and monetary systems.

Management buyout: See Leveraged buyout.

Margin: Cash or securities lodged with an exchange to collateralize an exchange-traded derivative, thereby eliminating credit risk exposure; initial margin may be supplemented by variation margin as the price of the reference asset moves.

Marginal cost of capital: The cost to the firm of each incremental amount of capital funding.

Market efficiency: The degree to which the market prices of securities absorb and reflect all known (public) and unknown (non-public) information.

Medium-term debt: Credit extended to a company via medium-term loans and securities with maturities ranging from 1 to 10 years.

Medium-term note (MTN): A domestic bond issued from a pre-filed "shelf" registration, allowing for quick and easy launch.

Merger: A process where two companies agree to combine their operations in order to expand market presence or take advantage of possible cost savings.

Monetary policy: The set of financial actions taken by a country, generally through its central bank, which allows it to manage inflation and economic growth.

Money: A fungible medium of exchange and store of value that is typically backed by government fiat rather than a hard asset such as gold.

Money markets: The national and global markets for tradable short-term liabilities issued by banks (e.g. certificates of deposit, repurchase agreements), companies (e.g. commercial paper), and sovereigns (e.g. treasury bills).

Mortgage loan: A loan granted to an individual for the purchase of a home, or to a company or investor for the purchase of a commercial or industrial property.

Mutual fund: See Open-end fund.

Negative equity: A state where the value of a company's liabilities exceeds the value of assets, indicating that it is technically insolvent.

Net asset value (NAV): The value of a fund's assets, computed as invested capital plus cash less current liabilities.

Net income: See Profit.

Net margin: A financial ratio indicating how much of each dollar, pound, or euro of revenue (from sales of goods/services) remains after removing the costs of producing the goods/services, selling, general, and administrative expenses, interest expenses, and taxes, which is typically calculated as net profit divided by revenues.

Net present value: A present value computation that also includes a net outflow at time 0, which represents the amount being invested in the asset generating cash flows.

Net profit: See Profit.

Net worth: The capital value of a firm, which can be computed in simplified form as assets minus liabilities.

Non-bank financial institution: A finance or leasing company associated with an industry or parent company that is engaged in the provision of specialized loans, leases, or other financial transactions.

Non-cumulative preferred stock: Preferred stock that does not provide for dividend accrual, indicating that, if a dividend is skipped, investors in the securities have no continuing claim on that dividend.

Non-diversifiable risk: A risk common to all projects/investments, meaning it cannot be reduced through diversification.

Notional: The reference amount used in the computation of certain derivatives, such as swaps and forwards.

Off balance sheet accounts: Contingencies or uncertainties carried apart from balance sheet accounts that may include undrawn/unfunded bank loans, financial guarantees, derivative contracts, and leases.

Offer: The price at which an investor in a security is willing to sell.

Open-end fund: The most popular type of investment fund, where a fund manager accepts without limitation capital from investors and uses the proceeds to buy securities. Also known as Mutual fund, Unit trust.

Open market operations: A tool of monetary policy where a central bank sells securities to financial institutions in order to absorb cash from the economy and raise short-term rates, or buys securities to achieve the opposite effect.

Operating cash flow: The actual cash impact (receipts and outflows) of the firm's normal operations, computed as net income generated by the business plus depreciation (which is a non-cash operating expense) plus/minus changes in working capital.

Operating income: A company's gross profit less selling, general, and administrative expenses, interest expense, and other income/expenses, which yields a taxable income equivalent. Also known as Pre-tax income.

Operating lease: A lease, typically with a maturity of less than 5 years, that is generally cancelable by the lessee and where maintenance and repairs on the underlying assets are the responsibility of the lessor.

Operating leverage: The degree to which a company relies on fixed investments and associated costs to produce revenues, often measured as the change in earnings before interest and taxes divided by change in revenues.

Operating margin: A financial ratio indicating how much of each dollar, pound, or euro of revenue (from sales of goods/services) remains after removing the costs of producing the goods/services, selling, general, and administrative expenses, and interest expense, which is calculated as operating profit divided by revenues.

Operating risk: The risk of loss arising from a firm's inability to sell its goods/services or obtain raw materials or other essential inputs required to support business.

Option: An exchange-traded or over-the-counter financial contract that gives the purchaser the right, but not the obligation, to buy (call option) or sell (put option) a reference asset at a particular price (known as the strike price); in exchange for this right, the buyer pays the seller a premium payment.

Ordinary shares: See Common stock.

Over-the-counter (OTC) derivative: A derivative contract that is arranged between two parties on an off-exchange basis, where each contract represents a customized negotiation of terms and conditions related to notional, term, reference market/asset, and payoff profile.

Over-the-counter (OTC) market: Any marketplace for trading in assets that is conducted away from a formal exchange, typically by phone or electronically.

Par value: 100 percent of the issued bond or the nominal value of shares issued by a corporation.

Partnership: A common business structure where multiple partners serve as capital providers, and where loss liability may be divided in equal or unique ways.

Perpetuity: A fixed cash flow that is paid forever, as in an endowment fund or perpetual bond.

Poison pill: Legal clauses that a company puts in place that trigger post-acquisition asset sales or other value-destroying measures in order to dissuade potential acquirers.

Pooling method: An accounting methodology used when two companies involved in a merger or acquisition exchange stock on a tax-free basis; the resulting "consolidation" is an addition of the balance sheets of the two firms.

Preferred stock: A form of non-voting, dividend-paying ownership capital issued by a company to investors. Also known as Preference shares.

Preference shares: See Preferred stock.

Premium: The amount an insured pays an insurer every year for specific insurance coverage, the amount an option buyer pays an option seller to purchase an option, or the amount in excess of book value (net worth) that an acquiring company pays shareholders in a target company for their shares.

Prepayments: Payments made by a company for goods/services to be received at a future time, classified on the balance sheet as an asset.

Present value: The value of one or more cash flows to be paid or received in the future discounted back to the current time through the appropriate discount rate or cost of capital.

Pre-tax income: See Operating income.

Principal: In the financial markets, a party that assumes risk by taking one side of the transaction (e.g. purchasing a security) and then either retains the risk, hedges the position, or separately arranges an offsetting deal (e.g. selling the security it purchased). Also known as Dealer.

Private placement: A bond that is exempt from regulatory registration, trades infrequently in large denominations, and is designed for sophisticated institutional investors that can bear more risk than the average individual investor.

Probability distribution: A graphical representation of the likelihood of occurrence of all possible outcomes across a sample or population.

Profit: The income that remains after expenses have been deducted, the difference between a company's pre-tax income and taxes paid, reflecting the true profitability of the operation. Also known as Net profit or Net income.

Profit and loss account: See Income statement.

Property, plant, and equipment (PP&E): The physical infrastructure that a company needs to run its business, such as computers, office buildings, real estate, warehouses, trucking fleets, factories, and so on. Also known as Fixed assets.

Proportional reinsurance: A form of reinsurance, enacted through the quota share (fixed) and surplus share (variable) structures, where the insurer and reinsurer have an economic interest in every risk written based on a prearranged formula.

Public company: A company that has issued stock to investors which is actively traded on an exchange.

Purchase acquisition: An accounting methodology used when one company acquires a second company; if no premium to net worth is paid, the consolidated balance sheet is a pure summation of the two companies, and if a premium to net worth is made, the consolidated balance sheet reflects the increment in the acquirer's goodwill account.

Pure risk: A risk that features only two end states: loss or no loss, meaning that there is no opportunity for a profit.

Put option: The right to sell a reference asset at a particular strike price in exchange for payment of a premium.

Puttable bond: A bond that gives investors the right to put (sell) the bond back to the issuer.

Quantitative easing: An aggressive, and generally medium-term, form of open market operations where a central bank, seeking to boost the local economy in a low inflation and low-interest-rate environment, purchases securities from financial institutions, thereby injecting cash into the financial system, lowering interest rates even further and encouraging more borrowing to occur.

Quick ratio: A financial ratio that measures the truly liquid portion of a company's balance sheet by dividing current assets (less inventories) by current liabilities.

Recapitalization: A corporate finance transaction that is used to restructure a company's capital base, generally by altering the mix and size of debt and equity.

Redemption: The sale of fund shares by an investor.

Refunding risk: The risk that interest rates will rise by the time a company has to renew or initiate a debt funding program.

Reinsurance: Insurance purchased by an insurance company from a reinsurance company to transfer a portion of the risk in its own operations.

Reinsurance company: A regulated institution that serves as an insurer of other insurance companies, providing risk transfer coverage to insurers that are writing primary coverage to their individual and corporate clients.

Rent right: In a corporate setting, the right granted to every investor to share in the profits of the company, either through dividends, capital appreciation, or both.

Repayment schedule: The manner in which the principal amount of the bond or loan is to be repaid by the borrower.

Repurchase agreement: A form of short-term collateralized borrowing, where a financial institution sells securities (the collateral) to another party for cash (the borrowing), agreeing simultaneously to repurchase them at a future time.

Reserve requirements: A tool of monetary policy where a central bank indicates the amount that banks must set aside in non-interest bearing assets (as a percentage of loans or assets) as a way of controlling the level of credit creation in the economy.

Restructuring: The process of buying or selling assets or entire portions of a company, or otherwise changing the composition of assets, liabilities, or capital, in order to increase enterprise value.

Retained earnings: A capital account representing a company's accumulated profits which are available to be reinvested in new projects/investments.

Retrocession: Reinsurance purchased by a reinsurance company from another reinsurance company as a way of managing its risk.

Return: The amount that a risk-taker requires in order to accept a particular type and quantity of risk.

Return on assets: A financial ratio describing how much profit the firm's asset base is able to produce, computed as net income divided by total assets.

Return on equity: A financial ratio describing how much profit the firm's equity base is able to produce, computed as net income divided by total equity.

Revenue: The amount of money earned by a company from the sale of its goods or services.

Rights issue: A secondary placement of shares that is offered initially to existing shareholders, effectively giving them the right of first refusal to invest in the new shares.

Risk: The uncertainty or variability surrounding a future event.

Risk-free rate: The rate of interest accorded to sovereign borrowers of the very highest credit quality, whose risk of default is essentially nil.

Risk identification: An analysis of the types of risks a company faces in its business.

Risk management: The process of creating a consistent approach to the management of financial, operating, and legal risks.

Risk mitigation: See Loss control.

Risk monitoring: A formalized process enacted to track a company's risk exposures over time.

Risk philosophy: An explicit statement developed by the board of directors and executive management that reflects the nature of the risks that the firm is willing to bear.

Risk premium: For risky borrowers, an increment added to the risk-free rate to compensate for the additional probability of default.

Risk quantification: A quantitative description of the size of a company's risk exposures (or how large they may become) and the magnitude of the profit and/or loss that might be generated.

Risk reduction: A technique of risk management centered on diversification (i.e. constructing portfolios of uncorrelated risks) and withdrawal (i.e. abandoning entirely certain risky activities).

Risk retention: The act of preserving a specified amount of risk before seeking risk management solutions.

Risk retention insurance contract: An insurance policy that transfers very little risk from cedant to insurer.

Risk tolerance: A quantification of the actual amount of risk that the firm is willing to bear.

Risk transfer: The process of shifting a specified amount of risk exposure to a third party or to the market at large, typically through insurance or derivatives.

Rollover: The process of renewing, or extending, short-term liabilities coming due.

Savings and loan: See Thrift.

Secondary offering: An additional issuance of common stock by a company, coming at some point after the initial public offering.

Secondary trading: Any trading in securities that occurs after initial issuance.

Securities/exchange regulator: A national regulator that is typically responsible for overseeing the financial soundness and operations of local securities and exchange markets, including marketplace stability, investor protections, and product disclosure. In some cases they may also be responsible for the activities of investment banks/securities firms, helping to ensure that they remain properly capitalized and keep leverage and liquidity at prudent levels.

Securities firm: See Investment bank.

Securitized bond: A bond or note that is secured by, and which receives cash flows from, a pool of assets, such as mortgages, student or auto loans, or receivables.

Selling, general, and administrative (SG&A) expenses: The non-production costs that a company incurs in creating its goods/services, generally taken to include marketing, advertising, occupancy, employee health benefits, salaries, and so forth.

Seniority: The priority of equity or debt capital related to claims on a company's assets in the event of default.

Share: See Equity.

Short-term debt: Credit extended to a company via short-term loans or securities, where maturities are generally defined to be less than 1 year.

Sole proprietorship: A business structure where the capital and liabilities are held by a single owner.

Solvency: A sufficiency of capital (or permanent/semi-permanent funds) to meet unexpected losses.

Speculation: Creating a risk position that has the potential to generate a profit or loss, depending on which way a particular market or reference asset moves.

Speculative risk: A risk that can end in one of three results: profit, loss, or no profit/loss.

Spin-off: A corporate finance transaction where a company sells one or more of its units or divisions to the public (in an initial public offering – IPO) or to a third party (in a private equity transaction).

Standard deviation: A risk measure that reflects the degree to which an outcome deviates from the average or expectation, generally computed by adding up the probability-weighted outcomes of the squared differences between expected and actual outcomes and then taking the square root.

Statement of cash flows: A cumulative reflection of a company's sources and uses of cash and its ending cash position at the close of the reporting period. Also known as Cash flow statement.

Stock: See Equity. In British English, stock also means Inventory.

Stock market: The national and global markets for common and preferred stock issued by corporations.

Style drift: Investment outside of a given area of expertise that can result in a misbalancing of risk/return.

Swap: An over-the-counter package of forward contracts of defined notional amounts that mature at successive periods in the future, until the stated maturity date, and which can be arranged on virtually any asset from any market sector.

Syndicate: A group of financial institutions joining together to launch a financing transaction for a borrowing or issuing company.

Takeover: See Acquisition.

Tax planning: The process of optimizing corporate operations to reduce the tax burden.

Tax shield: Tax deductibility on debt financing that arises because interest expense is paid from operating revenues, before taxable income is computed.

Terminal value: An estimate of a company's worth used in certain valuation models, often determined through liquidation value (e.g. an estimate of the proceeds generated through the disposal of a company's assets) or a multiple value (e.g. an estimate based on applying a multiple to earnings or revenues based on market comparables).

Thrift: A regulated financial institution that specializes primarily in the residential mortgage market, accepting retail deposits from individuals and using the funds to grant residential home mortgages. Also known as Savings and loan, Building society.

Time value of money: A financial concept indicating that cash inflows/outflows must be adjusted through discounting or compounding in order to properly account for the appropriate time horizon on which they occur.

Transaction exposure: Currency exposure arising from a company's individual cash flows that can be managed individually.

Translation exposure: Currency exposure arising from conversion of a company's local balance sheet back to the home currency for accounting and disclosure purposes.

Treasury stock: Authorized and issued stock that is repurchased by a company, through a periodic or one-time stock buyback.

Treaty reinsurance: A form of reinsurance where the insurer and reinsurer agree on underwriting criteria for specific risks, which are then automatically ceded and accepted up to an agreed-upon limit.

Turnover: See Gross revenues.

Unit trust: See Open-end fund.

Universal bank: A large financial conglomerate that acts as a hybrid of the commercial and investment bank models, providing clients with the broadest range of financing and advisory products and services.

Unlimited liability: A legal tenet of business structure indicating that owners and partners are responsible and liable for debts that they incur on behalf of their organizations and must repay claims from personal assets if insufficient funds exist within the business.

Upward sloping yield curve: The most common state for a yield curve, where short-term rates are lower than long-term rates.

Value maximization: A concept in a free market system where a firm undertakes actions designed to increase the worth of the enterprise.

Vertical expansion: An acquisition strategy where a company grows by acquiring firms involved in its supply, production, and distribution chain.

Weighted average cost of capital (WACC): The average cost of capital for a firm, based on the percentage attributions of the cost of equity, the cost of retained earnings, and the after-tax cost of debt.

Working capital: Current assets minus current liabilities.

Working capital management: The process of managing cash, other short-term assets, and liabilities.

Yield: The return on an asset, typically expressed as a percentage per annum.

Yield curve: A representation of the cost of borrowing across different time buckets (maturities), typically from overnight to 30 years.

Zero-coupon bond: A deep discount bond that pays no intermediate coupons but redeems at par value (i.e. 100 percent) at maturity.

BIBLIOGRAPHY

Banks, E., 2002, *The Simple Rules of Risk*, Chichester: John Wiley & Sons.

—— 2004, *Alternative Risk Transfer*, Chichester, John Wiley & Sons.

—— 2009, *Risk and Financial Catastrophe*, London: Palgrave.

—— 2010, *The Dictionary of Finance, Investment and Banking*, London: Palgrave Macmillan.

Bodie, Z. and Merton, R., 1999, *Finance*, Upper Saddle River, NJ: Prentice Hall.

Bogle, J., 2009, *Common Sense on Mutual Funds*, New York: John Wiley & Sons.

Bragg, S., 2012, *Business Ratios and Formulas*, 3rd edn., Chichester: John Wiley & Sons.

Brealey, R., Myers, S., and Marcus, A., 2013, *Fundamentals of Corporate Finance*, 11th edn., New York: McGraw-Hill.

Brigham, E. and Ehrhardt, M., 2013, *Financial Management: Theory and Practice*, 14th edn., Boston: Cengage Learning.

Bruner, R., 2004, *Applied Mergers and Acquisitions*, New York: John Wiley & Sons.

—— 2009, *Deals from Hell: M&A Lessons that Rise Above the Ashes*, New York: John Wiley & Sons.

Burton, E. and Shah, S., 2013, *Behavioral Finance*, Chichester: John Wiley & Sons.

Carey, D., Rappaport, A., Eccles, R., Aiello, R., and Watkins, M., 2001, *Harvard Business Review on Mergers and Acquisitions*, Boston, MA: HBS Publishing.

Carnes, W. S. and Slifer, S., 1991, *The Atlas of Economic Indicators*, New York: HarperCollins.

Cassidy, J., 2009, *How Markets Fail: The Logic of Economic Calamities*, New York: Farrar, Strauss, and Giroux.

Cox, J. and Rubinstein, M., 1985, *Options Markets*, Upper Saddle River, NJ: Prentice Hall.

Crouhy, M. and Galai, D., 2014, *The Essentials of Risk Management*, 2nd edn., New York: McGraw-Hill.

Cumming, D. and Johan, S., 2009, *Venture Capital and Private Equity Contracting*, Burlington, MA: Academic Press.

Damodaran, A., 1996, *Damodaran on Valuation*, 2nd edn., New York: John Wiley & Sons.

Darst, D., 2008, *The Art of Asset Allocation*, 2nd edn., New York: McGraw-Hill.

Davies, H. and Green, D., 2008, *Global Financial Regulation*, London: Polity.

DePhampilis, D., 2013, *Mergers, Acquisitions and Other Restructuring Activities*, 7th edn., Waltham, MA: Academic Press.

Doherty, N., 1985, *Corporate Risk Management*, New York: McGraw-Hill,.

Edwards, R. and Magee, J., 2012, *Technical Analysis of Stock Trends*, 10th edn., Boca Raton, FL: CRC Press.

El-Arian, M., 2009, *When Markets Collide*, New York: McGraw-Hill.

Emery, D., Finnerty, J., and Stowe, J., 2012, *Corporate Financial Management*, 4th edn., Upper Saddle River, NJ: Prentice Hall.

Fabozzi, F., ed., 2012, *Handbook of Fixed Income Instruments*, 8th edn., New York: McGraw-Hill.

—— 2012, *Bond Markets, Analysis and Strategies*, 8th edn., Upper Saddle River, NJ: Prentice Hall.

Fama, E., 1972, *The Theory of Finance*, New York: Holt, Rinehart and Winston.

Fight, A., 2004, *Syndicated Lending*, London: Butterworth-Heinemann.

Forbes, W., 2009, *Behavioural Finance*, Chichester: John Wiley & Sons.

Fridson, M. and Alvarez, F., 2011, *Financial Statement Analysis*, 4th edn., New York: John Wiley & Sons.

Gaughan, P., 2014, *Mergers, Acquisitions, and Corporate Restructurings*, 5th edn., New York: John Wiley & Sons.

Geddes, R., 2003, *IPOs and Equity Offerings*, London: Butterworth-Heinemann.

Gibson, R., 2013, *Asset Allocation*, 5th edn., New York: McGraw-Hill.

Grabbe, O., 1995, *International Financial Markets*, Upper Saddle River, NJ: Prentice Hall.

Graham, B. and Meredith, S., 1998, *The Interpretation of Financial Statements*, New York: Harper Business.

Graham, B. and Dodd, D., 2008, *Security Analysis*, 6th edn., New York: McGraw-Hill.

Harris, L., 2002, *Trading and Exchanges*, Oxford: Oxford University Press.

Haugen, R., 2000, *Modern Investment Theory*, 5th edn., Upper Saddle River, NJ: Prentice Hall.

Higgins, R., 2011, *Analysis for Financial Management*, 10th edn., New York: McGraw-Hill.

Horngren, C., Harrison, W., and Oliver, S., 2011, *Accounting*, 9th edn., Upper Saddle River, NJ: Prentice Hall.

Hubbard, G. and O'Brien, A., 2011, *Money, Banking and the Financial System*, Upper Saddle River, NJ: Prentice Hall.

Hull, J., 2014, *Options, Futures, and Other Derivatives*, 9th edn., Upper Saddle River, NJ: Prentice Hall.

Jorion, P., 2010, *The Financial Risk Manager Handbook*, 6th edn., New York: John Wiley & Sons.

Jury, T., 2012, *Cash Flow Analysis and Forecasting*, New York: John Wiley & Sons.

Kidwell, D., Peterson, R. L., Blackwell, D. W., and Whidbee, D. A., 2011, *Financial Institutions, Markets, and Money*, 11th edn., New York: John Wiley & Sons.

Koller, T., Goedhart, M., Wessels, D., 2010, *Valuation*, 5th edn., New York: John Wiley & Sons.

Lake, R., 2003, *Evaluating and Implementing Hedge Funds Strategies*, 3rd edn., London: Euromoney.

Lefevre, E., 2009, *Reminiscences of a Stock Operator*, New York: John Wiley & Sons.

Levich, R., 2001, *International Financial Markets: Prices and Policies*, 2nd edn., New York: McGraw-Hill.

Lhabitant, F., 2007, *Handbook of Hedge Funds*, Chichester: John Wiley & Sons.

McConnell, B., Brue, S., and Flynn, S., 2014, *Macroeconomics*, 20th edn., New York: McGraw-Hill.

MacDonald, R., 2012, *Derivatives Markets*, 3rd edn., Upper Saddle River, NJ: Prentice Hall.

Malkiel, B., 2015, *A Random Walk Down Wall Street*, 11th edn., New York: W.W. Norton.

Maness, T. and Zietlow, J., 2004, *Short-Term Financial Management*, Mason, OH: Southwestern College Publishers.

Melicher, R. and Norton, E., 2011, *Introduction to Finance*, 14th edn., New York: John Wiley & Sons.

Minsky, H., 2008, *Stabilizing Unstable Markets*, New York: McGraw-Hill.

O'Brien, T., 2005, *International Financial Economics*, 2nd edn., Oxford: Oxford University Press.

Pignataro, P., 2013, *Financial Modeling and Valuation*, New York: John Wiley & Sons.

Pozen, R. and Hamacher, T., 2015, *The Fund Industry*, 2nd edn., New York: John Wiley & Sons.

Resti, A. and Sironi, A., 2007, *Risk Management and Shareholders' Value in Banking*, Chichester, John Wiley and Sons.

Robinson, T., Van Greuning, H., Henry, E., and Broihahn, M. A., 2012, *International Financial Statement Analysis*, 2nd edn., Charlottesville, VA: CFA Institute.

Rosenbaum, J. and Pearl, J., 2013, *Investment Banking: Valuation, Leveraged Buyouts and Mergers and Acquisitions*, 2nd edn., New York: John Wiley & Sons.

Rosenberg, L., Weintraub, N., and Hyman, A., 2008, *ETF Strategies and Tactics*, New York: McGraw-Hill.

Ross, S., Leroy, S., and Werner, J., 2000, *Principles of Financial Economics*, Cambridge: Cambridge University Press.

Saudagaran, S. and Smith, M., 2013, *International Accounting: A Users Perspective*, 4th edn., Riverwoods, IL: CCH.

Saunders, A. and Cornett, M., 2011, *Financial Institutions and Markets*, 5th edn., New York: McGraw-Hill.

Schwartz, R. and Francioni, R., 2004, *Equity Markets in Action*, New York: John Wiley & Sons.

Seitz, N. and Ellison, M., 2004, *Capital Budgeting and Long-Term Financial Decisions*, 4th edn., Mason, OH: Southwestern College Publishers.

Stigum, M. and Crescenzi, A., 2007, *Stigum's Money Market*, 4th edn., New York: McGraw-Hill.

Stimes, P., 2008, *Equity Valuation, Risk and Investment*, London: John Wiley & Sons.

Subramanyam, K. R. and Wild, J., 2013, *Financial Statement Analysis*, 11th edn., New York: McGraw-Hill.

Taleb, N., 2007, *The Black Swan: The Impact of the Highly Improbable*, New York: Random House.

Taylor, A. and Sansone, A., 2006, *The Handbook of Loan Syndications and Trading*, New York: McGraw-Hill.

Vaughan, E. and Vaughan, T., 2013, *Fundamentals of Risk and Insurance*, 11th edn., New York: John Wiley & Sons.

Weithers, T., 2006, *The Foreign Exchange Markets: A Practical Guide to the FX Markets*, New York: John Wiley & Sons.

White, G., Sondhi, A., and Fried, D., 2002, *The Analysis and Use of Financial Statements*, 3rd edn., New York: John Wiley & Sons.

INDEX